Wiltshire Within Living Memory

Compiled by the
Wiltshire Federation of Women's Institutes

Published jointly by
Countryside Books, Newbury
and the WFWI, Devizes

First Published 1993
© Wiltshire Federation of Women's Institutes 1993

COUNTRYSIDE BOOKS
3 Catherine Road
Newbury, Berkshire

ISBN 1 85306 249 9

The cover photograph shows the Boulton and Routledge
families from Highworth, setting off on a day's outing
around 1904. The photograph is reproduced with
the kind permission of Michael Marshman.

Designed by Mon Mohan
Produced through MRM Associates Ltd, Reading
Typeset by Paragon Typesetters, Queensferry, Clwyd
Printed in England

Contents

Acknowledgements

Wiltshire Federation of Women's Institutes would like to thank all WI members who supplied material for this project through their local Institutes. We are grateful also to Mr Gordon Coles for material on the Swindon Railway Works, and to Mrs Nancy Harding for permission to use her father's memories from his book *The Drovers*.

Unfortunately we were not able to include extracts from every submission; to do so would have meant some duplication of content, and of course we had to take into account the total amount of space available in the book.

But all the contributions, without exception, were of value in deciding the shape and content of the book. We are grateful for them all. The result is a collective memory of shared experience.

Finally a special thank you to Mrs Judy Snowdon for the delightful county map.

Margaret Elwin
Co-ordinator

List of Contributing Institutes

Contributions have been received from the following Wiltshire Women's Institutes:

Aldbourne, Alderbury, Amesbury Afternoon, Amesbury Evening, Avebury & District, Barford St Martin, Bathford, Baydon, Beanacre, Bedwyn, Biddestone & Hartham, Bishopstone with Hinton Parva, Blackland Calstone & Calne, Bourne Valley, Bowerchalke, Box, Boxlea, Bradford on Avon, Bratton, Bremhill, Brinkworth, Broadtown, Brokenborough, Broughton Gifford, Burbage, Cadley & Marlborough District, Charlton & Hankerton, Charlton & Ludwell, Cherhill, Chitterne, Colerne, Collingbourne Kingston, Compton Bassett, Coombe Bissett & Homington, Corsham, Corsley, Cricklade, Devizes Evening, Dilton Marsh, Dinton & Baverstock, Donhead, Downton Afternoon, Downton Evening, Durnford & Woodford, East Knoyle, Edington & Tinhead, Ellendune, Fittleton with Netheravon, Fonthill Bishop & Hindon, Fovant & Sutton Mandeville, Gastard, Hannington, Hardenhuish, Harnham Afternoon, Heywood & Hawkeridge, Highworth Afternoon, Highworth Evening, Holt, Hook & District, Hullavington, Kilmington, Kington St Michael, Kington Langley, Lacock, Laverstock & Ford, Lea, Leigh, Luckington, Lydiard Millicent, Market Lavington & Easterton, Melksham, Monkton Farleigh, Monkton Park, Neston Evening, North Bradley, Odstock Nunton & Bodenham, Ogbourne St Andrew, Pewsey, Pewsham, Potterne, Purton & Braydon, Redlynch & District, Sandridge, Sarum, Seend, Sherston, Shrewton, South Newton Wishford & Stapleford, Staverton, Steeple Ashton, Sutton Benger, Tisbury, Tootlea Brook, Turleigh & Winsley, Upavon, Upper Stratton, Wanborough, Warminster, Westbury Evening, West Lavington, Whiteparish, Wilton, Wingfield, Winterbourne Gunner, Winterslow, Woodside, Wootton Bassett, Wootton Rivers, Worton & Marston, Wroughton Afternoon, Wroughton Evening, Yarnbury, Yatton Keynell.

Foreword

One of the joys of Federation Chairmanship is the opportunity it affords to visit Institutes and meet with members around the County.

To encourage them to reminisce is always a pleasure and so I am delighted to introduce *Wiltshire Within Living Memory* which brings together recollections from members in all parts of the County.

Wiltshire has always been a county of contrasts. The saying 'as different as chalk from cheese' originates here, referring to the difference between the chalk plains of the south and the richer land in the north supporting dairy cattle and cheese production.

But times change all too quickly and the old ways of life become just memories which, if not recorded, become blurred and lost in time. A landscape picture needs people to give it life – I feel sure that everyone's 'picture' of Wiltshire will be brought vividly alive by the memories of people recorded here.

Jan Morris
County Chairman

TOWN & COUNTRY LIFE

SOME TOWNS AND VILLAGES REMEMBERED

The Cavalry school at Netheravon; the lost village of Imber; the horse-drawn fire engine racing through Chippenham; the lamplighter on the streets of Salisbury – these are just a few glimpses of our towns and villages as they used to be, an introduction to a way of life which is still within living memory.

SALISBURY

'In late 1991 I was speaking to a gardening club in Hampshire. The chairman introduced me, saying we were at school together. I had not thought about Miss Falwasser's mixed kindergarten in Fowlers Road for decades, but this brought back the 1920s and a long-forgotten Salisbury, when I was seven.

We lived at Porton but Salisbury was the focal point of life. Market days were always exciting, with pigs, sheep, cattle and poultry all mixed up with fruit, meat and general stores, marvellous smells and muck everywhere. Another joy was the nearby Corn Exchange with its clean, sharp, all pervading aromatic odour. The market place really came into its own during the annual October Fair, with its swings and roundabouts, games of skill and delicious eats. We were not allowed to enter the fair, whether in school uniform or not. Dire threats of scarlet fever and measles actually had little effect if we had any money, but a penny a week pocket money did not go very far.

For present day shopping Debenhams cannot compare to the old local family firms, Style & Gerrish, Clark & Lonnen and Blooms where one could go up in the tiny jerky lift to the second and third floors. There was practically nothing except eatables which these stores did not sell and the staff knew what they were selling. Then there was Main's for animal feeds (smells again) and gardening equipment; Pinder's household corner store; Mrs Meager's general grocery, a dark hole of wonders, opposite the Guildhall; Eldridge and Young where we got our school uniforms; and for special holiday foods there was Stokes, a holy of holies. For real treats we went to Gullicks nurseries (Queen Elizabeth Gardens), where the ancient head gardener granted adult status even to small children and discussed shrub buying with a seriousness that warmed small hearts.

Salisbury Market Place in 1930 — an exciting mêlée of people, livestock and market stalls.

Many of the 1920s buildings still remain, but often the use has changed. The churches remain, though one is now an art centre and congregations have dwindled. From childhood distant views of the cathedral spire have meant home but the cathedral's grey, cold interior only holds miserable memories of chilblains in the chilly school services. Even today my heels tingle during services.

The High Street leading to the Cathedral Close, in addition to Beach's bookshop, had Harry Simmons' rather highbrow bookshop. Harry was a local celebrity and in spite of legs totally unsuitable for tights, ran the Dramatic Society, with its large repertoire of productions. Every year the Society gave a week's showing of the current Shakespeare examination play. No one who was lucky enough to be there will forget the wonderful evening when Harry as Macbeth clouted a servant over the head and knocked his wig off. The servant put it on back to front and played the rest of the scene peering through hair. But better was to come. Macbeth furiously fought Macduff and the castle walls fell gently round them, so they finished the fight wearing skirts of castle walling.

The theatre was then opposite the present bus station while the cinema was up Fisherton Street. Again, scarlet fever and measles were threatened as inevitable at the cinema, but one year when the family were away Kathy our nurse took me to see Charlie Chaplin in the *The Kid*. Absolute bliss *and* jelly babies. The consequent rumpus and poor Kathy's scolding did not matter. I had *been* to the cinema!'

11

'I have lived in Salisbury all my life. I was born in 1914, the middle one of three girls. We had wonderful caring parents, but my father was a preacher for the Wesleyan chapel so a little strict, especially on Sundays with prayers at every meal. We had to go to chapel in the morning, Sunday school in the afternoon and chapel again in the evening. We weren't allowed to "know or sew" on Sundays. In those days you were seen but *not* heard.

As a child one of the things I remember was the horse-drawn carts which used to come round on hot summer days and spray the roads with water. Incidentally, I never did find out why this was done unless it was to clean the mess from the horses – there were very few cars in those days.

I vividly remember also the gas lamplighters. They came round night and morning with long poles to turn on and off the street gaslights. There was no electricity in those days. What a warmth those lights used to give out.'

CHIPPENHAM

'I was born and grew up living over my father's chemist shop in the centre of Chippenham. I have many memories of the people and of the happenings in the town in the early part of the century.

Early every morning there would be a long line of waggons forming a queue down the Market Place, High Street and Bath Road waiting to deliver their load of milk churns to Nestle's condensery. The drivers would take the opportunity to do some shopping while they waited, and the shopkeepers opened their shops at 6.30 am to serve them, closing later for breakfast before reopening for the day's trade.

A fire was always a great occasion and most of the townsfolk turned out to watch and enjoy the spectacle. The fire station was across the road from my father's shop so I had a grandstand view. The horses were kept in the nearby Angel Hotel yard at night but were released in the daytime into the fields at Westmead. On one occasion the horses were not brought in at night when there was a fire call-out. Joe Buckle, the captain, was not best pleased by the delay caused by trying to catch the horses in the dark.

It was the duty of the first fireman to turn up at the station to light the boiler. The engine, with its red paint and polished brasswork gleaming, was wheeled out and the horses harnessed. The firemen wore silver helmets for fires, keeping their gold ones for Church Parade and similar occasions.

It was a wonderful sight to see the engine with smoke and flames coming from the boiler chimney going four in hand at full gallop down the High Street with the firemen hanging on for dear life.

Market day was on Friday and was the busiest day of the week, not only for the shopkeepers but also for the numerous pubs which were very well patronised.

The market was held in the Market Place. The bulls were tied to iron bull posts (removed in 1940 for war purposes) and outside St Andrew's church and the Angel Hotel they erected hurdles to contain cows, sheep, calves and pigs. Cages were brought round from the old canal wharf to accommodate rabbits, guinea pigs, cats, dogs and ferrets. Another line of cages was used for chickens, ducks and turkeys.

Market day would not have been complete without the travelling salesmen. My parents were right to warn me not to believe everything they said but it was great fun listening to their patter.

The cattle were driven to market on the hoof and there were several men who were employed as drovers. One of these, a well known and liked character, "Peggy" Wilkins, had a wooden leg and rumour had it that he was quite prepared to take it off and use it as a weapon if occasion demanded.

All the shops in the town were run by private traders and among them there were some very independent and interesting characters.

Joe Buckle, the fishmonger (also captain of the fire brigade), told a complaining customer that he was very sorry but he was sure that the fish she had bought had been a sick fish.

The two Misses Honeyball kept a china shop on the bridge. They were of uncertain age and always dressed in long black dresses. We were rather in awe of them. They kept an eagle eye on their stock to make sure that nothing was broken. We were not allowed to touch anything. It must have been an awful shock for them when one Friday a cow decided to have a look around their shop. Rumour had it that it walked right round their shop and out again without doing any damage. Obviously the Misses Honeyball could control much more than little girls.'

'As a child living in Chippenham I remember after lots of rain the anticipation of the river Avon rising and flooding the town bridge. This had the result of cutting the town in two as there was no other road crossing the river.

For people, particularly shopkeepers who had to get from one side of the town to the other, this meant catching a rowing boat which would ferry folk across, or taking a much longer train journey. One had to catch a Calne train and alight at Stanley halt, with a long walk back into the town to the area of the market place, and then return the same way.

As you can imagine, it was really exciting watching the "lucky" people being rowed across – us children were not allowed near. I'm sure this view wasn't shared by the shopkeepers, though, whose riverside shops were flooded by inches of water.'

AMESBURY

'Amesbury in the 1920s and 1930s was a pleasant little village with everyone knowing everybody and almost everyone being a character in their own right.

The village was dominated by the lady of the manor, of whom we were all terrified. She and her quiet, gentle brother lived in the Abbey and allowed us to have the annual flower show and tennis tournament in their extensive park. Siddy Hinxman was the head gardener, even then finding it difficult to make gardening ends meet. Siddy's house and the glasshouses were removed later to leave room for the central car park but someone had vision enough to not to chop down the cedars and they give a certain elegance to the throughway.

The main street had several notables; Mrs Cockle and her dame school, old Father Pethen the cobbler, Zebedee's the butcher's and one of the Tucker girls running a guest house. Many of us enjoyed their tennis court and summer hospitality.

The Eyres were another well known family, the most prominent of the brothers and sisters being Harold who drove his carrier cart to Salisbury on market days, jogging along amongst the increasing number of cars and motorbikes. At the weekends one could borrow the outfit to take the dusty road over Boscombe Down, no aerodrome, to Porton.

Two landmarks lost under development were the workhouse and the much respected war memorial. In the workhouse an old woman named Mary achieved fame by standing up to the governors when they came to inspect and hear complaints. Mary asked them to try the very hard dried peas which were frequently offered to the inhabitants. After complying, the governors agreed that "the peas were very hard for toothless gums". "And they've been through me," explained Mary.

For me the period was divided between the river and the concert party. My father conducted the *Messiah* in Amesbury's old church and, using the best chorus singers, ran the Amiables, a jolly little concert party, for several years. The fairly stable cast included the Attwaters, farmers from Vineys Farm, Bob Miles a smallholder, a Tucker girl, a Binns girl, the bank manager and my stepmother Kathleen. The programmes were very varied and popular; classics, comedy, sketches and one act plays. We also had an unreliable comic, the doctor's wife, who always brought the house down. Unfortunately she never managed to learn lines so the cast had to adjust to her ad libbing. Kathleen was the most successful at doing this and the two of them are still remembered for their duo *Two little sausages* and the hilarious one act play, *Between the soup and the savoury.*

For us children the river was irresistible. The Crook family, besides providing numerous farmers, included two girls, who with me went to school in Salisbury, first by the train (the station was where the NAAFI now stands) and then by bus along the Avon Valley. We learnt to swim naked in the river, hiding under the bridge when people came by. Mr Martin the waterkeeper was a great friend of mine. He knew all the best birds' nests and wild flowers and introduced me to Lord Allenby of Jerusalem who let us watch him fishing as long as we were mice quiet.'

THE CAVALRY SCHOOL

'The Cavalry School, which was very different from the present camp on the A345 to Marlborough, was established about 1900 in the grounds of what village people called the Big House, and seemed just an extension of the village. This formerly belonged to the Hicks-Beach family as did most of Haxton, Fittleton and Netheravon, as well as several miles of land surrounding them.

When this was all sold to the Government, village people had the option of buying the cottage they were living in for £50, which was a lot of money when the men, mostly farmworkers, were lucky to earn £1 a week. Few could afford to buy and most of the houses became War Department property.

For a number of years no married quarters were built at the Cavalry School though North and South Lodges, Church View and the stableyard were used as such, also a few huts on the southern side of the camp were later converted into homes. Soldiers who wanted to bring their families would try to rent a house in the village or find lodgings and become involved in village life. Sports, concerts and other entertainments were often held at the camp and villagers had an open invitation to attend if they wished, all free and sometimes free refreshments too.

Horses seemed to be everywhere at this time and the Riding School was built for their training. Most of the cavalry officers seemed to have plenty of money and were keen polo players. A polo ground was made on the downs about half a mile from the camp with a small grandstand, and the civilian grooms lodged at The Dog and Gun, the ponies being kept in stables in the garden of the inn.

There were no council refuse collections so people either burned or buried their rubbish and quite often articles such as an old kettle or saucepan could be seen partly hidden in a hedge. A roadman was employed by the council to keep banks, hedges and so on tidy and one never saw any litter scattered around.

Cigarettes were very cheap (twopence a packet, I think) and most soldiers smoked. When they threw the packets away they seldom bothered to remove the cards inside so village children used to walk up to the dump where a local man who was paid to clear the Cavalry School's rubbish used to dump it (above the Wexland Farm). I still have a few collected in that way.'

DONHEAD ST MARY

'In 1910 the village of Donhead St Mary comprised two or three large houses, farms and farm cottages, as it was a farming community. Most of these cottages had no running water, the water was either drawn from wells or from clear springs which began in the rectory garden. The privy was at the bottom of the garden and if you needed it after dark you went down with a candle-lit lantern.

Nevertheless, there were many facilities in the village. The cottage near Yew Tree Cottage was a little shop kept by a lady and her daughter who sold sweets and many odds and ends. Continuing along the Semley road there was the pub, The Carpenters' Arms, where many pleasant evenings were spent. Next the laundry where the laundry from the big houses arrived each week; there was always the coachman from The Burltons bringing an enormous basket in his horse and trap. Then there were the village allotments belonging to the church, no rents paid. Turning back to the main road there was the village butcher who delivered his meat regularly, always run by the Pike family as long as it existed. At one time there were two butchers at Ludwell. The rectory is now Shute House. Opposite the village hall was a small building called the reading room where men could go for a pleasant evening of games.

Then came Mr Sansom, the village blacksmith. He was willing to do all kinds of jobs; later it became his cycle shop and later still the sons moved to Ludwell. Mr Sansom was the mainstay of the church bellringers and he never failed to bring his five helpers to ring on the first Sunday in every month, and a practice night, once a week, so we heard the bells regularly. We come now to the village shop which was open all hours. It was also a bakehouse and the fresh bread could be smelled as you passed by. The bread was delivered in a horse-drawn bread van as far as Ebbesbourne, and you should have tasted the lard cakes they made!

In one of the three cottages on the top of the hill lived an old lady with an artificial leg. She made hard boiled sweets and you could buy five black and white bullseyes for a farthing. There was the market gardener at the top of the hill, and every Monday and Friday he got his vegetables ready for market. In the evenings they were packed into the horse-drawn van and early in the mornings he set out for the market in Salisbury. Then came the builder who employed a carpenter, a painter and a bricklayer; he was also the village undertaker. The Royal Oak was our second pub. One Sunday afternoon it was burnt down and until it was rebuilt the bar operated in the stables.

The Burltons was a fine house in those days, the family waited on by parlourmaid, housemaids and cook. As there was no transport to Shaftesbury, Miss Emma Dunstan kept a small medicine shop and when accidents or sickness occurred one could go for ointments, cough mixtures, etc. There were two dairy farms, neither of them dairy farms now, alas. There was also the chapel, Wesleyan in those days, Methodist today. Mr Jeffery, living at Sunnybank, was the auctioneer in Shaftesbury and Salisbury.

Donhead Hall was the largest estate, comprising cottages which went round the deer fence, the lodge at the top of a hill we called Shipton, the Mill House, the Farm House, Lillies Green Cottage, the lodges at the bottom of the drive, the two cottages opposite the back drive (which was a drive in those days, not a track as it is today) and two more at the edge of the estate. Many times when the bottom of Watery Lane was flooded we had to walk up the front drive and down the back, which wasn't too good if we were returning from a late night dance. Most of the cottages have now been sold and are private dwellings. The farm was a Jersey farm and Mr Blackburn himself strained the cream from the milk, and on a Sunday morning one could have a jamjar filled with clotted cream for a few pence. He had a room where he had an organ and a library; on Sunday afternoons he played the organ whilst we changed our books for new ones.

We enjoyed taking tea to the men in the hayfields, and the highlight of the evening was to ride home in the waggons. At this time there were no milk deliveries, the farmworkers took their cans to be filled up daily and others bought milk from the farm. My sister and I took bottles of milk to houses at the end of Wincombe Lane, this before walking to school. In the summer the farmer's wife would ask us to come and pick her soft fruit, then she took us as a treat to Shaftesbury in her trap to sell the fruit in the market.'

IMBER

'I·was one of the last generation of people to live at Imber, a village on Salisbury Plain. Now a ghost village, used by the Army for training purposes, I remember the time it was a thriving community with its own school, shop, post office, church and chapel.

Once a week a bus ran in to Warminster but the inhabitants had little need to leave the village. Everything was there and we were able to create our own amusements. The village had its own cricket and football teams, and concerts took place in the school. Hunting and shooting were enjoyed and tennis tournaments were particularly popular. In fact, I can remember a tennis tournament in which 72 couples took part.

Everyone knew each other, and the land was farmed by three families who were inter-related. The outbreak of war put an end to this leisurely, peaceful way of life and now only the gravestones in the churchyard bear witness to the generations who once lived and worked at Imber.'

'We moved into Oxendean Farm in 1918 when I was five years old. It was situated two miles from Warminster and four miles from Imber on the edge of Salisbury Plain. We were a mile from any other house except the farm cottage.

I and my brothers and sisters walked to school in Warminster unless it was wet when my father fetched us in the car.

It was a lonely road and Imber seemed very remote. There was a horse-drawn carrier from Imber once a week. I think on Thursdays. I often saw women carrying bags of shopping walking home.

Sometime later, Imber children were bussed into school in Warminster and about 1930 Mr White from Longbridge Deverill started a bus service on Saturdays.

I have very happy memories of Oxendean. There was a wood where we picked primroses and bluebells in the spring and hazelnuts in the autumn. A short distance away was Battlesbury Hill, an ancient earthwork. How I enjoyed walking along the ridges, and on the steep side of the hill there was a wood with terraced walks through it and lots of white violets grew on the edges.

On the hill on the farm was a barrow; we used to get letters telling us not to excavate it. On the barrow was a flagpole on which a flag flew when the Yeomanry or Territorials were shooting on Mancombe Range which bordered the farm.

We picked cowslips, moon daisies, scabious and several species of orchids. I especially remember a big patch of bee orchids in the field opposite the farmhouse.

We got our water from a windpump and about 1929 some men appeared who were surveying for water. They said there was an unlimited supply, hence the compulsory purchase of all the farms round about by the War Office in 1930; from then on we rented from the War Office till 1935.

About 1931 they set up a canvas camp between us and Warminster and from April till September each year various units of the army came to train in artillery shooting, each for a fortnight. They had horse-drawn gun carriages and often a band led the soldiers up to Imber Clump. It sounded cheerful across the fields.

It was a shock some years after the war to drive up to Imber and see all the buildings and army quarters built over the fields, and my lovely wood on Battlesbury had been cut down.'

POST-WAR SWINDON

'I slipped out of bed as quietly as possible, my bare feet pattering on the cold, cheap linoleum, and twitched back a corner of the curtain. My heart sank. The view was no better in the brighter morning light than it had appeared on our arrival the previous evening. Row upon row of marble or granite gravestones, crowned by cherubim, scrolls or other fanciful ornamentation, seemed to stretch out almost to infinity.

Although a few bunches of fresh flowers were strewn over the newly-dug graves, Victorian monstrosities of waxen white wreaths under a glass dome decorated several of the plots.

My husband of a few months stirred and then propped himself up on one elbow. "Well?" he enquired.

"It's dreadful," I moaned and then burst into tears.

This, after all, was meant to herald the start of a glorious lifetime together, our first weekend in the town which was going to be our home. We had married a few days after the end of the war while I was still in the WRNS and he in the Army Pay Corps. So time together was very precious and demobilisation eagerly anticipated.

When Barclays Bank informed Eric that his career, interrupted by six years of war service, was to recommence in Swindon, naturally we were anxious to see the town for ourselves. Very few hotels existed, many were little more than shabby commercial guest-houses. Through a friend of the family, we heard of two maiden ladies who put people up for short periods of time and lived within walking distance of the shopping centre. It didn't sound exciting but would serve our purposes for a quick initial survey of the town, we decided.

Miss Laura was small and shrivelled. Her sharp eyes behind her gold-rimmed spectacles darted hither and thither, missing nothing. Miss Ada, a complete contrast, was solid in the shape of a cottage loaf, with long coarse hairs protruding from her chin. Their house belonged to an earlier era. It was characteristic of the many hundreds of terraced dwellings which were built to accommodate the growing numbers of railway employees at the turn of the century.

The original stone cottages constructed close to the engine sheds in the 1850s were pleasing to the eye but those red-brick "two up and two down" abodes put up hastily in monotonous parallel rows had no redeeming features. Most opened directly on to the pavement outside or at the most had a narrow cement strip with a couple of stunted shrubs, but the back garden was quite often no more than a yard made even smaller by the tacked-on extension of a scullery and outside toilet. This meant we had to suffer the indignity of a china "pot" under the bed in our room. It wasn't possible to use the outside loo in the night when all had been locked up. Washing facilities were equally archaic and uninviting. A large china jug on a marble washstand sufficed for our ablutions. As the water was completely cold, my toilet at least proved very sketchy.

After that we had rooms in a more modern house on the edge of the town for a few months and then finally moved to our own 1937 semi by Christmas of 1946, but my spirits went on plummeting.

Oh yes, it was fun to possess a home of our own at last and spread our few items of furniture in it until we could exchange some more of our dated Utility dockets but we found it difficult, almost impossible, to make friends who would come and visit us there.

"Is your husband inside?" was the first question people asked on being introduced. In my naivety I imagined it sounded like a prison sentence but it merely meant, "Is your husband an employee of the Great Western Railway?" If he wasn't, they didn't want to know.

At that time the railway works, housed in huge camouflaged buildings straddling right across our view from the bedroom windows, were the largest employers of labour in Europe. Hooters signalled the time for the start of work and the breaks during the day. Hordes of workmen streamed out on foot or by bicycle at dinnertime and then clogged the streets again in the evening as they wended their way home.

It was a tightly-knit society with no space for intruders. Whole families of males had worked there for generations and many of their female relatives were employed in the offices. Not only engines were designed and constructed there but the carriage works turned out the passenger compartments as well. On Wednesday afternoons, people travelled from near and far for a guided tour of the whole industrial enterprise.

Even the school holidays were arranged round the works. In Trip fortnight, the first two weeks of July, the town became virtually empty as all the railwaymen and their families took advantage of their free passes and went off on holiday on as long journeys as possible. On Trip Wednesdays, all the shops in the town were shut for the day and I was caught out several times when I went to buy food. Very few homes owned fridges then so it meant a daily expedition for fresh items. I completely forgot the day as it wasn't a normal Bank Holiday.

Swindon was divided roughly into two parts. It was a town with a split personality. New Town comprised the railway works, other small industries and the main shopping and residential areas on the level plateau at the foot of all the hills rising up to Old Town. Regent Street, now a pedestrian precinct, only possessed two or three walk-round stores. McIlroys, the largest, was restricted because it housed the central Swindon Library in part of the ground floor. Anstiss, on the opposite corner, burnt down in a fire a few years later and was never replaced as such.

Most of the other shops were converted cottage properties with living accommodation above the business. Rows of tiny houses converged on to this main street which in the 1960s were pulled down to create the new Brunel Centre. Instead of the plush and glossy travel agents, estate agents and building societies which now comprise a substantial part of the area, there used to be good old-fashioned ironmongers stocking everything from a humble nail to a tin bath, bakers from whose premises wafted mouth-watering smells of fresh bread and cakes baked on the spot and small drapers still supplying packets of pins and darning wool.

The old GWR hospital on a site close to the works and set up by voluntary contributions from the railmen still served the needs of many citizens. It would be several years before the first phase of the new Princess Margaret Hospital would be built.

Climbing up any of the hills up to Old Town, one was conscious of a change of emphasis and atmosphere. This area was the alter ego of the town's divided personality. Houses were larger, more pretentious, with substantial gardens, occupied by doctors, lawyers, works managers and the clergy. A good many of the shops were long-established family concerns rather than just one more branch of a national chain. A few architectural gems remained from earlier centuries along Bath Road and the High Street. Trees lined the principal roads and the Town Gardens provided a welcome leisure area for families at the weekend. True, the GWR park in New Town boasted an equally large expanse of green sward but it mainly lacked the blossoming trees and well-stocked flower beds to be found in the Old Town gardens.

As befitted a railway community, two stations still existed, one in each half of the town. Another important feature was the weekly cattle market held on Mondays. Some of the narrow roads skirting the market were choked with huge lorries. Farmers in from the country congregated round the different stalls, chewing straws and prodding the pigs with the tips of their canes, while their wives enjoyed the unaccustomed luxury of a shopping expedition. Small townbred children tugging at their mothers' hands dragged them round the various groups of animals, agog with excitement at the unusual scenes around them.

None of the large estates which were later to be added on the perimeter of Swindon had progressed further than the drawing-board. Within minutes from the town centre it was possible to pick catkins, pussy-willow and bluebells in the spring and blackberries and crab-apples in the autumn. Our bread still came to us every day on a light cart pulled by a white horse.

Yet, the overwhelming impression that remains with me in those first two early years was of loneliness. I missed the close comradeship of Service life and the warmth of my Yorkshire friends and family. We were aliens on the fringe of that railway-dominated society. Nearly 50 years on, Swindon has sprawled out untidily over many of the surrounding green areas but it's much more alive, peopled by a cosmopolitan society. Instead of being dominated by one industry, blinkered in its outlook, it now provides a base for a whole variety of enterprises.'

THE KENNET AND AVON CANAL

'I lived in a lock house on the canal at Brimslade near Wootton Rivers from 1940 to 1952. At that time the canal was owned by GWR and derelict. The only traffic was the workmen's barge from Devizes and one owned by an old sailor, George Day, from Cardiff. The canal was covered in weeds and the lock gates falling apart. The stretch from Brimslade to Burbage Wharf was rented by the Swindon Golden Carp Club, and men came from the GWR works during the war as they were exempt from military service. I saw many large pike caught – one weighing 21 pounds.

The wildlife was abundant, with lots of coots, ducks and swans nesting. We watched the water wagtails nesting on the lock gates. We had a kingfisher too, and various owls.

My husband was called up in 1942 so I took over the Waterkeeper's job. I had a badge and a card and had to ask to see the men's cards and to watch for poachers.

The canal race started in about 1945 and there were not many canoes then. They had to carry the canoes round the locks and some stopped for the night – one entry came from Dauntsey's school.'

'The canal had not been prosperous for the last quarter of the 19th century so the present century can be summarised as decline, dereliction, revival and restoration. The canal was under the ownership of the Great Western Railway and despite limited maintenance work carried very little traffic. One section was declared closed in 1950 two years after nationalisation. Deterioration took place very rapidly, only parts still being usable, but an attempt to legally close the canal by Act of Parliament in 1956 was not successful in extinguishing navigation rights, due to public opposition that had grown over the years as various closure proposals had been aired. Even in 1927 a Pewsey Rural District Council representative had objected to a GWR closure proposal, not wanting "20 miles of stagnant ditch" in the area. Although not usable, the canal was kept supplied with water and when Crofton pumping station was closed in 1958 due to chimney deterioration and shortening, first a diesel pump and then an electric one maintained a limited water supply to the canal.

The opposition to closure led to the formation of the Kennet and Avon Canal Association in August 1951 and by 1962 agreement was reached with British Waterways that the canal should be redeveloped with some limited Waterways money and volunteer labour. From this achievement the association became the Kennet and Avon Canal Trust Ltd with charitable status and canal restoration really started. The Trust purchased Crofton pumping station in 1968, bringing it into working order with volunteers and the late Sir John Betjeman, the Poet Laureate, ceremonially reopened Crofton to the public in August 1970, with further restoration and development continuing to the present. It was the beginning of a new life for the canal which, with a great deal of hard work has now been restored to its former glory.'

LIFE STORIES

For most folk, life was not easy in the old days in town or country and these reminiscences make no attempt to hide the fact that money was scarce and amenities few. Yet people made the best of what they had, found humour and love where they could, and can look back today with some degree of regret for a quieter, more leisurely way of life.

PEA SOUP FOR A WEEK

'My father was born in 1901, the third child in a family of seven children. The youngest, one of twins, was born dead. His sister recalls how she saw this little boy, upstairs on the landing, in a shoebox or so it seemed, which was taken away at night and laid beside several others outside the church wall to be buried. She picked a few wild flowers on her way to school, and felt quite proud to put them on "her grave".

Although born in Marlborough, the family moved house and came to a small village, Milton Lilbourne, where his father was the village blacksmith. The cottage had no amenities, the tin bath hung up on the wall outside, along with strings of onions. The toilet was down the garden, a rustic affair with wooden seat, squares of newspaper hung on a piece of string and the whole place liberally dusted with a highly smelling type of disinfectant powder, of a very bright pink colour!

Money was very scarce, unless bills were paid up there were tight belts all round. Once they all ate pea soup for one whole week – dinner, breakfast, tea and supper! The forge was the centre of village life for the menfolk, who gathered together, old and young, to put the world to rights, those that chewed tobacco spitting into the fire.

Sundays were a day of rest, no cooking, which meant an exhausting Saturday on the kitchen range. If the wind blew hard, the fire was too hot, or it might turn and the bellows – or billases – were put into action. The chapel parson was always invited to tea, and the jam was reserved for him. There was always a prayer at the meal and woe betide any small person who fell asleep.

In the family field were chickens and a donkey, with a mind of its own. In the summer the boys slept out under canvas with a tent they had all clubbed together to buy, a 1919 ex-army one, and they often slept in the cart. All the water was drawn from the well, where in the hot summer days the milk and butter were lowered for coolness.

My father started school at four years old and left at twelve years old; although passing for the grammar school, he was needed to work and bring in money. From the age of nine he had to go to the big house and clean out ashes and clean shoes, before starting school.

There was always a special day with races and a flower show on Empire Day – an uncle who had club feet and lived in the local workhouse, was always brought out for the occasion. Christmas was a stocking with an apple, an orange and some nuts. His mother would make a doll from a wooden peg, and he took it to bed each night!

When working for the local baker, he was allowed to unharness the horse and ride it home at dinnertime. Ironmongery was the next job, delivering to all outlying villages, paraffin, soap, candles etc, again with horse and cart. He recalled one particular day when, calling into one village, no one bought anything. Someone had seen white horses in the sky, an omen that the world was about to end, in which case they weren't going to spend their money!'

WE WERE POOR BUT HAPPY

'Calne, when I was born in 1914, the year in which the Great War began, was a small market town. It was a busy prosperous place, no one earned huge wages but there were very few out of work and, as I grew up, it continued to be a pleasant place to live in.

My father was a cheerful, whistling postman. My mother was parlourmaid at The Grange, home of a member of the Harris family of sausage, pie and bacon fame. We were poor but happy.

In 1914 my father was on town delivery, but in earlier years he walked from Calne to Avebury, with his sack of letters over his shoulder (not so much post then). There he delivered, then collected Avebury letters in his sack and returned to Calne. After a short time he graduated to a solid tyre bicycle and then, after delivering the letters in Avebury, he worked a few hours in the vicarage garden, collected the Avebury letters again, and cycled back to Calne post office. After many years the people of Avebury presented him with a silver teapot, with his name engraved on it. Calne to Avebury is about six miles.

My very first memory is of screaming with fright at the sound of the tramp, tramp, tramp, of the prisoners of war as they passed our house into the quarry, which is now St Mary's school, to work on the quarrying of the stone and the working of the lime kiln. The prisoners were brought into Calne from Yatesbury by transport of some kind and deposited at their various places of work each morning, returning each evening. As I grew older the war, of course, ended, and the next thing I remember is the tramps, who passed on their way to the workhouse, which was also in the quarry but has now been pulled down. The workhouse was a strongly built edifice, not much comfort inside, and the floors were all stone – all, I expect, dug from the quarry. The tramps had to be at the lodge gate by six in the evening if they required shelter for the night, and before the meal that was provided for them they had certain jobs to do, and also again in the morning before they left. Most of them were respectable people who had fallen on hard times and my parents taught us to treat them with respect. There were several families residing in the workhouse and my mother would go to visit when possible and take a little treat of some kind. It was nothing expensive as we had little to spare, but she made lots of jam and cakes, which were a tasty addition to their spartan fare. As we children grew older, we were encouraged to go to the workhouse and entertain the residents with short plays and recitals of poems or songs. This is how I know how cold and uncomfortable the conditions were. There was a bell tower, and the bell would ring out every evening at eight o'clock when everyone had to be in bed. The children attended the Calne schools and so we met them quite a lot.

A little way past the workhouse was what we called the Fever Hospital. I spent six weeks in it with scarlet fever, being taken there from home in the horse-drawn Black Maria, a horrible black van. Years after the hospital was disposed of I was out hiking in the Calstone area and there it was, the Black Maria, dumped in a ditch against a hedge.

People who were not ill enough to be taken to hospital but at the same time needed a quiet environment, had sand strewn outside their houses. I remember seeing this in Church Street and we all walked silently past the house concerned as we made our way to school. There were few cars in 1919 and we children walked in all winds and weather wearing our black button boots, which we needed a button hook for on the days when the school nurse attended to examine us all.

On Saturdays we did chores. We cleaned the brass stair rods, cleaned knives with sandpaper and stain-removing paste, sprinkled used wet tea leaves on the carpets (if any) and swept them up with the dust adhering into a dust pan designed for the purpose. Grates had to be blackleaded, sticks chopped to light the fires for the coming week, vegetables prepared for Sunday lunch.

On Sunday, it was Sunday school in the morning, then on to

church, in the afternoon Sunday school and church in the evening. The family went together, all in our best finery, Father in his suit and trilby hat complete with walking stick and a flower in his buttonhole. In the summer, we would walk over two miles of fields to a country church instead of going to our own parish church. We always called in on Father's cousins on the way and they gave us home-made wine, watered down for us children.

We walked a lot in our youth and thought nothing of two and a half miles to reach the top of the Cherhill Downs, carrying food, drink and a tray on which we would slide down the green slopes, then climb back to the top, ready to slide down again.

In the evening, once a week, we were sent to Beehive. It was the junior branch of the Abstainers. All of us children signed The Pledge, vowing never to touch strong drink, then we were shown slides on a magic lantern. One thing I could never fathom out was the Abstainers' outing. Practically the entire town set off in a special train about six o'clock in the morning for a day at the seaside, returning home about 10 pm by which time all the men were very merry and they had lots of empty bottles in their coat pockets. The Abstainers' outing was very popular.

Once a year we had our Sunday school treat. We all clambered into huge farm carts drawn by strong horses and were taken up to Cherhill White Horse for a picnic. There we would scramble for sweets which the teachers threw into the air. They fell on the ground, into bushes and, if wet, into puddles; none of them were wrapped but how we enjoyed them.

To earn a little money, Mother took in a lodger. Usually it was a teacher from St Mary's school, which was next door to us. For several years though we had the French mistress from the grammar school.

As children, life was so secure and people so honest, it was quite usual for us to go to the town shopping, leaving the house empty and the doors unlocked. In fact, we very seldom locked doors.

Christmas time was sheer magic. On Christmas Eve the town band would divide into sections and tour the town. The handbell ringers also, and groups of carol singers, were about in each street until late in the evening. We would throw back the curtains, open up the doors, and wrapping up warmly we'd go out to join them. This is what I miss and all the possessions and modern appliances, central heating and so on, do not compensate for the joy and friendliness we experienced.

Times were certainly hard, and in the 1920s people earned their money as best they could. One great joy was to see the two young men on stilts walking through the town with a collection box in which we put farthings or halfpennys. They each wore a dark suit and a top hat and white gloves. They appeared approximately once a year and we understood they toured all the towns and villages for miles around. The stilts were very high!

One custom that seems to have died out is the Churching of Women. When my first-born arrived, I went out nowhere until I had been to church to thank God for her safe arrival, in a special service with other mothers.

On New Year's Eve we and friends would take our glass of sherry outside in the back garden and as the bells of the parish church and the Bremhill bells across the fields pealed out their hymns, we would all toast each other's health.

Sometimes during the light evenings each year the Postman's Supper was held at our house. My Dad would play his concertina, some of the postmen would sing, and we children were allowed to sit in the corner and enjoy it all. They were a happy crowd of people.'

WE WERE THE RIFF-RAFF!

'I came to Corsley in the spring of 1924, aged 19. I answered an ad in the local paper and was taken on at Woodcock Farm between Corsley and Frome to do general housework. I never wore a uniform and on my half day off in the week I would walk into Frome or wherever. The roads weren't tarmacked and if a horse and trap came past you got covered in dust. The buses started in about 1925. I earned £28 per year and got my keep; after a while they put it up to £30. I used to go to church on Sunday nights with a few of the girls after I got to know Corsley people and the boys used to be all outside and sometimes we paired off. There was a whole crowd of us and our favourite walk was out to Westbury crossroads. I did go hell for leather to get back by 9.30. I knew a chap in Dilton Marsh who had a motor bike but no side car and I used to sit astride on the back and hold on for dear life.

Bert (who later became my husband) used to work on the same farm and then he left, but when we got to know each other better we used to go to dances up in the Reading Room. A Mr Vaughan came to give us lessons – sixpence a night and his sister played the piano. Now and then, the farmers used to get up a dance for the better class people – we were the riff-raff. They charged two shillings and sixpence so they reckoned the riff-raff wouldn't go, but we saved up our money and went just the same.

Women never went to the pub in them days. If the old ladies wanted a drink, they used to carry their jug down to the Jug and

Bottle in the pub and get a drink called porter and put a tea towel over the jug and carry it home. I can remember going out for a walk with Bert's sister and her husband of a Sunday and the men went and had a drink and we stood in the passageway afraid of our dear lives of being seen having had a drink.

I got a job in Warminster for a year with a widow who kept a grocery shop. She'd come back for her dinner every day, but on half-day – Wednesday – she used to hit the bottle and I didn't like that much. Also she used to count the eggs and I'd never been used to that sort of thing. I said to Bert that I didn't like it much. Bert used to come into Warminster – not into the house – and we went to the pictures one winter for ten weeks straight off to be somewhere in the warm. The pictures were mostly with a piano. In the summer, we used to go on different walks – up on the golf course, out to Longleat. I'd made up my mind to leave and go right up country somewhere, but Bert said, "No, you ain't going away. We're going to get married." That was near on to 1933, so I wasn't in Warminster long.

Jill was born in 1938, which was the year that there were 15 girls born in Corsley and only one boy. When they were babies, there was a centre in the village where we used to get orange juice, before the war. We kept our own fowls and Bert used to go out rabbiting of a Saturday. He'd catch nine or ten and sell them to the butcher chap who came round with a van, for sixpence each. He'd keep a nice one and we'd have a rabbit once a week and a brother-in-law who was a butcher in Warminster used to keep us some back bones. We roasted them; they were lovely; I wish I could get some now.

Everybody was so hard up in those days. Mr Barnard, the grocer over in Chapmanslade, used to come round on a bike and take the orders and get one of the farmers to bring the orders round of an evening on his milk van. I used to walk up to Chapmanslade with the pram – if you had to do it, you did do it. I once owed Mr Barnard 15 shillings for several weeks and he came round and said was I going to pay it? I said I was going to get a job when Jill went to school and I got one in an ammunition factory in Frome making jerry can rings which you had to cut out of black rubber. I'd catch the 9 am bus in and the 4.30 pm back and sometimes I'd bring back a bag of those things and the kids used to do them of an evening to earn a little bit extra.

When things got tight on the railway, we'd only been married for three weeks and Bert was on the dole. Then when Keith was born and Bert went to get his dole we were supposed to get three shillings for the baby. The man said, "You can't have it. What's the child's name?" Bert said we hadn't named him yet and he said, "Well, you

29

can't have the money until you give him a name." He was a proper army man.'

CARDBOARD IN MY SHOES

'My grandfather worked as a gardener on the Badminton Estate for the Duke of Beaufort. He and his friends used to travel there by tricycle from the village of Nettleton.

My father and uncle also had bicycles but preferred to *walk* to Bath and Bristol – but as they feared being laughed at, they used to start off on bikes but hid them behind a hayrick outside the village. I didn't have a bicycle when I was young, but sometimes hired one from Acton Turville which cost sixpence an hour.

Most houses in our village had a pigsty and pigs. Someone would come and kill a pig and the meat would be sold to the villagers. Once a year the Duke of Beaufort would kill deer and the villagers, I was one of them, would go with a dish to collect the dripping – sixpence a dish.

My father worked on a farm, but also worked on the railway, helping to build the line at Badminton. He was a sub ganger. He kept his equipment – detonator, frail, etc, on a shelf in the kitchen. My brother and I dare not touch these things. He was often called out at night.

We lived in a house called Chapel House at Burton, where we had oil lamps and coal fires. We cooked on a kitchen range and had a boilerhouse in the garden.

My mother had a bad heart and never went anywhere without transport. She did work as an upholsterer and gave demonstrations at WIs around Wiltshire. I couldn't go out to work, although my friends went into service, so I didn't have many girl friends in the village. My mother needed me at home to do the housework and the cooking, but sometimes I would deliver telegrams when I was about 16, and would get one shilling and sixpence for a delivery. Sometimes they would also give me an orange drink and sixpence. I also earned seven shillings and sixpence a week (but gave my mother five shillings and was proud to do this). I helped at a poultry place with the fowls and chickens, feeding and cleaning, collecting the eggs and getting the poultry ready for going on contract to a hotel in Coventry. Feeding fowls in winter and having to break the ice for them to drink was not so good . . . also being poor I had to work with some cardboard in my shoes because of holes. Fridays I helped make butter and cheese. I saved up to buy a leather jerkin and a bike.

Sunday was a special day in our house – in fact the chapel used to be known as James's Chapel because there were so many of our family in the congregation . ... ladies in their bonnets and capes, men with their beards. One girl, Queenie, was always immaculately dressed, but her mother made her tuck up her dress when she sat down to keep it nice – the boys in the back used to giggle to see her underwear! The chapel was heated by a slow combustion stove. Music was played on a harmonium (I sometimes used to pump it) but I believe they had earlier used piccolos to accompany the singing. Mother took in preachers who stayed with us. We always prepared Sunday lunch on Saturday; meat and vegetables and the rice pudding were all ready for cooking the following day. After evening service my friends and I would walk around the countryside, stopping off at a friend's house. I *always* had to be home by nine o'clock.

Dad was a lay preacher and church secretary and Mother was Sunday school superintendent. I took a class of about 25 five year olds. The Sunday school outing was in the country somewhere, all taken on a farm waggon with plants on the seats and wreaths of anemones. It was held in a farmer's field behind the chapel . . . tables were spread, and water was heated in an urn.

Sometimes we had a travelling preacher with his caravan. He would stay one to two weeks.

I joined the Duchess of Beaufort's Girl Guides and we met in a hut at Badminton. I took my Cook and Laundress badges and the Commissioner from Weston-super-Mare came and stayed overnight to test me. I remember she dressed for dinner!

The doctor held a surgery in our house on Tuesdays and Fridays, although he usually called in most days just to see us. He would come by horse and carriage.

On Fridays the horse and brake came through the village on its way to Chippenham market. It cost two shillings and sixpence. We had to take an umbrella on dull days but were given a groundsheet to keep us dry. The mail came by horse-drawn vehicle.

I started school at six at Nettleton and Burton school with about 50 pupils. This was during the First World War and I remember the teacher had a big map on the wall and she would trace the movements of the German soldiers . . . it gave me nightmares.'

I REMEMBER THE TIME . . .

'Do you remember when . . ?' How many conversations between old friends have started like that – usually about characters of the past, or small events which left a lasting impression at a young age.

SNOW AND TRAMPS

'The first snowstorm that I recollect was in the year 1925 when I was six years old. The earth was enfolded in a blanket of white and silence. I well recall the beauty and wonder of it all. It caused concern to parents and brothers who worked in nearby Warminster. The blizzard had caused the Frome road to be blocked in many places making it impossible to travel to and fro until the snow plough could arrive and clear a single track. This was done at the earliest possible time, maybe a day or two after the storm. It was a time of excitement for my friends and I. We could not go to school and no doubt the schools were closed. Sheep were buried in the surrounding downlands and other cattle. Many birds died. There was no concern about electrical failures. Most homes were lit by oil lamps and candles. Heating and cooking were done on the old kitchen range. No doubt a very large area of the south was affected.

"I am so tired I could sleep on a clothes line" – how true! A boy of ten years in 1929, I was delivering papers in the early hours of the morning for the first time in Winchester Street, Salisbury. In this street was a lodging house where I had to deliver a paper. Mistaking the door where the paper had to be left, I passed through a side door into what happened to be a large outhouse with a brick floor. To my horror I saw lines stretched from wall to wall with men hanging from the lines sleeping. The lines were passed through the coat sleeves across their backs. I ran from this place at great speed without delivering the paper.

Later I learned that men on the road and tramps used the lodging house, a place to lay their bodies, costing one penny – the line one halfpenny.'

LLOYD GEORGE ON THE WALL

'At Box a local tenant farmer's daughter can recall the agricultural depression of the 1930s. Her father, throughout his farming career, was never "out of the red" and she can remember him taking part-payments of rent to the landlord, who would shout after him down the village street.

My mother recalls the first terrace of small houses with bathrooms built in Box by the Bath and Portland Stone firm. A visitor to one of these houses observed potatoes stored in the bath. This part of Wiltshire was a stronghold of the Liberal Party, and in the parlour downstairs a photograph of Lloyd George hung on the wall, framed in a polished mahogany lavatory seat.'

GRAMPS AND THE UMBRELLA

'When I was young we lived with my grandfather at Beanacre. He lived to be 92 and for the last few years he was bedridden, but kept us all at his beck and call by banging on the floor with a walking stick whenever he wanted anything (the stick being kept beside the bed).

I remember the time my mother decided his bedroom needed redecorating – this was at the time when ceilings were white-washed. Well, after everything was prepared, there was just one problem. What on earth was she going to do with Grandad? He certainly wouldn't appreciate being splashed with whitewash. The bed was covered with a dustsheet but of course she couldn't cover Grandad with it as well.

After some deliberation she went to the cupboard and came back with a large, long black object which she gave to Gramps to hold, and there he sat under his umbrella while Mother whitewashed the ceiling. Everything was going well when who should walk in but the Rev Hemmings, minister of the Melksham Baptist chapel, who never forgot the experience and must have raised many a laugh when relating this story to his friends.'

I'M NOT STOPPING LONG

'Just before the First World War my mother, a petite young lady from the Hants/Sussex border, was visiting her future mother-in-law in Wiltshire and went to the post office to send cards to friends at home. Whilst she was paying for the stamps the postmistress was busy reading her cards! As she was leaving the post office the post-mistress wished her good day and remarked that she was sorry my mother's stays were so short. When she arrived back she asked my grandmother (to be) if there was anything wrong with her stays. On explaining, my grandmother laughed and said she meant she was not stopping long. Over the years this has been a joke in our family – when anyone was leaving some wag would say, "Sorry your stays are short" in what we thought, or hoped, was a Wiltshire accent as we lived in Hampshire.'

MOTHER AND MINNIE

'In the 1930s there lived, in a neat little Victorian house in the centre of the village, an elderly widow with her middle aged single daughter whose name was Minnie.

They both dressed in a fashion more suited to the 1920s. They wore long beige or brown skirts with matching lengthy jackets and hiding any sight of chest or neck were "ecru" modesty vests. Their toques of layered velvet, liberally dotted with small jet hat pins, made their headgear look like Chelsea buns! Tightly furled umbrellas completed the ensemble and, to our childhood eyes, they looked very much like miniature replicas of the more stately Queen Mary.

Minnie lived a very closeted life – Mother ruled her completely, even to the extent of vetting the library books Minnie chose from those available at the little village school. However, once a month

The Seend Giant, Fred Kempster, stood 8 ft 2½ inches tall. He often frightened the local youngsters by chasing them with his stick!

Minnie escaped to attend the recently formed Women's Institute.

One November day, the rector paid his usual call and, over a cup of tea, Mother was regretting the long winter months in front of them. "I do not allow Minnie to go to the WC in the winter," she informed the puzzled and somewhat worried cleric. He was very relieved when his wife, the President of the WI, explained the mistake.'

THE SEEND GIANT

'During the First World War, when I was about six, I remember seeing the Seend Giant. His name was Fred Kempster and he stood 8 ft 2½ inches tall. His brother in law kept the Barge Inn by the canal at Seend Cleeve. When we youngsters came home from school, the Giant used to frighten us by chasing us with his long stick. He lit his cigarette from a gas streetlight, and could reach the bedroom windows from outside. No one remembers where he slept!'

CHURCH AND CHAPEL

Church and chapel were at the heart of every community, and Sunday was a day for rest and worship for the whole family (apart from the women who cooked the meals!). Children went to Sunday school, often twice a day, and the annual treat and outing was eagerly anticipated.

CRICKLADE CHURCHES BETWEEN THE WARS

'During the 1920s and 1930s with a much smaller population, Cricklade was well supplied with places of worship. The town was the proud possessor of two C of E parishes. St Mary's at the north end of the High Street was generally considered to be the "low" church. Its parish must have been one of the smallest in England, stretching as it did only as far as Gas Lane to the south and the canal wharf house and lock house to the north, together with the adjacent lanes. Most Anglicans who lived within that boundary attended St

Mary's. The church was well known to all children who attended Cricklade school between the wars. On certain Saints' Days, all trooped across the road to St Mary's for a lesson on the catechism which lasted for about an hour, after which all were allowed home for the rest of the day. This celebration of Saints' Days was a cause of annoyance to nonconformist parents, who regarded this as almost a popish practice!

The remainder of the town of Cricklade, together with Chelworth, formed St Sampson's parish. St Sampson's, with its massive tower dating from the Reformation, dominates the skyline of the town and surrounding area. Similarly it has always had a prominent place in the ecclesiastical life of the community. The vicar during the 1920s and 1930s was a colourful character, Dr Richards, who lived at the vicarage (now known as Candletrees) in Bath Road. At times he took students who were "cramming" for Oxbridge entrance examinations. These students were a useful asset to the Cricklade Cricket Club as they were often good players and an unknown quantity so far as local village teams were concerned! Dr Richards was an academic, suspected by some of Roman Catholic leanings. His flock arrived one Sunday morning to find all the choir stalls had been painted bright red! A furore resulted and he was eventually persuaded to restore the pews to their original brown. During the war he was also chaplain of South Cerney RAF station.

There were no less than four nonconformist churches, or chapels as they were then usually called. These included the Primitive Methodists, who built a chapel in Calcutt Street, now in use as a doctor's surgery. Victorians had a penchant for giving Old Testament names to nonconformist buildings, the name still to be seen over this building was "Pethahiah" (Whom Jehovah loves). The ethos of the Primitive Methodists was Evangelical and an annual Camp Meeting was held, often in a field in Gas Lane, where North Wall estate now stands. There a farm cart was used as a pulpit and Cricklade Town Band were enlisted to supply music for the hymns. This denomination was strongly opposed to alcohol, and for some years ran a Band of Hope when young people were urged to sign "The Pledge".

The Wesleyan Methodist church (1870) stood alongside the town bridge and the river Thames. My grandparents were members and had many recollections of rural Methodism. One story concerns Mr Charles Ockwell, founder of the gloving business still active in Cricklade. He was apparently a dignified person of considerable status in the town, on Sundays to be seen wearing a top hat and frock coat on his way to church, where he was the organist. His seat at the organ was immediately below the pulpit. A local preacher, noted for an excitable and demonstrative delivery of his sermon, at one point knocked over the pulpit bible onto the unsuspecting organist below. The preacher only faltered momentarily in his peroration to call down, "Don't worry, brother, it's only the word of God!"'

THE CLERGYMAN

'The clergyman occupied an important place in the rural community. Living in some style and comfort, they nevertheless were available in times of need. I remember one, a Mr Teasdale, sitting up all night with my sick brother. Another would spend Saturday evenings in the local pub. After spending some time playing games such as shove ha'penny and dominoes with the other customers, he would leave saying, "See you in church tomorrow!" This would generally have the desired effect. Albeit reluctantly, his drinking companions of the previous evening would take their places in the pews the following day.'

THE PARISH CLERK

'Thomas Pressey, my great uncle, was parish clerk (never known as verger or sexton) at St Nicholas's church, Baydon from 1896 until shortly before his death in 1939. In those days there were three services, plus Sunday school, every Sunday and prior to the 11 am and 6 pm services he regularly chimed the three church bells. This he did by having one rope in each hand while the third he manipulated with his foot in a loop in the end of the rope, so having to stand on one leg. Churchgoers knew how much time they had to get to the services as he stopped chiming the three bells ten minutes before the hour. He then chimed two bells for five minutes each, the second being of a higher tone that the first.

The church was heated by an underground solid fuel stove situated in the centre aisle, the heat rising through a long wide grating. Uncle Tom would light up the stove on Saturday and keep it going until after Sunday evening service. He took his own kindling wood and had to carry the fuel from a shed at the end of the churchyard. When the wind was in a certain direction the grating immediately above the stove would sometimes get red hot. Besides attending to the heating, the hanging brass oil lamps had to be filled, the wicks trimmed and the glasses and globes kept clean.

When a parishioner passed away the whole village knew, as he always tolled the bell. The number of times varied for man, woman or child. The bell was also tolled before and after the funeral service.

People showed their respect for the dead by closing their curtains as the cortège passed their houses and they also stood still with head bowed if in the street as it passed by. The coffin was always taken from the house to the church on a bier which was handled manually, the mourners walking behind. I think Uncle Tom was also the gravedigger. The graves were always mounded and in straight rows. The churchyard was mown by several men, using scythes and hooks.

Another of Uncle's jobs was to look after the church clocks, one being inside and the other outside by which the villagers set their own clocks. In those days very few people owned a wireless set, as it was then called, to get the correct time.

After Uncle Tom's death a cousin taught himself to chime the three bells in the same way as described earlier. He carried on doing so until prevented by ill health and old age.'

THE OLDEST METHODIST CHURCH

'Seagry Methodist church was built in 1825 by two brothers, John and Peter Carey, who also gave the site and a year later built their own cottage against it, and thus saved themselves the cost of a wall. The church was originally built rather low with square windows. In 1875 to celebrate its Golden Jubilee the roof was removed, the wall built six feet high, the present long windows put in and a new roof. Mr Isaac Tyler – 60 years a local preacher who died in 1924 – was heard to quote, "They gave the old lady a new bonnet". They also replaced the old box pews with the present pine seats, all for the grand sum of £82!

Extensive renovations were carried out in 1925 to celebrate the centenary and electric heating was installed in 1963. The organ was rescued from a farmhouse cellar where it remained for 40 years, in 1950. It was originally in Stanton St Quinton parish church. The electric chandeliers were made by a German metal worker in Hildesheim in 1946. They were made in sections and smuggled home in an army kit bag.

Among the worthies who gave life-long support to the chapel was Alfred Baker, who died in 1920 aged nearly 90. He liked to encourage the preacher by interjecting suitable remarks such as "Bless Him" or "Praise Him", as did many of the old timers. Towards the end of his life he became very deaf but this did not stop him. He would watch the preacher to see when he paused for breath then say something he hoped was suitable.

The late George Selwood, a local preacher for over 50 years and Church Secretary for over 40 years, used to delight to tell this tale.

One Sunday morning the preacher, a Doom and Damnation type, had been holding forth about three quarters of an hour and, getting warmed up with much thumping on the pulpit, had consigned all non-Methodists to a very warm and unpleasant future. He said, "And the Devil, that old adversary." He paused to take breath. "Bless Him, praise His holy name," cried Alfred Baker in a very loud voice! Of course, the naughty children started laughing and after a feeble attempt to "shush" them the adults started laughing too. The preacher (who had no sense of humour) proceeded to call down the wrath of heaven on them all for ungodly laughter and merriment in the House of the Lord, closed the service and never went to Seagry to preach again.'

SPECIAL SERVICES

'At Wanborough a service is held every year in February to commemorate Dobbin's Day. In the early 18th century a Mr Brind left a field to the church, the rent from which (plus a grant from two ladies) was to supply all the old inhabitants with bread at that service. People came from all around with pillowcases to collect the loaves. The vicar received a fee of ten shillings to preach the sermon. The service is still held but the loaves are now symbolic bread rolls. An old notice in the church porch still requests ladies to remove their pattens before entering.'

'On Sunday we went to Sunday school held in the village school. The vicar presided for prayers and then we went to various classrooms with our teachers according to our age where we would have our lessons, then proceed to church for Matins if we wished and sat with our families. In the afternoon there was a children's service in the church and we would sing the hymns we had learnt. The service we liked best of all was Ascension Day Flower Service, for we all took bunches of flowers, usually cowslips. They were plentiful then and we gathered them from the banks and my mother made them into cowslip balls which were hung on a ribbon. At the church service we took them up to the sanctuary, where the choirboys put them on large trays which filled the sanctuary floor. Whilst this was happening we all sang the hymn *All things bright and beautiful* as we took our flowers along. These flowers were packed in boxes and sent to the station and put on the train to Paddington and the Children's Hospital. The children here went to the vicarage garden and had a tea of jam sandwiches, seed cake and plain cake, then we played a few games before going home. On Whitsundays

Sundays were reserved for church or chapel, Sunday school, and the leisurely afternoon walk! Dressed in their best, the Telling family set off across Lyneham green.

the girls put on their best white dresses with a coloured sash around the waist, some boys would wear buttonholes in their coats, some flowers in their caps.'

'In most villages where they start a community project they clean out the village pond. In Leigh they moved the church.

For centuries All Saints church had stood in the middle of a field at the end of an unpaved lane, but with the passing vicars the village had radiated outwards and the church stood alone. The vicar in 1898, a forward-looking man, got the necessary permission and the church was taken down. Each stone was numbered so that when they had been hauled to the new site by horse and cart, the church could be painstakingly rebuilt exactly as it was before.

Eventually the work was finished and all that remained in the meadow was the chancel. Every summer on the site of the old church a service is held, attended by many old and new friends of Leigh, with the local silver band to add to the party atmosphere. For one day in the year the chancel loses its name of the "Loneliest Church in Wiltshire".'

40

SUNDAY SCHOOL

'As there was little to do on Sunday in the early part of the century (playing games was taboo!), children were dressed in their best and went to Sunday school. Boys wore black stockings to cover their knees, and stiff collars.'

'When I was a child in Corsley in the 1920s, we used to go to church every Sunday, and Sunday school. We went on Sunday school outings in an old open topped charabanc to Weymouth, for instance, and go on the beach. We'd all have our buckets and spades and we'd think it was marvellous. We used to wear hats to Sunday school and gloves and lace-up boots and black woollen stockings which had to be darned.'

'Most of my early memories are of Bratton Baptist church Sunday school. I think the earliest is of a trip to Orchardleigh near Frome. We infants were in a horse-drawn waggon. I hung my hand over the side to feel the bank of the narrow lane and stung it painfully with nettles!

Soon after, the Sunday school acquired a set of four swing boats which were kept at Reeves' Works during the winter. Then Frank Barnes overhauled them and come summer they were hauled up to the White Horse Hill with the Reeves' water cart and a portable boiler to make tea. There we had our Sunday school treat (it never seemed to be wet on that day!). It was always on a Saturday afternoon at 4 pm, when the Works men were free for half a day. A circle was formed with coffin boards from Reeves' saw mill to sit down on. The two Bratton bakers provided currant and plain bread and butter, currant buns and seed and other cake. Tea over, we could use the boards to slide down the chalk grass slopes of Bratton Castle. The older children dashed to the swing boats and swung together – trying to get high enough to see over the top of White Horse Hill to Bath. Everyone played ring games on the grass – I sent a letter to my love; Twos and Threes; Blind Man's Buff etc.

When it was time to finish, the small children were piled into the waggon while the older ones played Thread the Needle down the castle – a single line holding hands before and behind, trotting forward, the first two forming an arch towards which the last couple ran to pass through, and raise up their arch in turn; this was repeated ever faster until smaller children were being dragged off their feet, when it was time to proceed more soberly.'

'On the chapel Anniversary at Aldbourne every Sunday school

41

attender would say a "piece", and new dresses of white would be worn by the girls. There would be some rivalry between the Wesleyan and Primitive Methodists – their Anniversaries were one week apart! Choir practices lasted over six weeks and each thought they sang the special hymns and anthems better than the other.'

'Sundays were always busy in Salisbury with chapel, church and Sunday school, with one of the most exciting and nerve-wracking events being the Sunday school Anniversary – how big the congregation seemed as one's trembling legs carried one relentlessly up into the pulpit of St Mark's Road chapel and how hard it was to swallow the big lump in one's throat and say the well practised recitation. It was always the boys who were allowed to sing solos, a favourite being *Holy City*. Pretty summer dresses and little flower-trimmed straw hats were the girls' delight and were always kept for "best".

The other highlight was the Sunday school outings, before the war put a stop to them. Excitement grew as we packed trains and buses to be conveyed to the seaside at Bournemouth, Swanage or Weymouth. I still remember the feeling when we came to the top of a hill and saw the sea at Bournemouth, still there after another year! A chorus of voices shouted, "There it is!" I still get that feeling now if I reach the top of a hill and see the sea in the distance.'

'Before the war, Sunday school outings were grand – a trip to Weymouth by train from Bathampton station, but 1939 changed all that. Not many people owned cars then and those who did, unless they were on essential work, had their car upon blocks in the garage and covered with a tarpaulin.

However, in 1940 it was decided we should have our outing as usual. I was about ten years old then and with the others of my age group was given the job of cleaning up one of Farmer Lock's waggons in which we were going to be taken to Warleigh Manor, an afternoon trip with games and tea. The waggon was all spruced up and decorated. We spread the floor with the coconut mats we used when we did our drill (not gym) in the mornings at our primary school, which adjoined Farmer Lock's house and yard and dairy. It was his shire horses which were to pull the waggon.

Time to set off and we were lifted up into the waggon which was quite high. The adults who accompanied us had to walk. It's about two miles to Warleigh Manor from our village along a leafy lane through the woods and then down the drive to the Manor in the valley by the river Avon.

Miss Dorothea Skrine who owned the lovely old house met us

when we arrived. It was a lovely sunny summer day and we had races, games and tea on the lawn. We had little cakes covered in hundreds and thousands, and Eiffel Tower lemonade – no crisps, sweets or Coke in those days.

It's over 50 years ago now but I remember it vividly – not a grand occasion but how we all enjoyed it.'

GETTING ABOUT

When cars were a rarity, we got about by bus, train, bicycle or horse power – or we walked. The buses became regular meeting places for marketgoers and shoppers, as the only link between the towns and outlying hamlets and villages. Trains were our trains, when we knew the driver and the guard, who would hold the train up if they knew we were coming, and could set our clocks by them. And the country railway stations – now they are worth reminiscing about!

GOING TO TOWN

'In the early part of this century, up to about 1910, the only way to get to Salisbury from Netheravon was by carrier's cart. This was really a sort of covered waggon drawn by two horses. At the back it was fitted with hard wooden seats, holding up to half a dozen people. On Tuesdays and Saturdays it went to Salisbury, and to Devizes on Thursdays. It would leave Netheravon at 9 am and reach Salisbury at about 11.30 am, where it would park outside The Chough and the horses would be put in stables behind the inn. The return journey would start about 4 pm and on the way home a stop was always made at the George at Amesbury to give the horses a rest and a feed, and let the driver have some refreshment. The passengers also could stretch their legs and buy a drink if they wished.

Young adults often preferred to make the trip on horseback or bicycle, though the state of the roads made cycling a rather hazardous affair. During the winter when farmwork was at a minimum, farm labourers would be given the job of picking up the big flintstones that littered the fields and piling them up at the roadside. They would then be scattered over the muddy roads to be crushed by heavy farm waggons or occasionally a steam roller would appear on the scene. The sharp flints that resulted in this treatment caused many punctures, and no cyclist thought of travelling without a puncture outfit in his saddlebag. Until granite chips were used with tar to make roads, they were covered with mud in winter and a thick white dust in summer.

The return to town was two shillings, quite a lot of money to people when the average wage in the village was slightly over £1 a week.

A couple of years or so before the outbreak of the First World War, Mr Cave of Netheravon started running a bus to the towns. It was a large cumbersome vehicle, not very comfortable to ride in but, as the fares charged were the same as the carrier's, it always seemed to be full of passengers.'

'In the early days Donhead St Andrew had no public transport and people probably went to Tisbury rather than Shaftesbury. The first transport was bought by the lady of Donhead House. It was a brown bus so it became known as the "chocolate bus", and it travelled through Milkwell to the A30 to Shaftesbury. The bus could be hired by groups who wanted to go to dances or whist drives. Then Mr Blandford from the Brookwater post office bought a large car, almost a minibus, and this also went to Shaftesbury and could be hired like a taxi. It was a black car so we called it the Black Maria. Eventually the W&D began a service through the village which made travelling much easier, but today the buses are not very frequent.'

'I came to Biddestone village in the late 1940s. It hadn't altered much and transport was still mainly by bicycle. There was a bus service, in a vehicle with wooden slatted seats, ninepence return to Chippenham, and the driver knew all his passengers by name and if one lady was not at her usual stop he'd ask if she was alright.'

THE OLD FIRM

'It was in 1928 when at the age of eight I came to live in Wroughton, but attended a school in Swindon, that I came to know and love the local bus service. It was called "The Old Firm" and was privately owned. When I started my daily ride to school we called the bus "The covered waggon". This was because the driver sat in the front with one passenger and behind were two benches along each side, the whole being covered with a canvas top and you had to go up two steps to get in. Later on these buses were superseded by more modern ones.

The fare for a child was a penny ha'penny from Wroughton to Swindon Town Hall. Sometimes coming home we would walk up the hill to Old Town. From here to Wroughton was only one penny so we could spend the halfpenny on sweets.

The buses went every 15 or 20 minutes according to the time of day, starting at 7 am for the railwaymen to get to work and ending at 11 pm for the convenience of the cinemagoers. In those early days you could stop the bus anywhere and if you lived on the bus route even alight outside your own home. Staffing of the buses was mostly by the Hawkins family. The owner, Mr Ted Hawkins, had a large family and out of it four sons were drivers and two of the girls were conductors. During the war one of the girls became a driver.

It was such fun in those days and when I left school I worked in Swindon so still used The Old Firm. One got on the bus, looked round and sat by the person who looked the most interesting! Everyone knew everyone else then.

A big link with the past disappeared when The Old Firm was taken over by the Bristol Tramways and Carriage Company in July 1955 but the memories linger on.'

MISSING THE LAST BUS

'In 1940 the railway fare from London to Dinton was about £1 return, and the bus fare to Salisbury was one shilling and sixpence return. The single-decker was always packed and everyone had a good laugh and chat, meeting up with friends and neighbours.

In 1949 a friend and I decided we would like to go to the Salisbury theatre one evening to see John Hanson in *The Desert Song*. We caught the bus to Salisbury that evening, and enjoyed the show so much that we missed the last bus home at 9.30 pm. There was petrol rationing, but we managed to get a lift in a car (we wouldn't do that nowadays!) and we were dropped at Barford St Martin, at least three miles away from Dinton crossroads. We just had to put our best feet forward and walk, in high heeled court shoes. Nothing passed us on the road either way, and so we staggered, fortunately in the moonlight, along the woody road. The Dinton church clock struck midnight as we reached the beginning of Dinton village, and with our hearts in our mouths, expected our husbands to be out looking for us. But to our great surprise and disbelief, all were nicely tucked up in bed and fast asleep!'

CAR!

'When I was a little boy at about the time of the First World War,

The first petrol pump to be installed in West Lavington in the 1930s. Mr Holliday stored the petrol in two-gallon cans in a special shed in the garden, with a ditch all round in case of fire.

my brother and I were down by the ford near Barford St Martin bridge when this monster with two great eyes approached the bridge. I was so frightened I fell into the river and had to be rescued by my brother. It was a Scout car, actually made in Salisbury.'

'A great change over the years has been the volume of traffic. In about 1946 at Worton, the gate at Ibsens, next to the old post office, was recessed from the straight main road through the village. This made an admirable goal for the young boys to practise football. Worton had a football team in those days. If a vehicle came in sight there would be a cry of 'Car!" and all would scatter to the sides and let it pass. What an amazing difference from today, when the amount of traffic would make such activities completely impossible and very dangerous.'

WE SET OUR CLOCKS BY THEM

'In the 1920s at Purton, the trains were so punctual my grandfather set the clocks by them. I remember rushing along to the level crossing manned by friendly Mr Hancock just to see the beautiful Cheltenham Flyer at ten to four every afternoon.'

'I travelled on the eight o'clock train from Highworth to Swindon every day in the late 1920s, going to school in the "care" of older girls and boys. The train stopped at Hannington, Stanton and

46

Stratton St Margaret on the way, picking up schoolchildren and office workers. The earlier seven o'clock train was the workmen's train, the chief employer for miles around being the Great Western Railway. Those seven miles from Highworth to Swindon took one hour on the train, but it was a real service for the villages on the way and it allowed precious time for homework and help from older friends! The train was called the Highworth Bunk and I remember one morning being at least 200 yards from the station when the train was due to go. Everybody was waving at me from the windows and the stationmaster, Mr Mant, was shouting, "Come on, Margaret"; well, I made it and was hauled onto the train. I can't imagine that happening today!'

'I used to travel to school in Salisbury by train from Porton in the 1940s. Many were the times I had to run up Station Hill because I was late. The kind engine driver would whistle the train for me, laughing and joking as I made it. This was not a local train, but the train from London.'

'Travelling by train in the 1920s and 1930s was a great event. Living in Pans Lane, Devizes, I knew the time of every train throughout the day and one's life became programmed by them – 7.20 am up train: time to get out of bed; 2.30 pm up train to London: nearly time for dinner; 8.30 pm down train from London: in bed and lights out when the 9 pm Curfew Bell rang from St John's church.

Going to the station to meet a much loved aunt was a joy. Standing on the down platform with eyes fixed on the tunnel opening under the Castle mount, the signal going down would tell me the train was nearly in and then with a big puff of smoke the engine glided out of the tunnel pulling its long string of chocolate and cream carriages. Having been reunited with Auntie Kitty, the next scramble would be to obtain the service of the "Outside Porter" who would take cases and trunks on his truck anywhere in the town for sixpence a time.

In the mid 1930s it was possible to get the down trains from London to stop at Pans Lane halt, which was such a help to people living in the south of the town. One had to tell the guard before Patney Junction was left – I'm told it cost the GWR seven shillings and sixpence to stop and restart the engine for this service for passengers.'

'Our home at Pewsey was within easy walking distance of the railway station, and in 1951 we could go by train to Devizes 15 miles away for a morning's shopping, stopping at all the pretty country stations on the way, and get back easily before the children came out of school. If only it were still like that!'

CHIPPENHAM STATION 1945

'My father was a booking clerk on Chippenham station for many years. His name was Ben and my brother and I were known as "Ben's children".

At least once a week we were allowed to take my father his sandwiches, and when Dad knew there was a special train coming through, we used to do just that. It was so exciting to us. I am quite sure the children of today would never appreciate the anticipation and pleasure the whole thing gave us.

The journey to the station was not far, but even that was exciting – it used to take us (although I'm quite sure now it need not have done) through the churchyard and we used to go that way especially to see "Butler's Finger". I must explain this was a granite-type grave with a tall pillar, with just a hand on top with a single finger pointing to heaven. The name on the grave was Butler and we used to stand and gaze at Butler's Finger with great wonder; sometimes we used to pick celandines and put them on the grave. This spot gave my brother and I great pleasure. Then we would proceed to the railway station across the wooden bridge and wait for a train to come and all the steam would come up through the wooden slats on the bridge and we would laugh and shout in the mist.

On we went, down the steps to the station and finally to the ticket office, then we would wait in great anticipation until Father caught sight of us, and then again we would have to wait very patiently until we heard the keys rattle and Father would unlock the little wooden door and we delivered the sandwiches.

Sometimes we were allowed to stand inside and watch my father punch the tickets and take the money – I must explain it was nothing like the grand booking office of today. On the few occasions when I have returned I have had some difficulty in trying to decide where that small wooden office with the hand-punch ticket machine used to be, but my brother and I thought it was wonderful!

Then the porter used to take us onto the platform – the final climax, we were really excited by now, jumping up and down and then being really quiet listening for that whistle, the signals down and then we could hear the thunder of the train, the shaking of the ground and here it comes! – white smoke, loud whistle, thundering straight through the station.

Then, back to the ticket office we went, Father looking out of the little window telling us to go straight home and not to be late as

Mother would be waiting – and we would do just that, running most of the way.

I feel, perhaps, I should leave my story there but I can't resist telling you one more memory. Harris's of Calne moved some of their factory to Chippenham, it later became known as the Wiltshire Bacon Factory. This brought another little bit of excitement to "Ben's children".

Father said one day, "How would you like to see the pigs at the station?" "Pigs!" we said, "Pigs!" We just couldn't believe it. So down to the station we went, we never even stopped to see Butler's Finger, or to jump up and down in the steam. We just couldn't wait to see the pigs.

We went through our usual procedure and much to our surprise Father locked the little wooden office and came with us. What an occasion this was, down to the railway siding we went and we could hear the pigs squealing and squealing and we could see their pink snouts coming through the wooden slats. When we asked Father why they were making so much noise he told us they were excited to come and see the trains. Of course, when I got older (as we all do) I learned the horrible truth and it made my brother and I cry. We learned they had gone to be killed just to make bacon.'

BEDWYN STATION 1951

'I moved to the Bedwyn area in 1951 and my memories of Wiltshire begin then. I remember Bedwyn station in those days, a Victorian brick building containing ticket office, porter's rest room and passengers' waiting room. Adjoining this were two toilets, basic but adequate. On the opposite side of the railway lines were the signalbox and a smaller, less elaborate, waiting room. There were two bays/sidings on the up side. A great deal of goods were handled there. Local hay, straw parcels of all shapes and sizes and the important daily despatch of milk (in old fashioned metal churns). The local farmers made full use of the goods yard. At that time a station-master, two porters, a goods lorry driver and three signalmen were employed at the station.

During the cold weather a fire was lit in the waiting room. If this was not always burning brightly the porters would allow waiting passengers into their rest room which was sure to be warm. One could always walk along the platform, maybe admiring the flower beds alongside, or wave to the man on duty in the signalbox, who at quiet times would open a window and pass the time of day. The exit from the down platform was by a series of steep steps to the road above – I must explain there are two hump-backed bridges here, one that arches high over the railway lines and another that goes over the canal, drivers need to exercise extreme care on this piece of road. There was also a footway across the line to the main gate. I am not sure if it was strictly legal to use it but, of course, everyone did. It is not possible to cross the line at this point now, strictly prohibited and highly dangerous with electric rails in use. We climb a steep path, tiring and difficult if one is carrying shopping bags or pulling a trolley.

After the passengers had alighted, the train would carry on a few hundred yards, crossing the lines and reversing into a siding and then returning to the up platform of the station. Local trains still do this. In those days we could take a train and travel westwards from Bedwyn. Nowadays we go to Newbury and change, then back along the line and wave to Bedwyn as we pass through. Older inhabitants have told me they would take the train to Swindon on a Saturday afternoon, changing at Savernake from Low Level station. There they would be time to shop or watch football at the County Ground with a visit to the old Empire Theatre or a cinema in the evening and maybe some liquid refreshment before catching the train back home.

The station was staffed until 1964. Gradually the buildings were demolished, the goods sidings covered and new lines laid. The waiting room etc has been replaced by a flimsy shelter and we pay for our tickets on the train.

There is much of the old station memorabilia in the possession of local residents. One of the station nameplates hangs in a nearby house and wood from the steps has been used for wonderfully hard-wearing kitchen surfaces. Two semaphore signal arms now grace an entrance hall.

The late Sir Felix Pole, former Chairman of Great Western Railway, lived in the village for many years. His father, Edward Pole, was headmaster at Little Bedwyn and Great Bedwyn schools. The Felix Pole Trust Fund in memory of his father still provides a bible for each child when he or she leaves Great Bedwyn school. Little Bedwyn school closed some years ago.

Bedwyn railway won the National Award for Best Kept Station in 1962 and 1963. The linesmen also won an award for the best kept length of line between Bedwyn and Hungerford.'

HOUSE & HOME

THE WAY WE LIVED THEN

Though today many of them are picturesque cottages, yesterday's homes were far from comfortable. Overcrowding was common in farm cottages, there were no 'mod cons' and they could be very cold in winter. Yet we took such things for granted – though few would want to return to those good old days!

THE TIED COTTAGE

'I was born 71 years ago, in a small village called Winterbourne Monkton, only a mile away from Avebury and its famous stone circle.

Our cottage was a few yards away from our local pub, the New Inn, which is still there today, but greatly altered. Spirits of all kinds are sold there now, instead of draught beer from the barrels kept in the cellar. The floor used to be bare boards, with spittoons underneath the wooden seats for the men to spit in. The Jug and Bottle has long gone. It was a little square lean-to, on the side, where the women used to get their husbands' beer, in a jug or bottle. On Saturday nights, the villagers danced outside the pub to the strains of *Moonlight and Roses*, played on an accordian by one of the locals. There was very little money in those days and they had to make their own amusement.

The houses in the village were all farm cottages and went with the jobs on the farms. The consisted of one living room and pantry, one bedroom and landing. My sister and I slept on the landing.

Most of the houses were thatched. A large family lived in the end one from us, with six children. Four boys and two girls. They solved the problem by some sleeping at the top, and some at the bottom of the bed.

At the bottom of the garden was the toilet, or privy, which consisted of a long seat with two holes, one for adults and one for children. There were three of these, one for each house, but all the waste went into a large pit at the back which they called the vault. I can remember the men cleaning the vault twice a year. Digging out, they called it. Toilet paper was newspaper, cut into squares and hung on a piece of string behind the door.

When I was seven years old, the three cottages caught fire; I remember as if it was yesterday. My friend and I had been to the farm to fetch the milk, and then we were going to have our tea out in the fields. It was a boiling hot day in July and a lady came running over the bridge to phone the fire brigade. The farmers were the only ones who had phones in the village then. I rushed home terrified. The houses were an inferno, and the only water avilable was from the well.

My mother was sitting at the bottom of the garden with a few belongings around her which they managed to save. We lost all our clothes, and I still remember how shocked she was.

From that day I am still scared of fire. It was thought that maybe it was caused by a piece of glass on the thatched roof. Houses were very hard to get in the village as they were all tied with the jobs.

Shifting days as they were called were at Michaelmas and in March. But if you didn't suit the farmer you could be turned out without any notice. Thankfully, tied cottages are done away with today and other accommodation has to be found for the family.'

'I spent my childhood in a small farm cottage in the village of Charlton All Saints about five miles from Salisbury. Ours was the end of a block of four and was made of red brick with a porch around the front door. This led directly into the living room with the staircase facing you as you went in. A door opened with a latch to the stairs that were dark and creepy, up about three, then round a corner (with who knows what lurking there!) and on up to a small landing with three bedrooms leading off. All the rooms had a sloping cellIng with a dormer window set into the roof. All the windows in the cottage had diamond-patterned panes which took ages to clean in all the corners and made our fingers sore! The largest front bedroom had a small fireplace in one corner and when it was very cold or if either my sister or I was ill, Mother would light a fire and we would sit there wrapped in a patchwork blanket.

Back downstairs, the living room was L-shaped around the cupboard under the stairs, which housed the boots and shoes, coats, bags of potatoes, dustpans and brushes – and large spiders!

The floor of the living room was bricks and was made cosy with rag rugs which were made from old clothes cut into strips and threaded through sacking, these were lovely and thick and warm.

In the far corner was the blackleaded kitchen range above which was a high mantelpiece with a line stretched underneath where Mother would hang clothes to dry and where we would hang our long hand-knitted woollen stockings on Christmas Eve. Always on Christmas morning these would be filled with small parcels and in the toe would be an apple, an orange, a few nuts and sweets and a shiny new penny.

53

In the hearth Mother kept the flatirons that had to be heated on the fire on ironing day, and kettles would always be hot on top of the range.

To the right of the fireplace was a large dresser next to which stood the wireless with its valves and accumulators and things and we could listen to *ITMA* and *Dick Barton*. We also had a gramophone we could wind up and listen to old records. A couch stood under the window and a large table and chairs were in the middle of the room and two wooden armchairs stood either side of the fireplace.

A door led from this room into the washhouse with a copper in one corner and every Monday morning Dad would fill this with water and light the fire underneath before he went to work.

All water had to be carried into the house from an outside pump shared by all four cottages, and in winter this would freeze, even though it was packed around with sacking. Then the men would take turns to pump furiously while pouring in warm water, to start the pump working.

To the left of the washhouse was the pantry where the food was kept and also a large galvanised bath and three buckets of water which was our outdoor water supply. Washing up was done in a bowl on the kitchen table and bathtime was a large bath in front of the kitchen range while our "loo" was either a pot under the bed or a long walk to the bottom of the garden, which was not very pleasant on a dark, wet and windy night.

Father grew most of our vegetables in the large garden and Mother made lots of gooseberry and raspberry jam with the produce. Meat rationing was helped with rabbits and pigeons Father could catch on the farm and the occasional pheasant, or "long-tailed pigeon" as they were called!

It was an idyllic life for a child with long summer days spent mostly outside in the fields and meadows and cold winters tucked in bed with a hot brick or roasting chestnuts by the fire. Picking masses of wild primroses and violets to decorate the church at Easter and learning to swim in the river. Blackberrying and gathering nuts in the autumn and picking wild rose hips for syrup. Giving a few pennies to the hurdy gurdy man with his little monkey or the barrel-organ, or buying an ice cream from the "Stop me and buy one" man on his bicycle. Life was free and easy for a child in the country in the 1930s.'

A HARD LIFE

'I don't remember my childhood with affection. One of 18 children, 15 of whom still survive, life for me was hard and pleasures few. My

In July 1939 an advertisement offers to make every 'country woman's dream come true' – by installing calor gas for lighting, heating and cooking. Most country homes were still dependent on oil lamps or candles, the old blackleaded range and open coal fires.

father did nothing around the home, nor was expected to. This work was for my mother and the children. My spare time was spent working on the allotments in the evening, for our diet consisted mainly of vegetables. I was also responsible for drawing water from the well. In 21 years my mother had 22 children. No help came from the State, it all had to come from within the family.

The children slept eight to a bed, four at the top and four at the bottom. Often we were cold and hungry. The cottage was damp, the walls made of wattle and daub. Downstairs the floors were of brick. Such was the shortage of bedding that at night coats were placed on the beds to provide an extra layer. Only when the wind was in the right direction would the fire draw, and coal cost two shillings a bag.

My father's wages were 30 shillings a week. After rent and insurance, 26 shillings and threepence remained, of which he spent a shilling a day on cigarettes. We, meanwhile, had to eat stale bread as this was cheaper to buy. I well remember the pleasure of buying clothes once I became a wage earner. Those were the first new clothes I had ever worn.'

THE FARMHOUSE

'Our house was not as large as some Wiltshire farmhouses, but was wholly delightful. For one thing, it was in a lovely peaceful setting, with trees and hedges round the fields. It was built of stone from Ashcombe House which was being demolished. There was a handsome front door, an Adams mantelpiece in the dining room, and some fine panelling on the front landing. There were five bedrooms on the first floor and three good attic rooms. We had one bathroom on the first floor.

The kitchen was large with a brick floor and racks on the ceiling for storing bacon. There was an old dresser and a large kitchen range which had to be polished with blacklead every day. There was a row of bells in one corner – each of which would sound a different note. Next to the kitchen was a walk-in larder. We also had a fair sized cellar.

Washing was done in my grandmother's time in two large coppers in the back kitchen by a lady from one of the cottages. Beside the coppers was an old bread oven, under which was a long cavity in which a faggot could be burnt. This had not been used for many years. It would have baked many loaves.

At the back was a courtyard, and in the outside yard was the coach house, tack room, two large stalls and two loose-boxes with a passage in front. There was also the very old barn. It had walls about three feet thick. Twice I remember my grandmother having it rethatched. In the centre of the yard in front of the barn, was a 16th century timber framed granary – also thatched. Steps up to it made a useful mounting block.

The front garden was of lawns and narrow flower borders. I can still smell the heliotrope which one of my aunts planted there. The kitchen garden was large and had a wall at one side facing south. Here were old moss roses and right at the bottom two cucumber frames. Along the bottom wall with a gate into the orchard were plum trees – Victorias and green and golden ones. The other side backed the carthorse stables and at the bottom was the potting shed. Under the stable wall were black, white and red currants. We also grew several kinds of apples and pears, loganberries, cherries and gooseberries in abundance. It was such good soil and all kinds of vegetables did well. We won prizes for them.'

FACING THE HIGH STREET

'My father and mother and five daughters and son lived in a house which was once two thatched cottages, then later had a slated roof, with three front bedrooms facing the High Street at West Lavington, and two back bedrooms, one of which was converted to a bathroom and Elsan lavatory. The ceilings were low with a beam across the centre of each ceiling.

The ground floor had a front hall leading into a sitting room and dining-cum-living room, while at the back a passage led to the back door, kitchen and large walk-in larder. In the corner of the larder was a small alcove where there was a well, but this was cemented over in our day.

There was no damp course in the upright walls of the house except some ventilators at floor level in the front of the ground floor rooms. The outside walls of the back consisted of chalk and brick, and the kitchen floor was below ground level at the back; it had a square brick tiled floor. The flagstone at the back entrance and passage had a cement floor, the larder square flagstones, and the front entrance brick floor covered with matting. The sitting room floor was of wood, and there was an old fashioned fireplace and glass mantelpiece, a suite of chairs of oak and velvet seats and two armchairs upholstered. There were pictures on the walls of scenery, and lots of family photographs on the piano – removed when we had a sing-song together. The dining-cum-living room had large pictures on the wall. All the walls were papered up and down except the kitchen, and that was colour-washed. We had a coal range for cooking, with a boiler for hot water one end. Later we had a Valor cooking stove heated by paraffin oil, which had to be replenished every day. The dining room had a lamp suspended on the middle of the beam and gave plenty of light for reading, homework etc and games.

We all had candlesticks for our bedroom lights. My mother used to make a mark round my candle for I liked reading in bed and when the candle burnt down to the mark I blew the candle out. We all had candles, washbasins and chamber pots in the bedroom which were used at night. In the daylight and when we were up in the morning the outside lavatory was used. It was about twelve yards from the back door and was a two seater, one for adults and one for children which had a step on which to rest short legs. In the winter, especially if wet, it was difficult to keep a candle alight. When torches were invented it was far more convenient, but we did have a lantern hung over the back door at night which gave out a good light so far. The building was concealed by a lot of ivy around the path to it.'

THE DAILY ROUTINE

It was well said that a woman's work was never done! The household routine was adhered to in houses large and small – starting every week with that mammoth task of Washday. How many prayers must have gone up on a Sunday for a dry day tomorrow, as the treadmill of soaking, washing, blueing, starching, mangling, drying and ironing came round yet again.

WASHDAY

'Ask any housewife what she did on Monday and one could guarantee "the wash" would be her response. Planning the routine influenced the whole week. If you were lucky you'd a set of three – vests, pants, etc; the principle involved being a pair on, one in the wash and one ready to wear, all basic and functional in design and shape.

Regardless of weather, Monday was "the day". Preparations started on Sunday with soaking the mainly cotton garments overnight. They were collected following a sequence of family baths.

One prepared a fire under the copper or boiler and filled it with water in readiness for an early start. Bar soap was used, either grated for easy dissolving, or blocks for rubbing on to the clothes in readiness for knuckle rubbing or use on the corrugated wash board. The clothes were methodically rubbed up and down to clean them. I suspect this also speeded their wearing out. (Yes, the same contraption used by skiffle groups in the 1950s and 1960s.) Finish was enhanced by starch made in a similar process to custard – by blending starch granules, cold water and then boiling water until the starch grains burst and it thickened – and woe betide you if it was lumpy!

Rinsing was a cold laborious task made harder by hard water scum that automatically formed with soap, as we'd no soapless, powdered or liquid detergents pre-treated and specially formulated for the fabrics, wash and type of water hardness – in fact the quantity of soap used to gain a lather in hard water areas was considerable.

The type and design of garments reduced the wash. There were a variety of detachable collars and cuffs which were changed and so extended the wearing time of the garment. A shirt lasted several days and males tussled with front and back studs to secure the collars.

Easy care and modern luxury fabrics were unheard of. Some people had pure silk undies, and during the war parachute remains or pieces were greatly coveted, and fantastic creations designed. I remember so many of the pieces were on the cross weave.

There was a rather temperamental type of rayon termed "artificial silk" that we prized, but it needed careful washing and alas all too often an over-warm iron created a self shape hole in the garment.

Cleaned and rinsed clothes were wrung out by hand and then mangled. What an art! First keep your fingers clear, second fold the articles carefully around the flat buttons and feed them through the rollers. Inevitably some buttons always got smashed and mangles had the nickname of "button busters"!

On a good day if you'd been really efficient your clothes were billowing out on the line before anyone else's. Wet days were a steamy damp drudgery, as clothes were draped on clothes horse and pulleys, all in readiness for the ironing on Tuesday.

Ironing was quite a skill, flatirons being the order of the day. They were either heated on the range or cooker, or one put lumps of burning embers into an inner cavity that was locked in at the iron heel. Some modern town housewives had an iron on a flexible gas pipe with a controlled flame inside. All had to be kept burnished on the base by scouring on bath brick and polishing cloth. With no thermostats, irons were tested by a splash of water flicked onto the sole, and according to the degree of heat, a specific sounding spit or hiss ensued. They did a good job, being heavy and held in a padded iron holder. Thinking of iron holders, many youngsters learned early needlecraft stitches on such creations. But the dreaded iron mould was an ever-present threat.

Against all the odds housewives achieved excellent results and had every reason for pride in their work.'

THE VILLAGE LAUNDRY

'In a hut at the bottom of the garden at Cuckoo's Green was a laundry. This was owned by Mrs Caroline Bodman who employed seven villagers. All wearing clogs and coarse aprons, they started work by pumping water from an outside pump into buckets, filling two large boilers which were heated by coal fires. When the pump was frozen, water had to be collected from the brook at the bottom of the garden.

The clothes were wrung by hand before there were hand-operated mangles, then all hung out on lines outside to dry, but if it was wet there was a tin hut used as a drying room.

Next came the ironing. Twelve flat irons were in use, being heated on top of the stoves. Mrs Bodman did intricate ironing using a goffering iron; she also did all the sorting of the laundry before it was packed into wicker hampers and some small boxes.

Mrs and Mrs Bodman made all the deliveries by motorbike and sidecar to houses in Worton and surrounding villages, helped by their young daughter. All this in the days of no washing machines, no tumble driers, no electric irons!'

A WOMAN'S WORK

'My mother in law's childhood memories are dominated by recollections of housework. By today's standards cleanliness was an obsession. In her farmhouse home at Erlestone, near Devizes, carpets had to be painstakingly brushed every day with a dustpan and brush and rugs shaken. Every week mattresses on the beds were turned and swept. The blankets had to be shaken. In the garden nothing could be wasted and she remembers stirring jam for what appeared to be hours on end.'

'My mother had to help outside on the farm at Seend with the haymaking, with hand rake or hay fork for loading the waggons, and on the hayrick taking in the hay from the elevator whilst Father made the rick. Sometimes I would drive the two shire horses with the waggon – trying to make sure that they did not slip on my feet! Another of my mother's jobs was to wash all the dairy buckets or pails after the men had finished hand milking the cows in those days. This operation was done in a large tank or wash tub in an open sided shed – very cold in the winter. The water was carried from the boilers or hand pumped from the well. The milk was cooled over an open cooler with water from the well, which was ten degrees cooler than the spring water in the summer. In later years water from a spring which rose on the farm was pumped to the house or the yard for the pigs and cattle which was a great help to my parents. Before that I well remember having to take the cows, about six at a time, to drink from a nearby pond – after having to break the ice! They would then return to the sheds to be tethered all night, making use of the hay or straw for bedding.

Mother did all the cooking on a black range in the kitchen (how it smoked!) and made jams and chutneys. She made very good cakes – no temperature gauges in those days, she just tried the oven with her hand and declared it to be "just right" or not, as the case may be. Also the two boilers were in the corner and had to be filled with water from the pump over a well in the courtyard outside on the northeast side of the house. This we had to do in all winds and weathers. Every Monday was washday, so the boiler was filled early and the fire underneath stoked with various sticks and rubbish that had accumulated over the past week as no one could afford coal – that was kept just for the cooker. The very dirty clothes such as towels and Father's clothes – which were worn in the yard, milking cows, muck spreading and the like – were put in to soak overnight. These were all washed in galvanised baths before being put into the copper for boiling, then rinsed in rainwater when available, and later pegged out on the clothes line across the garden. Practically all the floors downstairs were stone and the kitchen had to be scrubbed twice a week. There were two rooms called a dairy and cheeseroom with shelves all around where the grandparents had made cheese – we only made butter, an arm aching job! Every room would be turned out for spring cleaning. The carpets were brought down from the bedrooms and put on the lawn and beaten, brushed or shampooed, rolled up and taken back in the evening. What a turn out!

The WC, or lavatory, was up the garden path. It had accommodation for three seats and Mother and I would sometimes be there together. We think Father would belatedly read the newspaper – no toilet rolls then! A cousin tells me that he lost many pairs of braces down that hole!'

'Washday was generally on a Monday and we knew that for dinner it would be cold meat from the remains of the Sunday joint and bubble and squeak, the fried leftovers of vegetables. Monday was really a hard day for Mother.

Stone sinks were used in the early days for washing up. I can remember how the grease from the pots and pans would coat the sides of the sink. We used to put soda in the water to remove the grease and you can imagine how careworn our hands would get.

Cleaning the silver (plated) was another chore. Every Saturday morning all the cutlery had to be cleaned – the worst job was the cruet set, all corners and knobs. The boys also cleaned all the household shoes and boots.'

'The household chores at our farm in Marstone included the making of the feather beds, which one shook every morning to make them level and comfortable. Then the pail was taken upstairs and all the pots and washbasins emptied. That was taken into the garden in the spring and carefully put around the spring cabbage plants (a nice drop of liquid).

Saturday nights were bath nights and during the week it was a wash in the bowl or sink in the kitchen. Our water came from a well in the garden.

The grates were cleaned once a week with blacklead – what a dirty job that was.

Monday was washday, and Tuesday was ironing day when the flatirons were heated on the range or on a trivet in front of the fire.

On Wednesdays the eggs were cleaned and counted in dozens and put in boxes ready to be taken on Thursdays to Devizes market in our pony and trap. Sometimes hens and a few wild rabbits would also be taken, as were calves, cows and pigs. The cattle market was held in Devizes Market Place. It was quite a large market in those days and Thursday was also the weekly shopping day with two bus companies running services from here.'

NO MOD CONS!

Before piped water and electricity came to our homes, we drew our water from a well, spring or pump, lit the evenings with gas mantles or oil lamps, and cooked on solid fuel stoves or open fires. Oh, the delight with which we greeted our first mod cons!

WATER FROM THE WELL

'The drinking water on our poultry farm at Baydon, near Marlborough, in the 1920s was obtained from a well of spring water 380 ft deep, which was drawn in eight-gallon casks. One cask went down as the other came up; it took eight minutes to reach the surface and this was done by hand. Another storage tank at the end of the house, which held 600 gallons for general use, was drawn by a pump in the kitchen.'

'I live in a house in Wingfield built in the 1880s. For a few years in the 1980s, I was lucky enough to correspond with the youngest daughter of the farmer who had originally built and lived in it. It was a smallish house, three up, three down, with eight people living in it – mother, father, and six children. However, each room has at least two large sash windows, and when I asked Arabella about it, this was her reply: "One thing pleases me, you don't have the windows covered, that would have pleased my Dad as he always said 'God sent us the light and a woman nearly always curtains it out', so no curtains – we had blinds but rarely used them."

Arabella, my correspondent, was born in 1898, and left to get married in 1920. She would write me three or four letters a year, and tell me about life there. When we first arrived in 1976 there was no pumped water, and no drainage. She writes in 1983:

"Now I'm wondering how you managed during the water shortage, is the old well still across the yard with a big elm tree just beyond it. [Sadly all the elms had died the year we moved.] That well is 80 ft deep and across some part down the root of the elm tree is across it, and many is the bucket that has been let down there and grappling irons as well. When my father first had the well we had it pumped up to the wash and dairy house but father said the pipes spoilt the taste of the good spring water so out had to come the pipes and we fetched all the water we used by rope and bucket and I can tell you when the cows were in for the winter also pigs and every other menagerie animal we had, we had to draw all the water up by bucket but it rarely went very low and nearly always a little stream came from it."

Of the privy: "I do so hope you've moved the lav as that to me when I grew older was very bad, as a child we had the wall hung with pictures and lace curtains tied up with ribbon and I remember us sitting in there banging our heels and just kicking up a noise till told to stop it. There was a shed there with a table on which we children had to clean our boots each week also knives, forks and spoons and stool outside the back door with always two buckets of well water, a big water butt round by that back window with rain water in."

Of the grindstone: "A ditch full of water at times ran by the well and downside the dairy under a home-made bridge of sorts from the yard and down the length of our garden past the back of the pigsties. There was a swill hole there and at the top of the garden was an old stone grinder that we kids used to turn the handle for our dear old Dad to grind all the edges of the tools, a tin of water poured on the stone at times with us generally fainting up on our knees worn out. I don't suppose such things are used now." '

'In 1941 it took 13 buckets of water to fill the copper in the outside

Drawing water from the well was an everyday chore for most people. This well at West Lavington was dug in 1912 and provided drinking water, rainwater being collected for other purposes.

64

washhouse on Monday mornings. Through the morning my mother would have refilled the copper at least twice, and kept the fire going underneath.'

BATH NIGHT

'Bath night began at three o'clock in the afternoon, when the water was drawn from the well and the copper was lit which was in the shed across the yard. Rubbish was saved up all week for the purpose of heating the copper. When the water was hot enough out came the large tin bath – we all had to sit down and stay still whilst the boiling water was carried in from the copper, and then more water was drawn to cool it. There were several of us so halfway through the procedure the bath had to be carried outside and emptied, and then begun again. Needless to say we only had our "treat" about once a month, usually our bare backsides were plonked on the scrub-top kitchen table and we were scoured from head to toe. Even then, there was an awful lot of fetching and carrying, and the room was full of steam from the constant boiling of kettles and pans. We looked like angels all clean and ready for bed but Mum was exhausted. Incidentally, the well was shared by three cottages at Aldbourne, up a cobblestone path at least ten yards from the back door.'

'On Saturday nights at Bromham in the early 1900s we always had a bath in front of the fire. It was lovely being dried in the warm. My sister and I had a lot of hair, which was washed every week, and every day my mother would go through it with a small tooth comb, because nearly all the girls had lice, but we never did due to my mother's care.

Four of my brothers were older than us girls and it was getting a problem about baths for them, so when Devizes prison closed down my father bought a bath from the sale and he built a little wooden room next to the boiler and installed the bath. By then we had a pump so it was easier to fill the copper which heated the water for baths. No one else had a bath in the neighbourhood. When the village football team played at home my brothers used to bring their mates home to wash in our bath – didn't they have fun.'

BATHS, BUGS AND BURYING THE DOG

'We grew up by candle and lamp light. One chore which I hated was cleaning and filling the oil lamp. The wick, which soaked in the oil-filled brass bowl, needed regular trimming and the cleaning of the glass funnel-shaped tube above was a most delicate operation. What a joy it was when Mrs Chant at the shop in Shrewton obtained for us children a gas-mantled lamp as a silver wedding present for our parents. On the odd occasions when we came in late at night and lit a candle, the floor would be alive with black cockroaches. I remember my father using a Beetle Trap – a shallow tin topped by small propellers across which beetles would crawl in search of the sweet substance placed in the centre. The beetle would be tipped into the base and dispatched of in the morning by boiling water, a method often used for pest control.

We had neither electricity nor running water. In each cottage garden there was a well. Some even had pumps. The clear, ice-cold water from the depths of the earth was life itself. The water was wound up in a large galvanised bucket attached to a thick rope. Quite often there would be a frog clinging precariously to the rim of the bucket. The water was then transferred to another, indoor, pail which stood on the stone floor of the pantry for domestic use. Much hard work was entailed in preparing the weekly wash or weekend baths. Pail by pail, the copper in the outhouse was filled with water and then heated by stoking the fire beneath with bits of wood and coal. When the water was hot enough it was transferred, again pail by pail, to the communal bath placed near the indoor fire. How cold we all must have been awaiting our turn. No electric blanket or hot water bottle for comfort was even heard of, let alone expected. Occasionally there was a fearsome earthenware pot of hot water, or a brick heated in the oven and wrapped in flannel, placed at the foot of the bed.

Because of the lack of running water, toilet facilities were most primitive – a little hut at the bottom of the garden known as the privy usually shared by two families. Inside was a wooden seat where one sat and "performed" into a bucket below. Some "super privies" would have three seats of various sizes. Nearby stood a pan full of ashes from the previous day's fire and it was considered polite to sprinkle these ashes after each visit. Those cottagers living near the lake had no problem in disposing of the unpleasant contents but most people dug a hole in the garden – usually described as "burying the dog". Cutting up packs of old newspapers was another regular chore. These were hung on the door in lieu of toilet rolls. I can only assume that newsprint did not rub off in those days! We must have had some inbuilt immunity as we often paddled and bathed in that polluted water as it meandered down through the water meadows on its way to the Avon. I might add that strong red Lifebuoy and Wrights Coal Tar soaps were always used for our ablutions. My grandmother, however, always used Pears

66

Transparent soap and what a thrill it was to be allowed to use it when I stayed at her cottage.'

THE SWAMP

'My sister and I were visiting with our friends at the other end of our small village in the 1920s. We went walking in the meadows near the river and found a large patch of kingcups. Naturally we had to pick some to take home. Little did we know it was a swamp and we got more and more terrified as our feet and legs sank deeper and deeper into the smelly mire. We eventually struggled out and returned dejectedly to our friends' home – minus kingcups – where we had to be more or less scrubbed down. Our shoes and socks were washed and dried and we went home with polished shoes. We had to make sure we scuffed them in the gutter on the way home or our mother would have questioned us! We never told her of this episode, as in fact we were forbidden to go near the river, and we found out later that the "swamp" was all the waste and sewage from the "big house" nearby which soaked away into the river.'

WAYS TO GO

'We lived in a large thatched farmhouse at Bishopstrow down the end of a long lane – the hedge met overhead so the lane was dark winter and summer.

We had no mod cons. We had a very large toilet with a long seat the length of the hall with a large hole and a small hole complete with large and small buckets, heavy iron ones with handles over the top and on the side.

My sister didn't like the dark and wouldn't go to the toilet on her own. If she asked me to go with her I always said wait until I want to go – we had to take the candle with us.'

'My family lived at Widdleys Cottages, where my father was a farm labourer at Widdleys Farm, at Sherston. One Saturday in 1928 the Beaufort Hunt went racing past the cottages and a little later there was a knock at the door. One of the ladies out hunting was dying to "spend a penny". She asked my mother if she could use the toilet but, only having an outside closet, Mother invited her to go upstairs and use the chamberpot. The huntswoman did so and gave Mother sixpence for her trouble. As she left the cottage she complimented Mother on her beautifully scrubbed stairs!'

THE COMING OF PIPED WATER

'My grandfather William was a great storyteller and this was one of his memories.

Before the days of piped water the people of Trowbridge had to get their water from public pumps provided by charitable benefactors. In 1865 it was decided to purchase land, bore a well and pump water into two reservoirs and lay pipes to supply the town. Unfortunately, lack of money prevented the work from continuing for some time so it wasn't until 1874 that Trowbridge had piped water. However, after the pipes had been laid and everything was ready for operation people began to be very sceptical that the power would ever be strong enough to get water to the upper storeys of the houses. To prove it would be, the Water Company decided to stage a special event.

A temporary fountain was set up in the corner of the town centre. The Water Company was sure that the power of the water would be strong enough to be guided and shot right over the parish church and into the street on the other side. They planned special celebrations and crowds gathered to see the spectacular event.

Grandfather was six years old at the time and his father took him from their home at Studley, a distance of some two miles, to see the great event. As William was so small his father hoisted him onto his shoulders to get a better view. The moment came, the fountain was turned on and everyone waited eagerly – but alas, the water did not go in the right direction. The wind was too strong and instead of going over the church it backfired and came down over the crowd. Poor grandfather was soaked and had to walk back to Studley dripping wet.

Success did come – the next day the fountain was turned on again and this time the water went in the right direction.'

'I was renewing a tap washer the other day when it occurred to me that I have 19 taps in this house yet the cottage I was born in at East Knoyle had only one, and that was more than a great number of houses or cottages in the village. Piped water was available throughout the village and its outlying hamlets, but to have water "laid on" in the cottage meant double the annual water rate. My parents paid ten shillings while those who had to trek anything up to 200 yards in places for their water only paid five shillings. The people who lived at the green or Underhill took their buckets to the well and of course that was free.

Even though we had an indoor tap, piped water had only become available during my mother's lifetime, as I can remember her saying

68

that as a younger woman she went to the village pump daily some 200 yards.'

OUR FIRST SINK

'When I married in 1934 and went to live at Church Farm, Wingfield, we had no electricity (oil lamps and candles) and no mains water. The drinking water was fetched in milk churns from a standpipe at the top of Church Lane. The rest was pumped by hand from a well – for the garden, buckets of water came from a pond at the bottom of the garden.

After a few years we did have electricity (just lights – no plugs, but wonderful). Some years later mains water came. Joy of joys, a *tap* in the kitchen – but only a bucket to catch drips!

About 1948 the old black kitchen range was replaced by a Rayburn cooker and we actually had a hot water tap at the side of the Rayburn – luxury indeed! But the most wonderful mod con of all was, eventually, a deep white porcelain *sink* in the kitchen.

That sink was the pride of my life. I had no fitted units at first but later a carpenter friend built some wooden ones under the sink and a wooden draining board.

Although, in our retirement, we do appreciate all the comforts of modern day living, I'll always remember the joy of our first sink.'

ELECTRICITY

'Electricity was first brought to the village of Neston in the 1930s. Before that cooking was done on oil stoves. Three light sockets were put in free by the Electricity Board, anything over this was charged for. I had three lights and one power point so was able to have an iron.'

FROM OLD TO NEW

'I was born in 1939 and for the first twelve years of my life lived in a small thatched cottage at Whistly Road, Potterne. The cottage, now demolished, had no mains water or electricity. Water was drawn up from a well for all cooking and household purposes. Our only means of light were candles and oil lamps. The radio was a large wooden affair that contained valves and ran on a very large battery and an accumulator. This was a glass container full of acid which had to be recharged each week. We took the empty one along to Sunny Strange's garage and exchanged it for a full one for sixpence.

The toilet was a wooden shed in the garden containing a bucket which had to be regularly emptied. My mother had four children by 1950 and the washing was done in another outhouse in the garden containing the copper, which had to be filled with water from the well and a fire built underneath.

The water when it was drawn up from the well contained insects etc which had to be scooped off before boiling it for cooking. Bathing took place in a bath in front of the living room fire.

In November 1945 my mother was expecting my next sister and I spent a lot of time with the elderly couple who lived opposite us. Their son kept rabbits (for providing extra food for the pot) and I was always going across to see these rabbits. We had had a lot of rain that autumn and on this day the family were drawing up water from their well and had left the lid off whilst taking the water indoors. I ran up the garden and fell straight into the well. As the well was full to the top I bobbed up again and held on to the brickwork around the top. The daughter heard my cries and came out and pulled me up. They quickly wrapped me in a blanket and in order not to frighten my mother, made out that I had had an accident to my clothes to get me dry clothing. We often laugh about this incident but it could have had tragic consequences.

When I passed the exam to go to the local grammar school I had to do my homework by the light of the oil lamps and if the wind was blowing and the door blew to, the glass would crack. This would always happen at weekends when you could not get a new lamp glass until Monday when the shop opened.

In 1951 the first council houses were built after the war and because the cottage was condemned because of its lack of amenities we were allotted one of the new houses at Blackberry Lane. For the first time we had electricity at the press of a switch, hot and cold water in the taps, and a bathroom and a flush toilet! My mother and father still live there.'

'The year 1935 was indeed a year to remember in the small village of Great Bedwyn. After great celebrations of the Silver Jubilee of HM King George V and Queen Mary, no sooner had the village resumed its everyday life than a crowd of young men on noisy motorbikes invaded it. These were wiremen employed by the Wessex Electricity Company who were operating a scheme to install electricity into homes of willing householders. Three lights and a plug were installed free, providing they agreed to rent for two years at the cost of eleven shillings and tenpence halfpenny per quarter and one penny per unit used.

There were some old die-hards who were suspicious of "thic there electric" until their dying day, but most people welcomed the wiremen with open arms and cake and home-made wine.

Wine-making was a popular pastime in the 1930s. There being no sewage in the majority of homes, "buckets" had to be emptied into holes dug in the garden, no easy task during the hard winters of those days! However, the gardens were usually very big, enabling a rotation system to be used.

The result was very heavy crops of vegetables and fruit, and the surplus was usually turned into wines.

The "modern" council houses actually had a bath installed downstairs, drained by a cesspit, and filled with water taken from a coal-fired copper built next to it. These baths, however, instead of being used for the right purpose were brought into use for fermenting carrots, beetroot, parsnips, potatoes or any produce surplus to kitchen requirements. The resulting wine was most potent!

What a difference electricity made to the lives of housewives of those days. Just to flick a switch on, instead of having to light paraffin lamps, duly trimmed and filled daily (what a dirty smelly job) or trying to keep candles alight in draughty passages and bedrooms. To have an electric cooker and wireless as well as coppers and irons.

It's nearly impossible to imagine village life before those young men came to Great Bedwyn in 1935.'

FOOD AND DRINK

Many of us produced our own food and drink in the past, men working long hours in the garden and on the allotment to keep the family supplied with vegetables. Nearly every country dweller seems to have reared a pig or two for the table – and wild rabbits were always a good standby meal. How many of us as children were coerced into picking dandelions and other hedgerow treasures for home-made wine?

SPARROW PIE

'In my mother's day, at West Harnham at the beginning of the century, she would set a sieve with corn underneath to catch sparrows to make a pie. You needed about two dozen. You could use starlings but you had to twist their heads off straightaway. Cruel, wasn't it.'

KEEPING US FED

'We always had a hot breakfast to go to school. We had porridge with salt on it and toast, and on Sundays when Father was there we used to get some bacon and egg – cut up, not a whole one. We made toast over the open fire on a toasting fork. Some days, we'd have a boiled egg.

We had a pudding midday with our dinner, spotted dick or ones in a basin with the treacle at the bottom, or jam, or those rolled up in a pudding cloth tied with a string at each end. We sometimes had marmalade pudding. Mother made jam and marmalade and we had a hive of bees. We had honey in the comb and the wax got on your teeth. There was always something hot for tea as well. Mother had a lot of washing to do, and did all the baking, cooking, everything.'

RABBIT STEW

'Every Sunday morning during the winters around 1945 my father and his brother set off on their bicycles with boxes tied on the back, containing their ferrets, and shoulderbags containing their nets. They used to go to Hebden Farm rabbiting.

The nets were placed over the rabbit holes and then the ferrets would be sent down to chase the rabbits out. Sometimes, if the ferret was a young one it would have to be put on a collar and long line so that it did not get lost. When the rabbits bolted out the men would get them in the net and then quickly pull their necks.

If the hunters had a good morning they would come home with the rabbits' feet tied together and perhaps they would have six or seven rabbits hanging either side of their handlebars.

My job, being the youngest of the six children in our family, was to deliver the rabbits to the various customers in Sherston at two shillings and sixpence each. Meat was rationed and so it was no trouble to find customers, but regulars always came first.

We ate rabbit stew with dumplings, stuffed rabbit or rabbit pie, hot or cold. So much so that I can't face a cooked rabbit now! I was lucky, if Mother was very busy I had the job of skinning the rabbits – and if I skinned them I was allowed to collect the sixpences which Walt, the Oil Man, used to pay for them. He delivered paraffin for the cooking stove and bought the rabbit skins as a sideline. I never did know what they were used for.'

KILLING THE PIG

'Lea was known as "Piggy Lea". From the turn of the century until the Second World War there was a Pig Club in Lea. Every villager owned a pig, for the price of a few pence. If a villager could not afford the few pence, the club paid for his pig and if for some reason a pig died the club replaced it.

When the pig was fattened and ready for slaughtering the owner would share the meat with two or three other households. As these were the days before refrigeration the sharing meant that no household went without meat. Of course every part was used and there were joints of pork, ham and bacon. Brawn and faggots were made and the trotters cooked — the saying was that only the pig's squeak escaped the pot!

At times "black markets" operated and there was a tale of one pig which turned up in three different households.

On a happier note one villager just before the last war is said to have treated his pig like a pet and would lift it on his wall to watch the carnival band go by.

Over recent years the pigs were confined to one farm — however, in the 1980s the pig sties and adjoining barn were sold and converted into elegant dwellings for the human race. At last Lea can drop its nickname.'

'When I was nine we had a load of baby pigs delivered at the farm at Bishopstrow. Then my father had to go into hospital and it was my job to feed the pigs before I went to school and when I got home. In those early days it was meal mixed with water to a very sloppy mixture. I coped when they were babies but as my father was in hospital for nine months, needless to say it was a battle towards the end. Most of the time the food left the bucket at the door before it reached the trough.

When they were ready for slaughter a little man from Moody's in Warminster came and shot each one. We kept our fingers in our ears until they were all dead.

They were cut in half and put in large silts in the dairy. The pork had to be rubbed with saltpetre twice a day and turned each time. The chitterlings were put in buckets and we had to clean and turn them every day, Faggots were made with everything that could be put in them.'

'A great day in our lives was the killing of a pig. A butcher would come and joint it for us. My mother made black puddings and we cleaned the henge and plaited it up and it was called chitterlings. I would like to taste some now. We had the liver and we melted down the flecks for lard which we used on toast. Then my father would salt the whole side of bacon, which hung on the pantry wall and kept us going all winter.'

'During our dinner breaks from school at Shrewton in the early 1920s, there was one horror which I remember vividly. This was meeting the local butcher, Austin Brown, striding through the village resplendent in straw boater and blue striped apron. Carrying a fearsome knife and with other mysterious instruments in a wooden trug over his arm, he would be en route to a garden where a wretched pig lay in its sty awaiting execution. I would creep into my bedroom with my fingers firmly plugging my ears and in floods of tears. The poor pig screamed for what seemed like hours as its throat was cut. In spite of this revulsion I was always fascinated at the final ritual. The corpse would be singed (a ghastly smell), hung, drawn and quartered, before being distributed to the various families who had contributed to its livelihood. Most cottages had pig hooks in the ceilings from which large portions of meat were suspended and gradually used until the next pig-killing session came round.'

DANDELION WINE

'My mother made wine. I remember we had to pick the dandelions from the fields, putting them in a clothes basket. You just used two fingers, putting them under the flower head. Our fingers would get stained as we picked. The flowers were put in the copper with water and boiled, then tipped into a huge washing tub, yeast floated on top and left overnight. We would dip our hands into the tub and suck our fingers to taste the wine, but it had a horrid taste then. It was bottled and kept until Christmas.

Jam was also home-made, such as gooseberry, raspberry, straw-berry, rhubarb, Victoria plum, purple plum and greengage, with fruit from the garden and small orchard by an allotment next to our fields at West Lavington. My father grew several beds of asparagus there, selling some to an hotel nearby.'

'On a hot summer morning in 1924 my grandmother had been making her renowned dandelion wine. It had been put to cool in a large earthenware pan, and was covered with the wooden lid of the copper. It was then put aside to rest in a corner of the kitchen.

In the afternoon my sister in her pram and I were taken for a walk by a young girl from the village. It was very hot and I was tired, and running indoors I collapsed on the lid covering the wine. Over went the lid, over went the wine. It was spilled everywhere, over me and over the floor.

I was not popular and to this day I dislike dandelion wine.'

SHOPPING AND CALLERS TO THE DOOR

Many villages were self contained communities in the days of small shops and local tradesmen – and regular delivery to the door of essentials such as bread, milk and meat was commonplace.

SHOPPING

'Before the Army took over Salisbury Plain, there were lots of farms up there and every Saturday night the farmers and their families came down to Market Lavington, as the shops stayed open until ten o'clock. The men went to the pub and the women did their shopping, caught up with the village news and visited their friends.'

'We were a self contained village at Shrewton as far as I remember, with Williams' bakery at one end and Chant's bakery at the other. Sixpence would buy a lump of dough to which my gran would add sugar, currants and fat to complete a luscious Wiltshire Lardy Cake.

Nine or ten shops lined the village street in those days and a great favourite for sweets was a little shop owned by the Misses Smith – Aunt Annie and Aunt Mary – near the Baptist chapel. To this day I feel a great pang of conscience remembering how I stole a farthing bar of pink and white nougat from a jar on the counter when the old lady's back was turned! All the shops sold a great variety of commodities from groceries to paraffin oil and gardening equipment. There would always be a taste of the cheese before buying it and a bag of broken biscuits on paying the weekly bill. Any clothing would be brought by Mr Chant on the old carrier van on approval from such stores as The Bon Marché, McIlroy's or Clark & Lonnen's in Salisbury.

The general store and bakery was an essential part of village life. Mrs Muriel Stone (nee Kail) at the door of Kail & Son in Porton in 1936.

The village was cut off for long spells in winter but we could always rely on the Withers brothers – Edgar the Milk and Oliver the Coal, so we were never short of food or warmth.'

'Nearly all the shops in Tisbury in the 1920s delivered, and there was a carrier who would travel regularly to Salisbury to undertake commissions for the villagers such as banking. The local baker cooked turkeys for anyone who needed the service on Christmas morning.'

THE MILK AND THE MEAT

'Our butcher at Wishford brought the meat each week in a horse-drawn vehicle and when he finished his round he called at the local inn. Later he would be put in the cart and the dear old horse got him home to the next village, Stapleford.

Up until the late 1920s our bread was brought around the village by a lad pushing a handcart. The bread was delivered to the outlying villages in a horse-drawn high van. I remember lamps with candles enclosed on each side for use when it became dark.

Likewise, the milkman came round with a churn of milk in his horse-drawn vehicle. He stopped at each house where a jug was left at the door on a table for him to fill.'

'Brought up in Dinton in the early 1930s, I remember the way the tradesmen delivered our food. The local dairyman, having hand-milked his cows, came through the village with two large cans of milk on the handlebars of his bicycle, and measured out the milk into one's jug with shiny copper measures.

Our meat was delivered by horse and trap. It came from Tisbury, some five miles away. My strongest memories of "Butcher Jay" are of him arriving quite late in the evening. His only protection in bad weather was thick sacking for his shoulders and knees, and the lights on the cart were two candles set in jamjars. It was always said the horse could find his own way back to Tisbury, after the butcher had visited the East End Inn!'

THE FAMILY BAKER

'We were a family of bakers and grocers, before and during the Second World War. We lived in Porton and when my father retired, my brother continued in the business. I was the youngest of three, and remember as a schoolgirl wishing I could stay up all night to help make hot cross buns! The night before Good Friday was very hard and hot work. My father always carefully selected the fruit and insisted on his own recipe. And oh! how delicious it was. All the staff came to assist, rolling the dough by hand. The cross was made by pressing a wooden cross. Oh dear me, how sore our fingers became by the continuous pressing. There was no machinery then. The buns were bagged up seven for sixpence and 14 for one shilling. When the first batch was ready and cool, I remember as a schoolgirl delivering locally, on a long trade cycle. One spinster would leave a rope hanging from her bedroom window, to enable me to tie a bag of buns on to the end, which she then drew up to her room to eat in bed!

Besides the first delivery vans, we had a good all round adaptable horse named Bob. I used to ride him, and he acquired a good knowledge of the country roads. My father used to do the deliveries as far as Gomeldon by horse and cart. He loved having chats with the customers, and the many cups of tea that were waiting for him. On some occasions Bob got tired of waiting and walked on to all the known customers, then he would turn himself and the cart around and head for home two miles away. We would hear him clopping into the yard, without my father, who found his own way home quite confident that the round had been done satisfactorily by Bob.

Frederick Baily was for many years builder and undertaker at Downton. The trades of carpenter, builder, wheelwright and undertaker often went together in the days when each village was self sufficient, even to the final journey.

78

Everyone loved him, he was such a sensible horse. I cannot imagine this happening with today's traffic.'

'John Hunt and his three sons, Oscar, Victor and Gilford were all bakers in Chippenham.

Oscar built the bakery at Lowden Avenue and the bakehouse still stands. There was stabling for a pony, and space for the covered cart beyond the ovens. Long wooden troughs were used and the dough mixed by hand, overnight. Work started early in the morning, weighing out the dough, 2lb 4ozs to allow for shrinkage, as the first loaves into the ovens became more crusty and lost weight. The loaves were set in the oven with a wooden paddle on a long stem, called a "peel". Only cottage loaves and cobs were made in the early days. Four loaves were a gallon, and two were a quartern. The flour came from various millers, one in Chippenham on the Town Bridge, but also some flour came from abroad via Cardiff. At certain times of the year the bread was dark, because the wheat was sprouting when it was milled.

The earliest price I can remember was threepence halfpenny made and delivered. We didn't make any fancy cakes, only dough cakes and lardies.

There was a discount of sixpence in the pound and most people took that as a Christmas cake. Dorothy made them and we iced them between us. Of course, we didn't get a day off on Christmas Day, people brought their poultry and large joints of meat to be cooked, and Mother charged a penny each to cook rice puddings.

The boys, Stanley and Francis worked in the bakehouse, but there were the deliveries to make, using Tommy the pony, and keeping an eye open for the Weights and Measures people who would stop and check the loaves anywhere in town. We delivered out as far as Langley Burrell but I can't remember how far we went in the other direction. Dorothy used to cycle about four miles to deliver four four-pound loaves to one large family.

When they were making up the road outside they put down planks for us to walk on, and Tommy (the pony) fell off and broke his leg, so then we got Kitty, but she was a bad-tempered pony and I didn't like her.

Later we got a hook, turned by a big handle, for mixing the dough, and tins for making sandwich loaves.

Oscar gave up the bakehouse when he was 79 years old, and Stanley went to work at Westinghouse. Francis went blind, and Dorothy continued to make cakes for "occasions" for many more years.'

THE BAKER'S VAN

'I left school in July 1939 at the age of 16 and, because of the international situation at that time, was unable to proceed with my intended career. Needing some sort of income I applied for a job at the village shop as a van assistant. This meant travelling each day with the owner delivering bread, cakes and ordered groceries to the surrounding villages. I later learned to drive the van myself and did the various rounds on my own. Each day had its own route and brought its own differing needs, problems and amusing situations.

Each day I arrived at 8 am and went into the bakehouse where I helped the baker, who had been there since 4 am, to take the bread out of the two ovens. There were tin loaves and oven-bottomed cottage loaves. These were taken from the large ovens by using what looked like huge paddles. The tricky bit was getting the loaves out of tins without breaking the tops off. When this did happen the baker would blame me for not greasing the tins properly. When the ovens had been emptied I would regrease the tins for the next batch and then go and get the van ready for the daily run.

Monday was a very busy day with three different rounds. After loading up with hot bread etc we would set off about 9.30 am and be back about noon. A quick lunch break – reload and off again returning about 4.30 pm. A hot meal was then provided and then after a third loading, off on the road again. This journey during the winter had its problems because with the blackout restrictions in force the vehicle headlights were masked and driving around the country lanes was hazardous. There was one house on this run that always had 20 loaves and my instructions were to off-load as much of yesterday's bread as possible with this order! The last house but one on this round the residents were always in their night clothes waiting to go to bed as soon as I had delivered their bread and groceries. The last house on the list the occupants were always in bed and their goods were put in an outhouse (I never did meet them). From there I had a two mile journey and would arrive at the bakery between 10 pm and 10.30 pm. In bad weather it could be as late as 11 pm. No wonder we were known as the midnight bakers!

Tuesday was a quieter day. There were two things I remember about Tuesdays. One house we went to had a tethered dog which could just reach you as you went round the corner of the house. The drill here was to take two stale cakes and throw one to the dog each way, turning the corner of the house while the dog was retrieving the cake. When I did my first Tuesday on my own I was told of one customer who must not receive goods unless she paid and I was to ask for one shilling off her outstanding account. This I did and was amazed to see her account was nearly £300! I often wondered if it was ever paid off.

Wednesday meant a later start and a totally different set of villages. Another dog incident comes to mind. In a farm yard was a dog on a very long lead which enabled one to walk safely past while the dog ran in a great arc snarling and barking. One day I arrived to see the lead lying on the floor with no dog. I crept carefully across the yard towards the gate which let into a small walled yard outside the kitchen door. As I opened the small gate there was a loud snarl and bark and the dog hurled itself towards me. I swung the large filled basket I was carrying towards the dog and it grabbed a corner in mid air. The commotion brought the owner to the door and her call to the dog was obeyed instantly. "He won't hurt you," she said! I looked at my basket in disbelief. Another farm we went to was down a long lane miles from anywhere. We went into a large kitchen where we waited until someone came in answer to our shouts. While we were waiting my boss lifted up a row of coats hanging from pegs in a corner to reveal several sides of bacon cleverly concealed (well over the allowed wartime quota!).

Thursday was free from driving, just a few deliveries on foot in the village. My weekly job on a Thursday was to clean and wash the van, inside and out. This completed I would then spend the next few hours in the bakehouse helping the baker. My jobs were legion – greasing bread tins, mixing the fillings for pork pies, making the fillings for eccles cakes, repairing the wooden boxes that the slab cakes were baked in, putting jam in doughnuts and rolling them in sugar while hot from the fat, putting jam and cream in cream horns ("Only put the cream on top and not inside," shouted the baker), jamming and rolling the swiss rolls (terrified of breaking them) etc. This was supposed to be my half day but I rarely got away before 2 or even 3 pm.

My main memory from the Friday round was a farmhouse where again I had to walk into a large kitchen, read a note and put the required bread on the kitchen table. What a joke that was, the kitchen table was completely full of all sorts of things. I mentioned this to my boss and he said to just push a few things away to make space for the bread. I did this each week and some things just fell off the other side and stayed on the floor, nothing ever changed in all the time I was delivering.

Saturday meant a lot of travelling with few deliveries – isolated farms etc. Lots of chatter at each place of call. One call I enjoyed was at an aunt's, this always meant a piece of home-made cake or pie!

One journey I shall never forget was during the 1939/1940 winter. A village had been completely cut off by the heavy snow fall. We set off with a large farm cart full of bread pulled by a tractor. There was the tractor driver, the boss, his son, my two brothers and myself. At times we were literally driving over the top of hedges and it was bitterly cold. We arrived outside the village pub and were surrounded by people waiting for bread. "Customers first," shouted the boss, "and then anyone can have some." The cart was very soon emptied and the boss went into the pub for sustenance. He sent we four "under-aged" a cup of hot Bovril each. It was the best Bovril I had ever tasted. I learned later that a port had been put into each mug to warm us up. The journey home as the daylight faded was very cold and we lay huddled under a tarpaulin almost in tears with the pain of the cold. I can still see the tractor driver – Bill – puffing away at his clay pipe as he found his way across the snowy fields, seemingly impervious to the biting cold.'

FROM THE CRADLE TO THE GRAVE

We were much more likely to be born, to suffer our illnesses and to die in our own homes in the past, medical attention being only a last resort and sometimes beyond the means of poorer families. An exception, experienced by hundreds of children between the wars, was a spell in the isolation hospital with one of those dreaded fevers, scarlet fever or diphtheria. For less serious afflictions, home cures were always popular, often handed down from generation to generation.

BAD LUCK

'In 1951 I came to Wiltshire with my husband, who was starting a new job as Public Health Inspector at Pewsey. One of my husband's duties was meat inspection, and the slaughterhouse which stood behind one of the butcher's shops in the village was used for slaughtering about once a week. Quite often the meat was not ready for inspection until late in the day, so some evenings I used to go with my husband to keep him company. It could be a long job – I sat in the small office and waited, or otherwise I watched what was going on, as I found it very interesting.

One of the slaughtermen did not approve. He was full of dire warnings because I was pregnant. He was superstitious and thought it would bring me bad luck, or that the baby would be affected in some way, so when I had to go off to hospital several weeks before I was due, he shook his head as if to say, "I told you so." Fortunately, our little daughter was not born with any animal-shaped birthmarks.'

'UNTIL I WAS OBLIGED'

'In 1947 when I got married my grandmother said she hoped I would be happy and to look after myself. She then went on to say she hadn't had her children "until she was obliged" − I have often wondered what she meant, but in those days you didn't ask embarrassing questions!'

APPROVED BY THE VICAR'S WIFE!

'In the village of Bromham, where I lived in the early 1900s, when a couple were married and a baby didn't arrive until nine months or more had passed, the vicar's wife would present the couple with a hand-made christening gown. I still have the one given to my parents, and it must be over 100 years old now.'

HOME CURES

'If we were sick when we were children, the first thing the doctor asked was, "Has she opened her bowels?" We frequently had Beechams Pills crushed in jam. They were awful. Syrup of figs when it came was an improvement.'

'In the 1940s our cowman made dock root tea for my husband who suffered with boils, which completely cured him.'

'Old country remedies were widely used in the rural areas for various ailments and found in lots of cases to be better than their modern counterparts. In the autumn, we collected grey tufts of sheep's wool from the wire fencing on the downs, and rubbed our burning chilblains with it during the winter months. Some swore that the only way to get rid of these painful swollen lumps was to beat them with holly twigs until they bled. We couldn't face the initial pain of this treatment and stuck to the sheep's wool. Later

"Snowfire" was to come onto the market, thick cardboard tubes of a greasy substance which had to be heated before application. When dried, this covered not only our chilblains but also our socks with a thick layer of green grease.

We flew to the "bluebag" when stung by a drowsy bee and held a boiled onion, wrapped in flannel, against an aching ear. I was always anxious to see if cobwebs would stop bleeding. The only ones readily available were the ones festooned along the inside of the granary roof. Laced with dusty barley meal, they looked far too unhygienic to put on a fresh cut.

We were all scared of putting our hands in water that had boiled eggs just in case we got warts. An old lady in the village could charm them away or so she said. We had doubts about this as her husband had a large one on his nose which had been there for years. According to her she could do nothing for him – to effect a cure, the patient had to have complete faith in her powers. Although I am sure I had not dipped a finger in the egg saucepan, I developed a large wart on my hand. I would have liked to enlist her help but doubted whether my own faith would be sufficient. In the end, I used the well tried method of a piece of cotton tied tightly round the offending brown blemish and, in the end, it dropped off.'

'We were rubbed with goose grease for colds etc. Sometimes it was put on a piece of brown paper and put on our chest. The goose grease was also rubbed round the edge of shoes and boots to keep the snow and rain out.

The middle of a boiled onion was put in our ear for earache. A syrup made from an onion cut up and put on a saucer with brown sugar, left on the range all night, was good for coughs. My dad would eat a basin of onions cooked in milk before going to bed to keep colds away.'

'I had a whitlow on my finger whilst I was at grammar school. It was extremely painful but a dear old lady living in the almshouses at Wishford, Tilly King by name, dressed it every day by putting lily roots under the bandages.'

UNDER THE DOCTOR

'I was not lucky enough to meet my great grandmother, who died in 1895, but heard many tales of her from my mother.

As a young woman living in Pewsey, my great grandmother used to assist the local doctor. In those days the use of anaesthetics was rare, and probably unknown in country districts, and on one occasion she had to feed a woman drops of brandy throughout an operation to remove her breast. History does not record whether the unfortunate woman survived this terrible experience.'

'When we had measles, no doctor called but medicine was sent, via the postman, from Melksham. When the doctor did visit in Seend, he came by pony and trap. Later, in the 1920s, one of the first cars in the village belonged to the doctor.'

'I remember having my tonsils removed by the local doctor on the kitchen table. I must have been about six or seven and this was in the 1920s. The doctor brought me an ice cream the following day.'

'My sister developed polio as a girl in the 1920s. To minimise the damage to her legs our parents purchased an electrical medical coil which plugged into the electric light. This antiquated treatment housed in a polished mahogany box has now been donated to Odstock Hospital Museum, Salisbury.'

THE FEVER

'Whilst visiting a children's ward in hospital recently I realised just how times have changed. Gone are the "fever" hospitals. In the 1920s I was unfortunate enough to spend two spells in the local hospital. Diphtheria raged in Trowbridge and it was a most serious disease, several of my little friends from the Junior School succumbed to it. In January I contracted it and was taken off to the hospital in the special brown ambulance reserved for infectious cases. As soon as I had left home the Sanitary Inspector moved in to fumigate the bedroom to kill all remaining germs.

The hospital itself, at present still in use as a geriatric hospital, consisted of two blocks, each with a ward for female patients of all ages, and one for males. I recall how dismal the stay there was – so many young patients and even, in some cases, whole families. The wards were overcrowded and the nurses overworked. Joy of joys, after three weeks I obtained the obligatory two "clear" swabs of my throat and I was allowed home but my brother was then hastily despatched to stay with grandmother for two weeks in case he caught the dreaded disease.

The health and school authorities were at last beginning to take the epidemic seriously and the school was closed for some time. However, came the summer, the diphtheria epidemic had subsided somewhat but scarlet fever was around, and, yes, I caught that next. So it was another stay in hospital – this time for six weeks. One or two vivid memories of that time stick with me to this day – how we all felt we were starving and as soon as the nurse had gone to the nurses' home one of the male patients took pity on the children and we went into the kitchen where he cut us slabs of bread and "scrape". That seemed like manna from heaven. Another memory was Friday evenings – round came the dreaded liquorice water in large tin mugs and we had to drink every drop – to keep us "regular".

During all the time I was in hospital, parents were allowed to visit only for a short time on Saturday afternoons. When I say visit, I mean they were permitted to stand outside the window and if we were still a bed patient our beds were moved so that we could talk to them through the window. The favourite man patient of ours also happened to be a friend of my father's so after visitors had gone he would go outside to my window and find the cigarette my father had left there for him which gave him a quiet smoke in the loo against all regulations.

Once again the time came to return home. This occasion I remember with great clarity. I was dressed in an assortment of clothes whilst my personal clothing was taken away to be disinfected and I was also to be "treated". Apart from the wards there was a tin hut, inside which was a bath of the hottest, steamiest water, smelling overpoweringly of carbolic. After a good wash all over in this bath I was allowed to dress in my own clothes and was taken to the Matron's office and reunited again with my parents.

How thankful we should be that children of today are safeguarded by immunisation.'

' "Whatever are you doing to that child?" cried Granny, as screaming I lay across Mother's knee while she painted the inside of my very sore throat with iodine. This was the treatment the doctor ordered for tonsillitis before the swab revealed that I was a further victim of the diphtheria epidemic of 1933.

Taken by ambulance to the isolation hospital three miles away I joined the 20 or so other children in a long ward heated by a huge black stove in the centre. Lying flat in bed with no pillow to avoid heart strain, sitting up was only allowed after improvement had progressed through one to two pillows.

Each day nurse came round and dosed every child with a spoonful of white emulsion from a large blue bottle, followed by a boiled sweet. Blunt knives and enamel plates were used for meals and the milk rice pudding served almost daily, seemed even to my childish eyes, very white and gritty tasting. Tea was enjoyable, all fruit brought in by parents being centrally shared out in the kitchen with each child receiving two pieces of bread and butter accompanied by slices of banana, orange and apple as available.

Visiting was allowed on Sundays and Thursdays when my parents could speak to me from outside the hospital window. Each week I wrote a postcard home but as I had only just started school this consisted of a jumbled series of letters of the alphabet followed by a brief report added by the nurse on my well being, then my row of kisses.

Meanwhile, at home, bedding had been officially fumigated and my sister, who had qualified in the scholarship examination, missed joining her new school term as she was in quarantine for three weeks. Sitting on the hearth rug she picked out all the best iced biscuits from the mixed pack to send to me.

Telephones were a rarity in the 1930s but a kind local solicitor set aside a couple of hours weekly to telephone the hospital on behalf of relations seeking news of their sick children. He made no charge for the service.

Six weeks passed and I was nearing the time to return home but when Mother visited on the Thursday she could not find me. I had contracted scarlet fever while in hospital and had been moved to another building, without any notification to my parents.

After a total of 13 weeks I returned home. My sister had passed on to me her doll's pram and I was allowed to trundle it round and round the living room. To my further delight there was a doll's house complete with furniture lovingly made in my absence by my father.

Did I suffer trauma from being whisked away for more than three months at the tender age of five? Not a bit. I had been amongst other children with kind nurses, visited regularly by mother and father, and had returned to a loving family home.'

'One December during the Second World War we were ill with scarlet fever. Kathleen and her mother were staying with us. Her mother took her to the doctor, and paid, who said it was tonsillitis. Mum had a very bad throat and struggled on. We belonged to a Doctor's Club, paying weekly. When I got the very sore throat Mum called a doctor. Dr M was a misery. He diagnosed scarlet fever and wanted to charge Kathleen's mum. My mum stood up to him and told him that if the other doctor had made a correct diagnosis it would have been easier for everyone.

The local isolation hospital was full so we were isolated at home in the best room. Although Mum was still ill she had to struggle to get the beds downstairs for the three of us. There was a sheet soaked in Dettol hanging on the hall side of the door.

Dr M came on Christmas Day, saw our little efforts to cheer ourselves up and muttered, "Huh! Christmas."

My toddler brother used to creep in to see us. If the doctor came in the back way he was quickly slipped out into the main room. If the doctor came in the front way John was pushed out of the back window. He never caught it.

When we were better the room had to be fumigated and sealed. Our books and toys were supposed to be burnt. The fumigator said it would be a waste to destroy them. He stood our books up open around the room so that they could be treated. As a bookworm I can remember being very grateful for his kindness.'

THE LAST JOURNEY

'My great uncle Frederick Baily was born at Charlton All Saints about 1866. As a boy he worked with his father in the building and undertaking business. He used to tell the story that in those days if you were too poor for a proper funeral, they would make a very plain coffin with rope handles and take it and leave it on the person's doorstep, paid for by the parish. He later went into partnership with his nephew as Downer & Baily, Builders and Undertakers.'

'Children didn't go to funerals in those days, but when my Granny died (1917) my aunt took me up to the bedroom window to watch. There were all these men coming down, carrying the coffin on their shoulders. They had a marvellous bier, varnished, at Horningsham church. It was given by the landlord in memory of his daughter and it was sold and one or two of the parishioners got it back. One of them said to me, "Now mind, Dorrie, if that bier ever do go, you fathom out where it is gone and you do get it back." The last time I was in the church it was gone.'

'My father's funeral in 1937 cost less than £10, which included the coffin, church service expenses, and interment.'

'A coffin table on wheels, still in Holy Cross church at Seend, was always used for funerals. Families went to church for several Sundays after a funeral, and sat in the front row of the pews. Some families still do this.'

CHILDHOOD &
SCHOOLDAYS

TOWN AND COUNTRY CHILDHOODS

Whether we grew up in a town or a country village, we shared a freedom in the past that today's children sadly will never know. Life was often hard, with large families and little money coming in, but somehow we found pleasure in small things, made friends of other children and adults alike, and rarely found life boring!

KITTY'S CRICKLADE CHILDHOOD

'Emily Caroline Holloway was born at 78 High Street, Cricklade at 12.30 pm on Sunday 6th November 1904. She was always called Kitty.

One of her earliest memories was of walking with her parents and older sister, Olive, across the fields to the tiny church at Eysey for the afternoon service. She also remembered being taken out onto the North Meadow to pick bunches of fritillaries, which she was certain were more plentiful than they are today.

Both her parents came from Tockenham near Wootton Bassett, so there were family expeditions to visit the grandmothers. She was told that on one occasion her mother walked the whole way to Cricklade, pushing her baby son in a pram, but usually the family travelled by train, first to Swindon, then another train to Wootton Bassett, followed by the long walk to Tockenham. Kitty could still hear her own plaintive voice asking her mother how much farther it was. "Not far," was the reply, and Kitty complaining, "But you keep telling me that.".

It was to her father that Kitty turned for affection in her childhood. Her mother was strict, with quick intelligence and formidable willpower. Asenath Holloway worked all her life and carefully saved every penny she earned with the single minded intention of buying property. Her money went into a box kept in the house, and the great moment came in 1931 when she was able to purchase 78 and 79 High Street, Cricklade.

There was a coal-fired range for cooking. Lamps burned oil and glowed softly through glass chimneys. The grate needed black-leading each Saturday, and the brass fender and other objects were polished too in preparation for the Sabbath. Kitty rubbed spoons, and her brother Jim cleaned knives. There was a family joke that her brother Arthur was once told to get sixpence worth of "elbow grease" for those knives. Sunday was strictly kept in this family. Church meant St Mary's where Kitty was christened, confirmed and married. In those days it was a popular and well filled church, and folk came from as far away as Purton for the services. Kitty sang in the choir for 30 years. Once when she was about twelve years old a stranger asked one of the choirboys how they all sang so well. He replied, "Oh, we all watch Kitty's mouth."

Asenath always insisted that her family should be indoors by seven o'clock; no late hours and getting into trouble. Kitty recalled games of snakes and ladders and ludo. There were rags to be cut neatly into strips for rugs, and stories told by her mother; Kitty particularly liked stories about fairies.

But there was work to be done even during schooldays, and not only tending the rabbits, ducks, bantams and chickens. Kitty was responsible for feeding them and bringing in the eggs. Even while she was quite small she was sent with her brother to collect baskets of laundry from Calcutt before school at nine o'clock. It could seem a very long way when the basket was heavy. Kitty was brought up to work. Occasionally she was kept home from school to help her mother clean a pig's carcase.

At the age of twelve Kitty was "chosen" by Miss Johnson to go to work for the local doctor. She would start work at 7.30 am filling and carrying six boxes of coke and one box of coal for upstairs, and a large box of logs. She cleaned the shoes, rubbed the steel knives on a brick, swept the front and polished the door brasses. For this she earned two shillings and sixpence a week and her breakfasts. These were oatmeal porridge with plenty of sugar, toast and butter and tea, and she often had to hurry in order to get to school on time. On Sundays she was up at 4.45 am with her brother to deliver newspapers in the town while her father was out around the surrounding villages.

In summer there were walks to gather the plentiful wildflowers down Fairford Lane and blackberrying later out along Gas Lane. On one awful occasion Kitty caught her foot on the stile and spilled all of twelve pounds of the hard won fruit into the cowpats. Kitty believed firmly in Father Christmas until she was 14. Till then she had delighted in the excitement of discovering oranges, nuts and a few tiny gifts on Christmas mornings. The great thrill of the day came when Mrs Cuss knocked softly on the door after morning service with a huge hamper filled with delicious treats of fruit, nuts, dates and figs.'

FROCKS AND RINGLETS

'I was born in the Manor House, Barford St Martin on 13th August 1908. My parents were disappointed to have a second boy when they wanted a girl. Accordingly, I was dressed in frocks and had long ringlets. Mr Clark, the barber, cycled out from Salisbury and I remember sitting in a high chair in the courtyard having my hair cut short.

My brother and I were taught at home by a governess, Miss Mangin, who was very kind to us. I later went to a small private school in Wilton, The Moat House in North Street. This was during the First World War when the road from Wilton to Fovant was being reconstructed to take all the heavy traffic to the army camps at Fovant. It was nearly impossible to walk along the road, so we went across the fields. If the weather was bad we were taken by pony and trap to Dinton station to catch the train to Wilton. Sometimes I used to beg some cobbler's thread from Mr Birchall, the harnessmaker in North Street, to catch trout from the stream that goes under the road by the Moat House. Once I was nearly caught when the water keeper came along, but I pleaded innocence and got my fish after he had gone.'

THE HOUSE IN ROUNDSTONE STREET

'It was 1912 and I was just three years old when I went with my parents and little sister to live in Roundstone Street, Trowbridge, but the house itself was over 100 years old. It had been built at the end of the 18th century in the paddock of the farm which had been demolished when the adjacent Rodney House was built. It was a tall Georgian town house, three storeys plus attics; semi-detached, with a passageway running from between the two front doors right through the house to the garden at the back.

To the right of the front door was my father's tailor shop, and in the windows were two wire blinds with "Culverhouse – Tailor" on them. It was not quite a shop as such, for customers had to ring the bell and my mother would come to the door and let them in – so she always had to be neat and tidy whatever household task she might have been engaged in. Inside the shop was a high mahogany counter; this was the cutting table, and under it were two boxes. In one were collected the cloth cuttings, and in the other the lining clippings. When these were full they were taken to the rag and bone man in Back Street.

My father, the master tailor, used to sit in the traditional tailor pose – cross-legged – on a table in his work room to do the hand

Holidays were few and far between for most but these lucky children were all ready for a family charabanc outing to Bournemouth c1930.

sewing. But it was not all hand sewing. He also had a treadle sewing machine. He employed four girls full time and both men and women outworkers. Two of the women outworkers lived in Bradford, and my sister and I had to cycle out to take the work to them and then bring back the finished waistcoats they had made. Through ability and hard work my father had prospered. He had left school at twelve to be apprenticed to a Trowbridge tailor. Having learnt his trade, he became a master tailor with his own business, employing hands and able to rent and eventually to buy the large house where we lived. He was happy in his work, proud of his creations and exacting in his craft. He particularly enjoyed making the prestigious, beautifully tailored clothes for the Wylye Hunt. He would never do any gardening for fear of roughening his hands and thus being unable to sew smoothly. He did make beautiful coats for his children, but had to be badgered into doing so.

We had lots of books in our house, as my father loved reading. When my sister was small, every lunchtime while he relaxed before returning to work, he would tell her the next episode in the "Gwendoline Story". Gwendoline was a little girl very like her, who had remarkable adventures which he made up daily for her delight.

My parents slept in the second-floor room fronting the street. In those days Trowbridge was busy with cloth mills and my mother used to be woken in the morning by the hooters, the chatter of the

93

mill girls and the clatter of their boots on the cobbles as they went by. There was among them one girl who always had a lot to say for herself and one morning my mother was both fascinated and appalled as she heard her proclaim to all and sundry, "'Tis my last day at mill. I'm giving up. Today I be vinishin'." "You never are," said her shocked companions. "Yes I be," was the reply. "What's the good o' workin' – the more thee's earn the more thee's spend, so thee bisn't no better off." My mother often saw her after that, "walking the town".

On market days the gate of the passage was kept locked, for the cows, driven by a cowman with the unlikely name of Clara, wandered all over the roadway and on to the narrow pavement outside our home, Clara meanwhile urging them onwards while playing his penny whistle for all he was worth.

One day the gate was not shut. An adventurous animal sidled in, meandered along and found herself trapped. The cow was fat, the passage was narrow, so she couldn't turn round. Then she saw a door ajar, leading into the house – and pushed. My mother within the room heard a noise, looked up and saw this great black horned face staring at her with its lustrous eyes. My mother was quite safe, for the door was secured on a very heavy chain – but she was terrified of cows. Screaming blue murder, she dashed over, slammed and bolted the door in the cow's face, and then had hysterics. I never knew what happened to the poor bewildered cow.

Washdays I hated. The kitchen was quite given over to it and it lasted all day. My mother was helped by the very needy wife of the cowman Clara. In the corner the fire was lit under the full copper. The room was full of steam, the flagstoned floor was wet and slippery, wet clothes hung from the rafters and dangled in my face, and over all was the horrid smell of washing soda. Lunch on washdays was usually cold mutton and the grown-ups' tempers were always frayed.

But my sister and I loved our garden. It was not very big and had a wall enclosing it at the bottom. There in the overgrown remains of what had been a shrubbery was our summer playground, a lonely, secluded and secret hiding place. We called it "The Shade". Two clearings amid the yews and the laurels became the two rooms of our Shade House. There we played with our cooking stove and our tea set, and put our dolls endlessly to bed in their cots and prams – happy in the glorious summer days of childhood.'

NOT ANOTHER ONE!

'My grandfather Mr E A Lucas was a smallholder with a small field

94

allotment a mile or so out of Cricklade. He kept one or two cows and had fruit trees. The produce he carried round with a pony and trap. He had several hives of bees in his back garden in straw skeps.

His house in the middle of a row was stone-built with a stone-tiled roof, and with a small shop at the front. At one time he had a fishmonger's shop, but I only remember the big posters of different salt and freshwater fish on the walls.

Grandpa used to go crayfishing in the river Thames at night with iron-hooped nets baited with bloaters. When not in use the nets were hung out to dry on the shed wall in the backyard. When he came home the crayfish were put in a galvanised bath until he was ready to boil them. We children used to get a plank of wood and make the crayfish "walk the plank" back into the bath.

I was one of twelve children, nine of them boys, and after this Mother had twins, one being stillborn and the other dying at 18 months old. That was the saddest Christmas I can remember.

My mother was always occupied with us children for a new baby came along every 18 months or two years. How she managed I'll never know, but in spite of a chronic shortage of cash, we always had enough food. The boys had to wear patched and darned clothes, and we girls had hand-me-downs. Our aunts and grandmothers were very good and helped as much as they could, in fact Aunt Win took me in and brought me up for two or three years as Mum had her hands full. I remember being in bed at Aunt's one night when cousin Paul came in and said, "Madge, are you awake? You've got a little brother." My reply is said to have been, "Not another one!"'

LIFE WAS NEVER BORING

'Born near the Victoria Park in Salisbury, in a small house we shared with five other people, the family – my baby sister, mother and father and I – moved to a house in a quiet cul-de-sac. Here the large kitchen had a range for cooking, a copper with a fire below to heat the water for washing the clothes and the bath. My mother sat the baby on the wooden table, strapping her to a hook on the window sill.

Most days we would walk to the Cathedral Close, to meet our father who worked in the Diocesan Registry Office. Here we usually saw the burly Close constable, of whom I was quite frightened. As my father was very musical and played various instruments, we had many friends who would come to spend an evening around the piano. Also he had three wonderful musical boxes, which introduced us to some fine tunes. I could pick out tunes on the piano, so I started to have piano lessons when I was nine. We all went to

St Thomas' church, and my eyes were always drawn upwards to the Doom painting, a truly terrible sight. I also went to Sunday school at the Congregational church, and then to Dews Road Primitive Methodist, all on the same day. Friday evenings was Christian Endeavour, a kind of social club for children and very enjoyable.

The milkman with his horse-drawn vehicle called to fill our milk jug from a can, while the baker brought dough cakes and lardy cakes as well as bread. But Fisherton Street was full of shops for almost all our requirements and the picture house was very handy, when we were allowed to go. Mr Bridle, the hairdresser, gave me my first shingle, and in a nearby empty shop we children were invited to come and sign a pledge never to touch alcohol. There were at least six sweet shops, one where you could see the lovely boiled sweets being made in the window. Two very small dark shops we frequented, as we were able to buy halfpenny bags full of odd sweets and black locust beans, sherbet bags, aniseed balls and broken chocolate.

Aged six, I was walking by the Infirmary wearing my new coat and fur-trimmed bonnet when said bonnet was taken from my head by a horse. My mother retrieved a rather frothy object, and the horse remained in line with the rest of the horse-drawn cabs or "taxis".

The various smells of my childhood return when I think of the water cart, that on hot days would go slowly past, leaving the street delightfully fresh. The clean smell of tar when the roads were resurfaced. The balsam scented poplar by Church House in Crane Street. Lastly, our favourite walk by the river, over the town path to Harnham, where we would pass the bone mill, from which came a truly horrible smell and we held our noses.

My first school was St Thomas', where we were sometimes allowed to play with large wax dolls that had to be kept away from the central stove in case they melted. Learning the times table was easy. We all said it in a sing-song way, twice one are two etc, never to be forgotten. A nearby part of the river was used by the children for a swim, but it was very cold. Next was St Paul's school and then South Wilts, and one had to pay a toll of half a penny crossing the river by the toll gate, to go by bus was one penny.

Salisbury Market was always crowded with stalls as well as cattle, sheep and chickens. Business was usually still brisk at nine o'clock at night when one could buy anything at a knockdown price. In October the fair came to town and it really was wonderful: the shining brasses on the steam engines powering the luxurious roundabouts, with the music and beautiful figures, the cake walk, boxing booths and attractive caravans.

Life in Salisbury was never boring.'

OUR FRIEND RON

'In 1926, during or just after the General Strike, we had a young out of work miner to help on the farm. Ron quickly established himself as a favourite with Peg and I – we loved him dearly, spending all the time we could with him whilst he was at his farm work. We sat on the curved side of the empty waggon and rattled over the bumpy ground to the haymaking field with Ron leading the horse. If we were lucky, we got a lift back to the rickyard on top of the load of hay, bowing our heads when Bonny and Trooper thundered through the gateway of Moremead, to avoid the overhanging elm branches. We went with Ron to feed the young cattle in the Long Ground, riding back in the empty tip-up cart afterwards. Sometimes we stood on the bed of the cart, peering over the high headboard, pretending we were pigs on the way to market, or otherwise sitting on the floor of the cart, where all we could see were the dark pitted boards, smelling of cow cake and manure.

Ron had a fund of stories of life in the Somerset coal fields. Midsomer Norton seemed miles away, another world in fact. We sat on the bottom rungs of the steps leading from the stables to the tallet whilst Ron was cleaning the harness and thought how wonderful it would be if he could stay on the farm for ever and not go back to the mines. If we pleaded with him, Ron would sing *Two little girls in blue* in his soft Somerset accent. I don't know whether this song was his entire repertoire but that was the only song we really wanted to hear – we were convinced he had written the words for us.

In the summer Ron followed the fairs around – he was an expert at the coconut shies and always came away with a prize. His bedroom in the small cottage where he had lodgings was full of china ornaments, plates, glass etc and was a veritable Aladdin's Cave. When he had a Sunday off, he spent his time cleaning and shining his trophies. However, the time came when Ron returned to the mines and Peggy and I wept at losing him. We thought of his face, brown from the summer's sun, growing pale through long hours underground, and we wept fresh tears for him.'

SUMMER HOLIDAYS

'When Dad said, "We're going to Wiltshire on Sunday and you can stay for a week", I knew the summer was really here. Although I had been born and brought up in the East End of London, where my parents had a dairy, Wiltshire was an important part of my childhood. Although I never knew my grandmother, I came to know some of her brothers and sisters and their families through holidays spent in Wiltshire as a young child in the 1930s.

We set off as soon as the milk rounds were finished on the Sunday and my mother, father, two older sisters and myself would travel in our roomy old car. Not much traffic on the road in those days so we could speed through London and soon be well on our way to Dad's cousins in Landford. A warm welcome always awaited us from Auntie Annie and Uncle Bill. When our parents went back home plans would be made for the week's stay. Auntie Annie's house, though not large, stood in its own grounds with a good size garden and vegetable plot and orchard beyond. Their youngest son, still living at home, kept pigeons and rabbits and, joy upon joy, there was a swing in the garden. What a contrast to our London backyard with its milk churns and dairy paraphernalia and not a flower in sight! Just to play in the garden was pleasure enough but I still remember cycling along lanes with the smell of honeysuckle in the air, and going with younger cousins to fish or walk to Nomansland.

Auntie Annie was a very busy lady but not too busy to have time to arrange special meals and treats for us. Best of all was her Summer Pudding with all manner of soft fruits gathered from her own garden. As Landford was halfway between Salisbury and Southampton we walked to the end of New Road to catch a bus in either direction. We sometimes went to Southampton, especially interesting if any big liners such as the *Queen Mary* were in dock. At other times we had a bus trip to Salisbury Market and sometimes tea in a lovely old teashop with Margaret Tarrant illustrations around the walls.

Auntie Annie was always dashing off, either to "Colonel's" where she worked two or three mornings a week, to her WI or on some other errand and usually on her bicycle. A local event was the Melchett Flower Show. One day Dad arrived as everyone was about to make their way there. He filled the car to capacity and my young cousin and his friends rode on the running board with their hands holding on to the car through the sunshine roof. I remember it was a very big event involving surrounding villages with every kind of entry from schools, individuals and organisations.

When war came in 1939 I, like many other schoolchildren, was evacuated to Wales to escape the London bombs, and so several years would pass before another Wiltshire holiday could be enjoyed.

After the war, though many things had changed for so many people, some things were constant – especially our Wiltshire welcome . . . and Auntie Annie's Summer Puddings.'

ME AND LADDIE

'I was born in February 1942. My parents had been bombed out of London in 1939 and were billeted to Calne.

One of the earliest recollections of my childhood must have been about 1946, when I was four years old. We lived on the outskirts of Calne in the lodge of Vern Lease and in those days the milk was delivered by a young man called Ken, with a horse and cart. I was allowed (by my mother) to ride with him just up the road to Mile Elm and back – I felt very grown up and proud.

I think it was 1947 that we moved to the "old black hut" in Station Road, Calne. There were two big chestnut trees in the front garden and I can remember my mother digging a hole under one of these trees to put an old biscuit tin in the ground to keep the milk and butter cool in the hot weather. There were no fridges then, or perhaps we just couldn't afford one.

As I grew up there, I spent a lot of my time going to the railway station with my doll's pram and my dog Laddie. I was otherwise alone (I couldn't have been more than eight years old at this stage). I can remember talking to all the staff and particularly remember going to the signal box to "help" pull the signals! I couldn't, of course, they were much too hard.

I was given a special treat at other times when I was allowed by the driver to go up into the engine, help stoke the fire and ride to the end where they turned the engine around ready to go back to Chippenham – it was a marvellous experience and one I shall never forget. I still recall that wonderful smell that came with the engines.

I can also remember going over the road to the wharf. There were stables there. I cannot remember whether the horses belonged to Wiltshire's The Family Store or Harris's Bacon Factory but there were a lot of carts (they were canvas covered and quite tall). They took all the waste from the factory in these horse-drawn carts and they passed where I lived on their way to Whetham at the back of the station. I think they made glue there, sometimes the smell was awful. I managed to cadge a few rides but my dog was more cunning; he would lie on the side of the road as though he was exhausted or injured and, occasionally, a driver would throw him a bone or something from the cart.

I think most of my time, and Laddie's, in the warm months, was spent going over the road, across the old bridge and down a slope to paddle in the little stream that led into the river Marden. I would catch tiddlers and sticklebacks by waiting for ages until they swam into my hands. I was always coming home with a jamjar full of these fish but my mother always made me put them back.

One year I was given a young duckling. He was so sweet – all fluffy and yellow. I remember putting some string around his neck and taking him for a swim. He loved it, although sometimes I had a job to get him back again.

There was another memorable occasion in my favourite place. I met an old man, who seemed such a nice man to me. He told me had no home or family. I felt so sorry for him that I went to ask my mother if he could stay with us – we had a spare bed and room. I think she was rather diplomatic and said he would probably be happier being a "gentleman of the road". Of course, I didn't understand that he was a tramp. How things have changed – who would let their children out on their own nowadays?'

TREATS, GAMES AND CHORES

Most children had to do their chores before pocket money was handed over – but oh, the pleasure those pennies gave us! Outings were few and far between and the better appreciated for that, and our games were fairly simple and followed a seasonal rotation well known to every child. For more organised entertainment, we joined clubs and societies.

TREATS AND OUTINGS

'My mother, born in 1884 in Aldbourne, was one of the many women and children who waited outside the church to see the first "white" wedding in the village in June 1891.

When she was 16 she was taken to Bath where Queen Victoria was to open an exhibition. She was near enough to get a good look, but was so disappointed at the dowdy little old lady who alighted from the carriage dressed all in black.

Once a year the family (my mother was one of 14) were taken to Swindon to buy new shoes, which took all day. Their other "outing" was to be taken by their father on a picnic where they slid down the Downs on a sack. The child who was still on the sack at the bottom was given a penny. They seldom were!'

100

'During the summer holiday at Bromham in the early 1900s, several families would get together and walk to the top of Roundway Hill, Devizes, about two miles away and spend a day there. The children took tin trays with them, and we used to sit on them and whizz down the hill. There was a dew pond built by Smiths of Market Lavington, which we all paddled in. Once my grandmother decided to have a go.

Unfortunately, she slipped and sat down in the water. We helped her up and she calmly took off her wet knickers and hung them on a bush to dry, much to the amusement of all us children. Late afternoon we lit a bonfire and fetched some water from a barn at the bottom of the hill and boiled the kettle for tea. Afterwards we cleared up all the rubbish and wended our way home, tired but very happy.

In my childhood days, the roads weren't like they are today. I can remember heaps of large stones by the side of the road and a man with a long-handled hammer and dark glasses to protect his eyes, cracking the stones. That was quite a common sight.

In the holidays our father would drive us to market in a pony and trap. Near the bottom of Dunkirk Hill is a farm called "The Ox House" and in those days there was a large figure of an ox over the front porch. Our father told us that every time the ox heard the clock strike twelve, it would come down and go in to dinner. We used to beg our father to be passing at twelve but, of course, he never would. I wonder what happened to the ox, but it's still called Ox House Farm.

Market day was quite different to what it is today. The market place would be filled with rows of cages containing rabbits, ferrets, ducks, hens and cockerels and there were pens for animals, all to be sold by two auctioneers shouting against each other. If we were lucky we were treated to faggots and potatoes (no frozen peas in those days!) at a little shop in Northgate Street owned by Wordleys, I've never tasted faggots so good as they were.

In my young days the girls had wooden hoops and the boys iron ones, and we used to trundle them for miles. We played hopscotch, marbles, whip tops and tag. In the evenings my father taught us all sorts of card games and then we had ludo and draughts to amuse us.

In my teenage years I went to dances and in the beginning it was the quadrilles and polka, and then we moved to the valeta, waltz, foxtrot and lancers. I loved being swung off my feet in the lancers, it's so different today. If we went to Devizes to a dance we all had cards and the young men would write their names down for the dance they wanted. The girls all wore long dresses.'

'During the mid 1930s I well remember that the young children of

Co-operative Wholesale members in Devizes were annually treated to a New Year party. First of all we were taken to the Palace Cinema in Devizes to a film show. I remember there were always cartoons and usually a Western film starring cowboy actor Ken Maynard. After the film show we would go to the Corn Exchange for tea and further entertainment.'

'I was about seven at the time, in 1910, and I had never been in a car. On returning to afternoon school, I met my father at the gate. He got off his bike and called me back. I, having been tricked too often by his teasing, ran on. Coming home at teatime, I discovered that he had hired a car to go to a large country house to give an estimate for removal. He took Mother, a great treat for her, and would have taken me as well!

A year or two before that, at a different house, I remember going out into the street to see my first aeroplane that was due to fly over Salisbury at eleven o'clock that morning.

Some 30 years later I watched hundreds, all lit up, fly over Salisbury on the way to France on D-Day. What a century it has been.'

'My grandparents played an important role in my young life. They lived in a thatched cottage which is near to the church in Heddington. We used to walk over the downs from Devizes, past Cromwell's Castle and down Kings Ploy to the back of their garden. The fields were full of cowslips and sheep and if you were early you could pick field mushrooms. My sisters and I used to fantasize about the battles between the Roundheads and Cavaliers and were told you could hear the bloodcurdling cries of the horsemen if you kept silent.

Sometimes my grandfather set off at dawn to shoot rooks. Later my grandmother produced a pie which I felt sure contained some birds. I could not eat it because I thought of the rhyme "Four and twenty blackbirds baked in a pie". My grandmother worked extremely hard in the house and garden but still found time to help to deliver babies, lay out the dead and play a part in village life. Her pantry was well stocked with home-made preserves, bottled fruits, eggs in isinglass and medicinal wines. Before walking home she gave us a glass full of blackcurrant liquid to warm us on the journey. I do not know what the alcoholic content was but we glowed and sang, tramping over the downs.

I have a 92 year old aunt who lived in Beckhampton when I was young. The farm where my uncle worked bordered Fred Darling's stables. It was great fun to watch the sheep being dipped. We used to take large baskets containing bread and cheese to the men shearing sheep by hand. The sheep were difficult to catch and after shearing gave a terrific leap before bounding off. We used to walk to the top of Silbury Hill, avoiding patches where no grass grew. We believed it was a massive burial mound and blood would gush out of the bare patches if we walked on them. Sometimes we picnicked amongst the stones at Avebury, playing hide and seek or imaginary battles.'

'I grew up in Salisbury in the 1930s. I first remember seeing the Salisbury Giant in the celebrations for George V's Silver Jubilee in 1935, as he was paraded through the streets. I was so frightened of him Mum had to take me home – to a six year old he was enormous and I was terrified.

When my Mum was in Salisbury Infirmary having my youngest brother I took my two friends Joy and Basil down to the sweet shop at the junction of Fowlers Road and Milford Hill owned by Mr and Mrs Tapper, and on Mum's account I bought three sherbet dabs at a penny halfpenny each. Needless to say, I was in terrible trouble when Mum came home and found out. I shall never forget the taste of those sherbet dabs – sheer heaven, and worth the good smack I received.

On Sunday evenings different bands used to give concerts at the bandstand in Victoria Park. Sadly, the bandstand is no longer there.

Sheep fairs used to be held in the field between Old Sarum Rings and Fairfield Road. We would wake very early in the morning to go and watch the sheep arrive and then make a mad rush to get to school on time.

During the war we used to go to Old Sarum Rings and watch the planes take off and land at Old Sarum aerodrome. We would take a tin tray with us and slide down the steep sides. What fun we had. It did not cost anything, we would be gone most of the day, and then we would wend our weary way back across the two fields to home, tired, dirty and hungry.'

'TWAS HAPPY TIMES

'My childhood memories of Luckington village are of long hot summer holidays from school which seemed to go on for ages. If we were lucky we had a day trip to Weston-super-Mare.

We had a tan house down by the source of the river Avon where all the village children used to gather and play. We built pretend houses and found so many old bits of china etc, which today might be Treasure Trove – who knows!

Several of our fathers, or grandfather in my case, worked as the village roadmen. Then all our villages were tidy with all the verges and ditches clean of rubbish; the church path was always tidied each Saturday specially for church on Sunday. Our job through the holidays as children was to take the mid-morning lunch to the roadmen, thick slices of bread and cheese and bottles of cold tea. Our local lockup, called "The Blind House", became the roadmen's house where they kept their tools, so at lunchtime they all gathered there. I can see them now swigging away at this cold tea straight from the bottle, a Thermos was a luxury then.

The Tar Pot seemed to arrive to tar the roads during the school holidays, a curse to our parents. What a sight to watch the old Tar Pot being fired up and getting the tar ready to spread by big brushes on the road, then gravel was thrown over by hand. Then the steamroller came to roll it in. I can remember one village boy falling headlong into the newly spread tar.

We had not returned to school long in 1939 when I remember one of the roadmen, Mr Saunders, who was a big man, tapping at the school window telling us the war with Germany had started. We all had to stand and pray for peace. Miss Webster was the schoolmistress. What a hoot to the boys at school, she kept her hankie up her bloomers' leg. Many of us had fathers and brothers called to join the forces. Three of my brothers were in the army. The village women used to chat and cry about the war at the garden gates, my mother amongst them.

The monthly visit of the district nurse to school remains clear in my memory, when Sister Lewis, or as the children called her, the Nit Nurse, examined our heads. I can feel those nails of hers digging into my scalp now, and see her doing the throat swabs using the *same* spatula dipped into horrible pink disinfectant; this would not be allowed today. She was a very straight lady, with ruby red cheeks and bright lipstick, and her large white cap always immaculate. She was the local midwife as well, of course.

We had a bit of fun as children. Queen Mary came to stay at Badminton House, and would often drive through the village and give us the regal wave.

We also played on all the roads with whips and tops, and large hoops from top to bottom of the street to see who could roll the hoops the furthest. No cars to worry us then! As the Wilts saying goes, "There 'tis, 'twas happy times" for most of the children, though some were very poor and not in very good health. There were no expensive toys, just old bikes, dolls' prams, and most of the time just pretend.'

'Until I was eleven years old I lived in Reybridge, a hamlet within the parish of Lacock. There were 18 houses in the close vicinity of our house and the number of children was 35 so we had plenty of playmates. The games we played came in strict rotation. Who decided when playing hoops stopped and hopscotch started, I couldn't say but no two games overlapped. Skipping followed on from these, individually or joining in with a long rope turned by two people, then came rounders and whip tops. Getting string for these was a problem, expecially if one had a flyer. This differed from the dumpy top and was mushroom shaped and when you got one going you would make it fly! The broken windows were proof of this.

When the weather got warmer we took to the river, soon learning to swim. First of all on a small raft of rushes at a place called Dresnews, graduating to Newhall where you could touch the bottom, then down to the waterfall where overhanging trees made good diving boards and the waterfalls a chute. But we never ventured to Devil's Hole – reputed to be bottomless and a very dark, sinister, still pool in a bend of the river. I shudder at it even now. We got very proficient at catching crayfish, cooking them on an open fire.

When the days got cooler we played hare and hounds. Then on really cold nights out came the charcoal tins. These were cocoa tins with a wire handle and holes pierced in the bottom. The fuel was from the rotten branches of elm trees. These were lit and to make it draw the tin was swung round and round overarm until the whole lot glowed red, and then flung into the air. Woe betide a child who got in the way of any descending – it was everybody for themselves.

The smallholding opposite us had a derelict cottage attached to the main house – today it has been restored into a second house – and we played in there a lot and took refuge when the shout went out, "Here's Uncle's hound dog coming". Why we were afraid of him goodness only knows, as he took no notice of us. We were frightened, too, of two white bull terriers called Punch and Judy who were taken out on leads every day for a walk. They took no notice of us either! Marbles we played out in the lane, seldom disturbed by passing horse-drawn vehicles.

Our house was just above the flood line but the people who lived in the Square had to take to living upstairs when the river flooded and the children couldn't get out to go to school. We were so envious of them. The Square comprised six houses forming two sides of a square, the gardens completing the other two sides. When the river was flooded and completely covered the surrounding fields we would get our wave-cutters. These were likely looking pieces of wood collected whenever we saw it, tied on to pieces of binder twine – easy to get hold of if you knew where to look. Hurled into the rushing flood water then pulled back in, this created a wave. Why no one ever fell off the bridge and into the torrent is a mystery. Another daft thing we did was to run and jump over a small abandoned gravel pit. We usually made it but the boy who missed and jumped into the water is still known today as Soppy.

We knew the best orchards to scrump in and to make a quick getaway, the best fields to go for mushrooms and all the birds' nests for miles around. We logged them but never stole eggs.

Dad worked on the railway after coming home gassed and wounded from the First World War. He was a great naturalist and at one time I knew the name of every plant and bird. But, alas, my memory is fading, I'm getting forgetful but I'll never forget my happy childhood.'

CAUGHT IN THE ACT!

'The village bobby is sometimes remembered with affection and quite often with fear.

My brother Jack was well known for his pranks – mostly quite harmless. Living in Sutton Benger in the 1930s was a Mr Harris (known to everyone as "Beaver" because of his distinctive beard). Beaver, who was a market gardener, owned a horse called Blossom which was used to pull a small plough. It was not unusual for the village children to catch Blossom and take turns in riding him around the recreation field. The village policeman, aware of this fact, was intent on catching them. He thought his luck was in when he caught brother Jack riding Blossom. "What are you doing with that animal?" he shouted. "You come with me and return it to Mr Harris this instant."

A sheepish Jack led the horse back up the lane to its owner with the policeman following to make sure it was returned. Jack walked up the long path to the front door and the policeman waited at the gate. Imagine the relief, not to mention look of sheer delight, on Jack's face and the dismay and disbelief on the face of the law when Mr Harris said, "Thank you, Jack, for catching my horse and returning him – he has a habit of escaping from his paddock," and presented Jack with a shiny half crown!'

A PENNY'S WORTH

'I was born in 1917 in Bemerton. I well remember the days when we could skip and play hopscotch, hoops and tag in the road without any fear of traffic. Mrs Young's shop along the road was very popular with us children as we could buy sherbet dabs, liquorice sticks and other small packets of sweets for a halfpenny or even a farthing. We could also ride on the open top of the bus to Wilton Square from Skew Bridge for a penny and many are the walks my parents and I, my brother and the dog made to Grovely Woods and the race plain from Wilton Market Place.'

'We lived very near the shop and bakehouse at Wishford. We were able to buy pennyworths of sweets from big glass jars with lids on and they were put into little triangular bags. Every Monday Happy Jack called with his big basket which held an amazing assortment of safety pins, needles, bootlaces, and even special little books we could paint.'

'In the summer of 1937, while walking across a field at Stratton St Margaret, I found a sixpence, which seemed a fortune to a youngster. We even thought about taking it to the police station, but instead with this little sixpence I bought five Woodbines for my Dad, two ounces of lime juice sweets and an ice cream. How times have changed.'

HOOPS AND PIG KNUCKLES

'There were no tarred roads when I was a child and the dust in the side of the road was marvellous for marbles, marking out for hopscotch, skipping and hoops. We were only disturbed by the occasional bicycle bell or pony trotting by.

I had a wooden hoop, and always wanted an iron hoop like my brother's, but was told quite firmly that wooden hoops were for little girls and iron hoops were for boys.

I was twelve when I had my first ride in a car. An uncle appeared with this wonderful big motor. It was a high old-fashioned car with a big horn where you pressed the rubber ball. Much to my annoyance, he only drove us up the lane and back. I would have loved to have gone through the village so I could have waved to my friends!

We walked for miles across the fields picking flowers. A popular walk at Easter time was to go the four miles across the fields to Horton, picking watercress.'

'We used to play tip-it – draw a circle in the earth, hit the end of a small piece of stick with a larger piece and see who could get nearest the middle of the circle. Then there was five stones, using the knuckles of a pig's foot, scrubbed. We always had a wooden top, which we coloured on top and flicked with a whip, as well as playing hopscotch and marbles.'

'In the 1920s at Winterbourne Monkton we played different games each school term – whip and top, ball games, yo-yo, marbles and hoops. Every Saturday we had a rag and bone man come to the village, and if we were lucky he gave us two pennies for bones and bits of iron we found, and he also paid for mole and rabbit skins.'

FISHING FOR STARS

'My love of the country and all wild animals stems from being born in a cottage in the middle of a field between two woods, between Sheldon and Corsham. All our spare time as children, and there were seven of us, was spent in playing in the woods and exploring the local area. One very interesting spot was in a meadow about four fields away, the place called Holywell. A stream ran through the field but it came out of the bank in the middle of the field, where it rose quite steeply up to the next field. Here we fished for stars. Where the water came out of the field were large boulders and in the bed of the stream at this point we used to fish and find stars . . . well, very small stone stars, which even today can still be found. I took my own children to find them and they in turn have taken their children, my grandchildren. I have never found out what causes these perfect star-shaped stones, not much more that a quarter of an inch across.'

CLUBS AND SOCIETIES

'Wiltshire has always been active in Guiding. To celebrate the 21st anniversary of the movement in 1932, Lady Baden-Powell visited Trowbridge Park. A large cardboard "cake" was cut from which sprang hundreds of Brownies.

In 1933 Mrs Caillard invited all the Bradford on Avon district Brownies to hold their revels at Wingfield House. This was her home and she was their District Commissioner. In 1935 a collection was made for a Margaret Caillard Memorial. This was to be a "quiet room", ie the library in Wingfield House. It was opened by the Duchess of Beaufort and dedicated by the Bishop of Salisbury. Sadly, Wingfield House has now been divided into several houses.'

'I kept chinchilla rabbits for show and had 30 breeding does which had to be fed before I walked to school. I belonged to the junior section of Warminster Fur and Feather Fanciers Club. We showed locally and as far away as Manchester.

My father made me special boxes to carry them with my name and address painted on them. We had to take them to Warminster station

108

on Friday evenings and put them on the train, then with great excitement picked them up on Sunday afternoon, and if you were lucky you found attached the prize cards you had won.'

'During the 1930s my sisters and I lived on a farm at Kington St Michael, which is about four miles from Chippenham. In 1932 we all became members of Chippenham Young Farmers Club. This club was the first of its kind in Wiltshire, started in 1930.

In those days membership was quite different from what it is today. As I recall, there were about 20 members. Each member had a two to four week old heifer calf to rear and look after. These calves were kept for about 14 months, from February. Originally the calves were brought by a cattle dealer by the name of Frank Drury, who would take between 20 and 30 calves to the back yard of a public house in Chippenham where the animals would be allocated to members of the YFC by a draw from a hat. We would then each take a calf home. During the following months we had to feed and care for them. We had a record book, into which we had to enter details of food and other aspects of the calf's growth, also all costs involved. All this had to be done on a weekly basis. Periodically someone from the County Agricultural Office would come to the farm and together with the club leader, would inspect the calf and the record book.

At that time the County Agricultural Office showed great interest and would also attend the monthly meetings of the club. This was largely done to help and guide clubs and their members.

During the 14 months we learned how to put a halter on the calf and lead it onto the public highway, and they also had to be groomed each day. My sisters and I would walk the calves around the local roads, hoping we would not meet many cars. Our problem was that if the calf became frightened it would jump about and sometimes land on our feet and this would be extremely painful. If the animal should get loose, it would upset the others or else run away like a mad thing. It can be imagined that it was with great difficulty, at the ages of nine to 13, we were able to catch them again. However, peace was usually restored after a lot of chasing, shouting and giggling before we reached home.

After the 14 months the YFC held a show and sale of the calves. This was quite an event. Held in May, the show was at the Angel Hotel yard and the sale at the cattle market in Chippenham. At the show, members were divided into classes by age. Prizes were silver cups given by animal feed manufacturers; there were also money prizes. When the judging was complete, we all walked our calves down to the cattle market for them to be sold by auction.

During the run-up to the show and sale, we spent many hours

109

grooming the animals and trying to teach them to stand properly to show them off to the best advantage, rather like dogs at Crufts. The day before the event we were very busy washing each animal to make its coat feel and look good for the judges. We also plaited their tails and left them overnight to make them nice and curly in the morning. Their hooves and horns were polished with linseed oils to make them shine. After all this we put the calves in a large shed lined with tons of straw for the night, hoping they would keep clean ready for the next day.

The following morning we were up early to get ready to walk the calves into Chippenham to arrive by 10 am. From home it would take us over two hours.

This trip was always rather traumatic as the animals would sometimes get a bit frisky, especially when we arrived in the town and had to walk them straight up the High Street to the Angel Hotel, taking into account the traffic lights which were on the town bridge in those days. Fortunately, we had an experienced male helper with us from our farm who, being knowledgeable, was able to help us to prepare the animals for the show and during the walk to the show managed to keep the traffic clear and in order as we walked one behind the other.

When the animals were sold we had to repay our parents the costs

The First West Lavington Girl Guides, formed in 1921. Guiding was a popular pastime for many Wiltshire girls.

of feed and rearing the calves, as per the details recorded in the record books, but any profit we kept.

My sister and I were chosen, with our calves, to go to the 1937 Royal Show, which in those days was held at Windsor. As far as I know, no other Wiltshire YFC member has been chosen for this. It was the year of the Coronation of George VI and Queen Elizabeth. We were very excited when during the day they, together with the two young princesses, drove right by us.'

'During the 1940s I joined the Westbury Girls Training Corps (GTC) and I have very happy memories of those years when I was in my teens. The Girls Training Corps was an organisation for girls aged 14 to 20, run similarly to the Air Training Corps and Army Cadets for boys. We wore a uniform of white blouse, navy skirts, ties, navy shoes and forage caps. We enjoyed taking part in marching, cycling, sports, carnivals, learning first aid and cookery, and meeting other girls when we attended large rallies.

Once a year we all travelled to London for the weekend to attend a rally at the Albert Hall – this was quite an experience for us in those days! We slept in Clapham Underground shelters which had been used as air raid shelters during the war. There were rows and rows of three-tier bunk beds and hundreds of girls from all over the country who were members of the GTC joined us. We attended the rally on the Saturday afternoon and then usually went to a theatre in the evening, which had been organised for us – several theatres were taken over by the GTC so not all of us saw the same show. I can remember Max Miller at the Victoria Palace (not quite the show for teenage girls to attend!). However, one weekend we spent in London we were lucky enough to go to the Adelphi Theatre where we saw *Bless the Bride*, a lovely musical written by Vivien Ellis.'

SCHOOLDAYS BEFORE THE FIRST WORLD WAR

Wet clothes steaming on the guard in front of the stove, writing in a sand tray, little girls dressed in white pinafores with frilled shoulders – memories of schooldays in the first years of the 20th century, and ones that most people who grew up in those days will share.

SKATING TO SCHOOL

'My maternal grandfather was a manager of the Public Benefit Shoe Company (later to become Lennards shoe shop), Regent Street, Swindon, but the family lived in County Road; this was from about 1908 – my mother tells me that in winter she often used to skate to school on the Wilts & Berks Canal into the town where College Street School was. This is now Fleming Way.'

WET CLOTHES AND COCOA

'Quite a number of children at Brinkworth had to walk a long way to school and often were wet through on arrival. Their coats would be put to dry on the guard around the stove and I still remember the smell as they were drying! Some children who brought their lunches also brought cocoa powder and sugar. Two of the older boys would be sent to fill a bucket from the pump at School House and this was placed on the top of the stove to boil so that the children could have a hot drink. As they were allowed an hour and a half for dinner a lot of the children went home.

If any of the children felt unwell they would have to lie covered over on chairs outside on the grass until they all went home after school, as of course there were no telephones or motor transport in those days. In the spring there were often outbreaks of chickenpox and German measles.'

'When the time came for school at Bowerchalke, we had a long walk. Footpaths, no hard road, our food for the day packed in a satchel, we wore lace-up leather boots. There were no rubber boots then and our feet were often very wet but no one seemed worried. In winter

The top class of eleven to 14 year olds at Dauntsey's Elementary School in 1909. Pinafores were everyday wear for girls before the First World War.

we always wore lots of clothes, as it was cold on the hills.

The school was in the centre of the village, two rooms, the large one divided by screens. There were two fireplaces, with open coal fires surrounded by an iron guard. We sat in long desks, rather close to one another at times. Attendance was usually in the seventies. An attendance board was kept on the wall.

At the back wall of the school was a large bell which one of the children would ring for a while in the morning. This made sure we were on time. We then formed into lines and walked into school in a proper manner.'

WRITING IN SAND

'I went to Horningsham school when I was five; there were about 108 pupils between five and 14 with three teachers. There was a small room for the infants and we transferred when we were about seven. I used to enjoy the needlework. We had writing books but in the infants we had a tray full of sand and a stick to draw in it. I often think what a silly thing to give to little ones. My first day at school – we had little tables with four chairs and about 20 of us in the room – the boy opposite me, I suppose he didn't like the look of me, upped with his tray and flung it at me. My hair, my face, everything covered in sand. Oh, didn't I ever scream! He hasn't forgotten it to this day – we still start laughing.'

'I had a happy childhood and enjoyed my school days at Winsley, which started at the age of five and finished at 14. We had a wonderful infants teacher who, with great patience and kindness, taught us to read, write, spell and do our sums. What would the children of today think of the bead frame on which we learned to count, our slates, and the sand trays in which we drew pictures? Most of the girls wore white starched pinafores over their dresses as there were no uniforms in those days, so we more or less looked alike. Once a year we were measured and weighed, examined by a doctor and a dentist. The district nurse came very often to see to the children who unfortunately had lice in their hair, poor things.

Eventually we moved into the big classroom where things were much stricter and the headmaster was too fond of using the cane. When he retired the new one was much more free and easy and very popular with everyone. When school was over, out we went to play with our hoops, marbles, skipping ropes or tops. I loved my top most of all, once it was spinning I could whip it all down the road and keep it going for ages. In the summer we would take our dolls and prams up to a field where we had hidden bits of china in the hedge to use as tea things. How we enjoyed playing in the hay fields and riding back to the farmyard on the hay waggon. A picnic in Conkwell woods was a great event. Everything was packed into a wheelbarrow and off we went, mums, dads, aunts, uncles and all the children. What pleasure we got from such simple things.

When I left school the headmaster gave me a fountain pen as a prize for being a good pupil. I was very pleased to receive such a gift, as you can imagine. Later in life he told my brother that I had brains but was too lazy to use them! He was probably right.'

STARTING AT THE DAME SCHOOL

'During the late 1890s the daughters of a local family businessman (milling and farming) started their education at a little village dame school, walking a mile each way unescorted. There they learned the three Rs and some sewing. One little girl's sampler dated 1898-9, produced when she was eight years old, is still in her daughter's possession. The schoolmistress and her mother also ran a small sweet shop on the same premises where a good pair of liquorice bootlaces could be purchased for a halfpenny.

Secondary education followed at a local boarding school, where life was much as portrayed in the works of Angela Brazil.

114

Compulsory French was spoken at mealtimes and anyone lapsing carelessly into English was passed a black ribbon bow, which tended to circulate like a sedate game of passing the parcel. The girls travelled home every weekend by train (Box to Corsham) and were transported to and from the station in their father's horse and trap. Acute homesickness often set in at these weekends, as the standard of food and general home comfort was very different to that of school. In winter it was not unusual to have to break the ice on the jug of cold water provided for washing.

It is interesting to compare this education with that of another little girl who lived with her mother and aunt in her grandfather's isolated cottage. He was a shepherd on a farm about three miles from the village. During the 1920s she walked daily unescorted to school, unless lucky enough to get a lift on the back of her aunt's bicycle.

At the village school the children sat in rows (persistent chatterers in the middle of the front row). One little girl remembers frequently having ink on the end of her pigtails, the boys in the row behind having dipped them in the inkwells. She also tells a dramatic story of a boy throwing an inkwell at the headmaster. It made a big splash across a map of the world hanging on the wall – evidence which remained for several years.'

TO SET AN EXAMPLE

'Fanny was born in 1905 in Chippenham and started at Westmead infants when she was three and a half years old. She recalled the little ones falling asleep at their desks during the afternoons at school as they were so tired.

The headmaster was a very strict cruel man. He would pull the girls' hair as they passed him in the corridor, or jab his finger in their ribs. The boys were prodded as well. He appeared to enjoy using the cane for the slightest reason, even to punishing the boys who did wrong outside school. When he died the children were asked to bring a halfpenny each towards a wreath. She was pleased to relate that no money was taken for this purpose.

Two boys caught some hens and pulled some feathers out, and let them run around with bald patches. The farmer reported them to the headmaster who thrashed the boys very severely in front of their class to set an example. This thrashing could be heard all over the school.

Fan hated art lessons, as she was a practical person who could not draw and could see no sense in doing what she was hopeless at. One day the headmaster came in, looked and sneered at her effort and put it up on the wall to shame her. It did not worry her at all.

During the First World War the Neeld Hall in Chippenham was used as a military hospital. The girls at Westmead school learnt to do patching and mending, repairing the bedding and mending and patching clothes. They always had to use a darning mushroom to darn the socks, but often found that the holes were bigger than the mushroom. Sheets were patched and turned sides to middle. Fan thought this was better to do than art and usually volunteered to do mending. The older girls enjoyed taking the mended goods back to the Neeld Hall.

The children went through all the crazes of iron hoops, whipping toys, and skipping to school. Their father whitewashed the pig sty for the girls to play in as they didn't keep a pig.

There were fields, called Englands, behind their home, and they walked miles during their spare time. They crossed the canal by clambering across the lock gates. They fished for evets (newts) in pools with worms on a bent pin on their line. The boys often caught the girls round the face with one as they pulled it out.'

WHAT WE WORE

'I went to school at four years of age in Swindon. In those days girls often wore white pinafores over their dresses to keep them clean; they looked quite pretty with frilly bits on the shoulders. I can remember wearing white calico knickers with a back flap that unbuttoned when needed, but my buttons had a habit of falling off! It was much better later on when we wore bloomers, at least we had somewhere to put our handkerchief. We also used to wear bodices called stays which buttoned down the front and later on when stockings were worn suspenders would be attached.

Laced boots to the knee were worn. My father used to repair our footwear and to make them last would put steel studs on the toes and heels.

I always had a Sunday best dress, a winter and a summer one. The summer one was made specially for Sunday school Anniversary. We wore hats in those days and I remember a special one, a cream straw with a wide brim and a ruched white silk lining under the brim and a lovely bunch of cherries hanging down one side. Gloves were always worn, cotton or silk in the summer. In winter we wore little fur necklets and had a muff to match to keep our hands warm.'

'The children did not wear uniforms at The Academy, a private school I attended in Tisbury, but we did make uniform dresses for the orphan girls of Dr Barnardo's. The material was of a stiff and coarse texture in black and white check, not the most cheerful type to sew or wear.'

116

OVER THE FIELDS

'My first recollection of Donhead St Andrew was when I went to its school in 1918. I walked through the fields when fine with a group of Donhead St Mary children.

I was terrified of the headmaster, he had such a loud voice and he often had to punish the boys severely. Quite a lot of the work was done on slates and facts of history and geography were learnt like tables (such as, "a lake is a piece of water surrounded by land" and the opposite fact).

There was no main drainage in the village so the toilets were buckets. When a certain mistress came to be interviewed for the headship and had to stay for one night, having lived in a town all her life she was amazed that the toilet was over the river – she never forgot. The village was later collecting for the church bells to be restored and the rector asked her for a donation. She refused saying, "My money goes for providing sanitation for the school and when we can pull the chains in the school I shall leave," and he replied, "And when they can ring the bells again, I shall leave" (and they both did).

In those days no sports gear was available from the County, but Lady Pender from Donhead House provided balls, skipping ropes, hoops, etc. She also gave the children a tea at Christmas and I believe each went home with an orange and a bun. The field around the school was called the Church Meadow, it was kept in good condition and the area facing the school was used as a school playing field up to the time of the school closure. St Andrew's Day was always a special day. In early days there was a tea party in the school to which many visitors came, followed by an entertainment. The schoolchildren had a holiday after a short service in the church.'

SCHOOL BETWEEN THE WARS

School life had not changed much during the 1920s and 1930s, there were still only minimal amenities available and the parents of this generation would have felt quite at home in the classrooms their children now attended!

FIRST DAY AT SCHOOL

'I lived on a remote farm two miles from the nearest village and did not see many people. I was like an only child as my sister was almost grown up and I had no small playmates, only an imaginary friend with whom I played lots of pretend games; it was a wonderful carefree life and I was never bored.

At the age of five I was sent to stay with my grandmother who lived in the village for the school week, bring driven on a Monday morning in a pony and trap by one of the men who worked on the farm. I well remember asking him if "he could make Friday come quickly" and he would say, "All right, I'll have it here about Wednesday," and I firmly believed that he would. He deposited me among a classful of infants, none of whom I had ever set eyes on before and frankly I was terrified. There was another little girl who was almost as frightened as me and was attracted, she told me later, by the brightness of my woollen hat and decided there and then to be my friend. Afterwards I loved that school but always looked forward to going home at the weekend. The friendship of that same little girl who started at the infants school with me has lasted all our lives without a break.'

'Play school had not been introduced in 1919 so at the age of five I started my education at the village school at Shrewton. How well I remember those first few days, sitting in the classroom which was heated by a monstrous coal-fired stove. Tears trickled down my cheeks as I gazed up at a poster of the Tonic Sol-fa and wondered what it was all about. The teachers were mostly kind. One diminutive lady known as Dotty Dimmer, although not much bigger than her pupils, certainly exercised great discipline. Another, Jinny Dawkins, terrified me with her threat of being sent down to Hell Fire if we misbehaved. My mother suffered many troubled nights at the frequent nightmares I had following these threats! Playtimes were great fun though, with games such as "A hunting we will go" and "The farmer wants a wife".

A great transformation took place when the new headmaster and his wife arrived – the introduction of school uniform of which we were so proud. Our education might not have been very comprehensive – the three Rs, good discipline and, most importantly, plenty of sound commonsense – but we were carefree and knew great happiness.'

THE WAY TO SCHOOL

'I came to Wiltshire in 1921 at the age of five, when my father was employed as a wheelwright and carpenter on the Manningfold Bruce Estate.

The village school – now a private house – had 20 to 30 pupils in two classrooms, run by a head teacher and a pupil teacher until 1927 and coping with children up to the age of 14 years. After that year over-elevens were transferred to Pewsey secondary school.

The way to school was along stony roads, broken by "pot-boilers", springs bubbling clear cool water, some of them quite high, lovely to sink one's face into and drink on a hot summer's day of childhood. Imagine kneeling in the middle of the road to do that in these traffic-filled days. Quite deep ditches ran down both sides of the road to reach the young river Avon. These were lovely to paddle in and find frogs, tadpoles, minnows etc causing many a late arrival for lessons. If you wanted to play hookey from school you could hide all day under the bridge where there was a two foot wide concrete strengthener, and be lulled to sleep by the gently flowing water. Tranquil days of childhood then.'

'Neston school was about a mile from our house. We sloshed through the puddles to school in the winter, and in the summer it seemed to take forever. One dear lady about halfway to school always had some cups on a bench by the well. How we children loved a drink of that cool clear water when the weather was so hot.'

SCHOOL IN SALISBURY

'I was born in 1915 in Belle Vue Road, Salisbury, and my first memories are wartime ones – of my aunt looking after me as my mother had gone back to teaching because the men had gone into the army, of syrup in my cup of cocoa when the sugar had run out, and the lights of the horse-cab that brought my father home safe at the end of the war.

119

The first school I went to was St Mark's elementary school in Wyndham Road, then all ages, later Wyndham Park infants school. At Christmas, the attendance officer, a Mr Matthews, came to entertain us with conjuring tricks – most mystifying! When I was seven, I went to Bishop Wordsworth's School Preparatory Department which was in what is now the school's big music room in Bishopgate. We walked back and forth twice a day, no school dinners then. The best day was Tuesday, when we walked through the market place to see the hens, ducks, calves, pigs and sheep where now the cars are parked. Needless to say, we were sometimes late for afternoon school.

At ten I got a scholarship and went into the "big school" (WWS was then co-educational). The younger girls' classes were held in the School of Art in New Street. These premises are now solicitors' offices. I remember huge Greek statues in one classroom, masters coming round from the boys school to take Maths and Science, and running round to Exeter Street for chapel on Wednesday mornings. Then in 1927, the new South Wilts Secondary (now Grammar) School for Girls was opened and we transferred to Stratford Road. I well remember the first day – a bright September day – everything new and smelling of paint and varnish, and the thrill of each girl being given a pen, pencil, rubber and ruler. The playing field was rough ground and we spent our dinner-hours picking up stones so that it could be levelled for us to play lacrosse and rounders. Miss Moore, the first headmistress, gave the school a fine tradition which is still continued.'

'The High School for Girls was founded in 1876 and was in the old London Road near St Mark's church. When I joined the school in 1933 the Misses A and N Reid and their sister Mrs Vipond were joint principals and the school brochure included "Games, Music, Art Examinations from Local Universities and London Matriculation", but "as we value the formation of character and development of healthy bodies no attempt is made to press examination work."

Uniform was strictly adhered to and woe betide any girl who did not wear her uniform panama hat in summer or velour in winter – how daring we felt as we grew older and made deep folds in the velour hats which made them perch on the backs of our heads! Perhaps summers were warmer in those days, for we always had to go back for the summer term in short white socks, cotton dresses with tussore collars, blazers and panama hats. In all photos of me at an early age, my hats seem to engulf me. At the kindergarten stage boys were also pupils but they went on to St Probus or the Modern School at seven years of age. The teacher had a wire-haired terrier,

Bing by name, and he spent all day by her desk and made me long for one of my own.

Concerts and prizegivings were held in the Victoria Hall behind the bus station in Rollestone Street or in the Assembly Rooms above Smiths. I remember us all having to wear white dresses and take part in a concert. In the summer our concerts were in the grounds of the Brambles opposite St Mark's church and we danced, sang and acted, popping in and out from behind the bushes and shrubs. Winters always seemed to have enough snow to prevent the country girls from getting in by bus and we town ones used to be sent home for an unexpected holiday to play in the snow.'

EASING MY WAY IN

'Unlike other children, I never really "started" school, I more or less "eased" my way in. Let me explain. We lived opposite the school at Lyneham where my mother kept the village shop so I spent many hours in the front garden watching the various comings and goings. In time I crept across the road to the school gate. This was the 1920s remember, cars were few and far between on that road and the fastest thing on wheels was often a bicycle, on legs it would possibly

Boys outside Wishford school in the 1920s. Short trousers were worn until the boys left school at 13 or 14 years of age.

121

be the farmer's two horses, off for a day's work in the fields. If I was lucky I might find myself hoisted on to the back of Blackie and be taken for a short ride as far as Hobbes Cottage, there to be off-loaded and to wander slowly home.

Gaining courage, I eventually braved the boys and their football and crept on to the smaller playground at the back to hang over the wall and watch the skipping games or the Ring of Roses, Drop the Handkerchief and Oranges and Lemons. Ball games too, of course, and in the summer, handstands against the wall.

Soon I was inside the wall and joining in and then came the day the teacher, coming out to collect her class, put me on the end of the line and let me follow the rest inside. There I was given a desk and a sand tray and was soon happily "drawing" pictures with some implement or other. After this I spent an idyllic year. I could stay in our garden if I wished but if I was a least bit bored, over the road I went and spent a few hours in school. By the time I was four and a half I had been put officially on the register and was happily chanting "The cat sat on the mat" with the rest of them.

My memory of the infants room is that it was on three levels with each level being quite a step up; no doubt the intervening years have heightened that step, I never remember anybody falling, anyway.

My next move was into Miss Martin's class. She had part of the "big" room, separated from the top class only by a screen so that we were soon used to hearing the bad boys next door being caned on the hand by Mr Willoughby. This was part and parcel of schooldays and nobody was any the worse for it.

It was about this time that I first became aware of the dinner-time line-up, the dozen or so children from poorer homes who were deemed by the school doctor to be in need of extra vitamins and were consequently fed a spoonful of cod liver oil. The sight of that oily substance in the big bottle made my tummy turn over but they seemed to swallow it quite happily before dashing back to the playground.

By the time I reached Mrs Hutchins' class we were expected to have mastered the basics and were being introduced to more exciting things such as sewing! French seams and running fells became part of our vocabulary, to me they were a waste of valuable reading time, nevertheless I am thankful now for Mrs Hutchins' patience.

Punctuation was also part of her curriculum and I can vividly remember writing out the Lord's Prayer complete with commas, full stops etc in the correct places. One mistake and you started again.

Our workbooks too looked more interesting as we were encouraged to decorate our geography books with wrappers from tins to illustrate which country the product came from; cuttings from

The Children's Newspaper could be fitted in when applicable and it certainly made us use our eyes more. I had a big advantage here as I could scour the shop shelves for likely material and encourage my mother to cook this or that if I fancied the label.

By the time I gained another teacher, Mr Willoughby had left and his place was taken by Miss Webb who happened to be Mrs Hutchins' sister. They were not alike in looks or temperament and one suspects they did not always see eye to eye. I started at a disadvantage as, when about to cross the road one Saturday morning with my dreamy sister, she started across without checking for traffic and who should turn the corner in her car but Miss Webb. I had reached out to grab my sister but was too late so I dashed forward and hauled her across to the other side whereupon this ferocious woman leapt out and berated me! Couldn't she see it wasn't my fault I thought, but it was as well I kept quiet as I recognised her instantly on her first day at school and no doubt she recognised me though nothing was ever said.

Miss Webb was a great one for manners and the boys soon found themselves raising their caps to the staff in the morning and we all found ourselves standing when anybody came into the room, something never done before. She was also very musical and we learned a wide variety of songs; although she played the piano for us we didn't dare to muck around when practising as she had a picture placed strategically over the piano and could watch our every move. It took us a while to realise this.

Some days the class was quite depleted as a number of boys went off to Wootton Bassett to woodwork classes and girls to cookery. I was very envious of these fortunates as my mother never had much spare time to teach me and my own experience of cookery was to peel the potatoes or watch the milk until it began to rise so that she could dash out and finish making the custard.

Too soon came the news that I was to sit an examination at Chippenham secondary school and after a few months I was being kitted out to begin a different kind of school life. Immature I may have been but my early years in a small village school were no handicap I found and I shall never forget my happy years at Lyneham school.'

THE BRITISH SCHOOL

'We had two schools in Marsh, the church school and the British school. As we were chapel, where my father sang tenor in the choir, I went to the British school. I started school at three and a half and used to be pushed down in a pushchair by a kind older girl who lived nearby. The infants were in the care of Miss Miles, a loving, caring but firm teacher. Our room was square, the walls painted dark green at the bottom and cream at the top, and heated by a huge tortoise stove. If you sat near it you were cooked, if you sat by the cold walls you were half frozen so Miss Miles tried to get us in a semi-circle for reading lessons. If it was very cold she would open the little trapdoor at the bottom of the stove so that we could see the red glow. That stove was blackleaded and polished until it shone. The caretaker, Mrs Doughty, lived near the school and worked very hard keeping the school clean and carrying in the huge buckets of coke from the yard. We all wore boots to school and kept them on so the floors got muddy. She also had the lavatory buckets to empty. There was a row in the girls' playground with trapdoors at the back so the buckets could be removed, presumably the boys had the same. I can't remember where they were emptied – maybe on someone's allotment and dug in to produce prize winning vegetables.

Most of us went home for our midday meal as our dads worked at the tanyard, Boultons, or on the farms. The children who lived outside the village at Old Dilton, Standerwick, Stourton Bushes or Happy Land had to stay to dinner and when it was very cold they made cocoa on top of the stove and lifted up the little trapdoor and toasted thick slices of bread. There was no school bus, no buses at all in fact, and these children had to trudge several miles to school and if they got wet coming to school there was nowhere for them to dry off.

I don't think there was a lot of absenteeism – we were too afraid of Pa Insley, the attendance man. He was a tall man with a sad droopy moustache who came regularly to check the register. Another regular visitor was the Nit Nurse! It was a terrible disgrace if you had "things in your hair", but as we girls all had long hair and sat close together it was small wonder that dirty heads were found. I had nits once – fortunately my mother found them and not the nurse – that would have been too shameful. But life was a misery for days. My head was raked with a fine tooth comb several times a day until it felt as if all the skin had been raked off. As my hair was long and mousey coloured the nits were difficult to see but my mother and I both suffered in different ways until my head was clean. Sometimes the nurse would give a girl a note to take home and she would come to school, her hair smelling of paraffin for a few days. Once a girl came back with close-cropped hair!

Another unwelcome visitor was the dentist. She had to use Miss Miles' room and the infants were all put in the big room for a couple of days. The sight of the dentist's chair with its white sheet used to terrify us and we dreaded having a tooth out. The dentist was a redhead with a brusque, rough manner. We were sent to school with a clean hankie pinned to our white starched pinnies and clutching our sixpence and another big hankie. Perhaps she had to do a certain number of extractions in a day and couldn't afford to be held up by a timid child but thanks to her I have always dreaded visiting the dentist.

Much less terrifying was the doctor. We were sent home with a note for our mothers to attend. I always had a bath the night before and all clean clothes – it was a point of honour to be clean for the doctor, a practice that followed us into adult life. Again we were herded into the big school room to wait our turn nervously to see the doctor. It was consoling to see our mothers waiting in the passage-way with the other mums and babies in prams. It must have taken a long time for each examination as we wore so many clothes – a warm vest, padded stays (pre-liberty bodices), a red flannel petticoat, a white starched petticoat and a skirt. We also wore bloomers, high-legged lace-up boots and thick socks. If the doctor found anything wrong with you, you had to go to the clinic in Trowbridge. I was supposed to be a bit chesty so if it was very cold my mother would slap a layer of Thermogene – bright orange cotton wool-like substance – on my chest. When I had my weekly bath in front of the fire she would put the Thermogene in the oven to revive it. Some really chesty children were sewn into a little Thermogene bodice all winter!

At school we had a thorough grounding in the three Rs but not much else. Sometimes a map of the world was put on the blackboard but it didn't mean much to us – our horizons were very limited – we knew the pink bits belonged to England but that was all. When you were eleven you sat for the scholarship to Trowbridge Girls High, which was a world away. We used to have singing at the end of the afternoon and then a closing hymn and prayer. We always started our day with a hymn, a prayer and a scripture lesson. I think that was nice, it gave a sort of order to the day like saying grace before your meals when you were a child. We did have some very good poetry books at school – I can remember reading *Hiawatha* at an early age. I can also remember reading *The Lady of Shalott* though I don't suppose I understood half of it, but I used to be so wrapped in this reading I never knew that the boy in the seat behind was dipping the ends of my long hair in his inkwell which left ink drips on my white starched pinny and made my mother very cross. She never seemed to realise I couldn't help it.

When we grew older we were allowed to ring the school bell. Sometimes two of us would do it, sitting side by side on the back seat pulling on the bell rope, knowing the sound of the school bell

125

would send the slowcoaches pelting down the road – no one liked to be late for school.'

'MISS'

'I had to walk nearly three miles each day to school, up Blunsdon Hill and then down into the village.

During the afternoon we had to lie on the floor on rush mats, for a rest. The teacher used to stride over us, so of course the children would go home and tell their parents what coloured knickers Teacher was wearing that day, usually pink.'

'Miss Mills taught at Kington Langley school from about 1938. She drove out from Chippenham. She was a church organist so was rather heavy on the school piano keys. She taught the infants and was very strict. The forefinger had to be straight when holding a pencil or a size one knitting needle, or the edge of a ruler was brought down across the offending digit.

She wore hand-knitted bouclé suits. She would often sit knitting in class while the children worked quietly. She hated the smell of oranges and was cross if we had one with our sandwiches. She would cook her dinner on the coke stove in the corner of the classroom.'

'YOU'LL GO TO A REFORMATORY!'

'Early memories of childhood and schooldays go back to 1937, to a small infants and junior school in a village near Salisbury. Just one classroom, one teacher and anything up to 48 children between the ages of five and eleven, all under the strict control of Miss Clark. Any rebellion or misbehaviour was put down by threats of being "reported to Trowbridge" or sent "to a reformatory". We were not sure what it meant but it didn't sound very nice.

Sand trays and cast-iron desks were the order of the day and Miss Clark's only equipment consisted of a blackboard and chalk and a cane, but very few pupils were unable to read after the first six months. No mod cons, just two electric lights and a tortoise stove at the side of the room, very useful for thawing the frozen milk on frosty mornings. The three Rs were the main subjects, the tables being learnt by the continual chanting method with mental arithmetic very much encouraged. There was Poetry once a week and Religious Instruction or "Scripture" as it was then known, was taught by means of large coloured pictures on canvas that were unrolled and hung on the blackboard and the relevant story told. We

126

were also taught needlework and knitting; the school speciality, at least of us boys, seemed to be dishcloths knitted with string on wooden skewers.

There was no playing field, just a small asphalt playground, the main games being hopscotch and marbles, and conkers in the autumn. But the most daring "game" was to abscond via the back door and through the playground having been kept in after school hours for some misdemeanour. This escape was possible due to the school door opening immediately onto the road and it was usually necessary for Miss Clark to make sure it was safe for the children to go out. This would unfortunately result in severe retribution on return to school!'

SCHOOLS DURING THE WAR AND AFTER

Memories of schooldays during the war belong more properly amidst our recollections of life in war and peace, as evacuees came to crowd us out of our classrooms and we learned to cope with gas masks and the threat of air raids. However, one school in Salisbury gives an example of how school routine was disrupted for many children. Otherwise, here are memories from the other side of the desk, so to speak, from those who taught in schools in the post war period.

TEACHING IN THE VILLAGE SCHOOL

'Having undergone my education in Wiltshire, I became an infants teacher and started my teaching career in the local village school in 1942. It was a school with only two teachers, and children attending from the age of four to 14 years in the same building, unless they were clever enough to pass the scholarship exam to the local grammar school eleven miles away. This meant becoming a weekly boarder in the town, as our nearest station was four miles away, a journey which had to be made on a bicycle. No school transport then. With the scholarship, parents were given a grant either for travel or lodging, not both.

In our school we still had quite a number of evacuees, but a great many of them had gone back to London, as they did not really fit in to village life. The only entertainment in the village was what we made for ourselves – dances, social evenings, whist drives and the occasional concert of local talent. A great deal of time and energy was spent in this way, raising money for National Savings, Wings for Victory etc, and later on a Welcome Home Fund for the forces men returning home. Two of my brothers were in the army but happily, they both returned safely.

One morning a local lady was heard weeping loudly at her garden gate with any neighbour who spoke to her, as her husband, who was in the navy, was reported missing. The local taximan who stammered said to me, "Oh, y-you kn-ow a b-bellowing c-cow s-soon forgets its c-calf". Fortunately, the gentleman returned home safely.

At the school we ran a Junior Young Farmers Club and our club won the shield for All England for the best JYFC. We duly travelled to London to The Friends Meeting House in Euston Road to receive the shield. Fourteen of the older children accompanied the headmistress and me, first to the station in the carrier's bus, with seats around the sides, leaving room in the middle for parcels collected from the town once or twice a week. No buses in those days in outlying villages. Most of these children had never been on a train before, let alone gone to London, so you can guess the excitement. Each child carried his or her own tube train tricket and one boy, having lost his, crawled past the ticket collector. Of course, he was more conspicuous that way, but the ticket collector was only amused.

In 1947, which was the year when we had deep snow from January until late March, my sister and I moved to a village at the Gloucestershire end of Wiltshire, the other village being on the Hampshire and Berkshire borders. We were both appointed to the village school, my sister as head and myself as assistant. My father, who was by then retired, came with us, as my mother had died. It was a lovely little school, a real Miss Read place, with charming children but the school building was only one room, with movable screens between the two classes and heated by an iron tortoise stove in the middle. No electricity, just oil lamps. This was not very easy for timetables but we managed very well with quite favourable results.

School dinners were then the new thing and they were brought each day in metal containers in a van. They brought full containers and took away empties. The meal was eaten in the same classroom, served by my sister and myself. The washing up was done in a lean-to shed which served as a cloakroom and had a sink at one end for washing up etc. Of course, in each of these schools the toilet, if that is what one could call it, was "across the yard".

A strange little lady was the school cleaner and general washer up etc. She rather resembled a witch, as she was very small, four ft nothing, and she always wore black and a floppy felt hat, and had one rather protruding tooth. One very small boy of five loved to help washing up. He said to her one day, "Mrs T, you are very old, aren't you?" "Well, Leslie," she said, "I suppose I am getting on." "One day you will die," said Leslie. "Well, yes, I suppose I shall," she said. "Then," said Leslie joyfully, "then I can do all the washing up." One day Mrs T gave Leslie twopence. He looked at it in his hand. "Twopence – twopence," he said, "you can't even buy a packet of crisps for twopence."

We had whist drives, quiz nights etc, in the school. At one "fur and feather" whist drive at Christmas I won a goose, with all its feathers on. No one wanted to pluck it as it was so near to Christmas, so Cliff, who is now my husband, helped me to pluck it in our garden shed. It took us two hours, because when we had got rid of the feathers we had to start again on the down. My sister then prepared it for Christmas dinner and it was very good.

I mentioned the tortoise stove. One day when all the children were quietly working, three baby rats came from under the floor and played by the stove. We watched them for some time. Later, the Pest Officer came and put some poison down, and then the floorboards had to be removed to take away the bodies owing to the aroma.

Our school house was joined to the school, and we had a communicating door in between. When I was married we laid out our wedding presents in the school. It was a very versatile building and is now a bungalow. It was next to the village church. Needless to say, it was a church school and we had visits from the vicar regularly. The church had a fine peal of bells and one school afternoon it was the funeral of a well known local man and a "muffled" peal was rung. The clappers of the bells had a leather shield on one side, making the second peal sound like an echo. I shall never forget the hush which came over the children.'

SIRENS AND FARMING

'My schooldays in Salisbury were greatly affected by the Second World War, which broke out a year after I'd started at the South Wilts Grammar School for Girls. We had to share our school with the Portsmouth High School which was evacuated to Salisbury. The tennis courts were dug up and air raid shelters built where we would assemble whenever the sirens sounded the alert. The assembly hall of the school, cloakrooms, and common rooms were commandeered by the authorities and fitted up as a first aid post in case of invasion by the Germans in 1940. Fortunately, it never had to be used.

During those war years, the school "adopted" a farm at Wishford in order to help plant and harvest potato crops, there being no men available for such work. In spite of being dirty, back-breaking work most of the girls were glad to get out of lessons for a morning or afternoon, and also earn some money into the bargain! Depending on age the pay ranged from threepence to fourpence halfpenny per hour, so no great fortunes were made. Even today the smell of tractor engine oil brings back memories of trying to snatch a few minutes rest on an upturned bucket, before the tractor came around again and unearthed another patch of potatoes. During the summer holidays we would help with the harvest of grain crops, stooking sheaths of wheat, barley or oats.'

MUM'S SCHOOL

'From 1942 to 1967 my mother was headmistress of the village school at Hilmarton, near Calne. I only attended the school for a short time when I was four years old. We didn't live in the village so at five years old I transferred to my local school – my mother considered this to be beneficial to both of us.

Hilmarton school was very small, just three classrooms, a staff room and two lobbies. There were probably no more than 70 pupils who came from the village and from surrounding hamlets and farms. Ages ranged from five to eleven and were split into three groups. My mother was a working headmistress, in other words she taught as well as taking care of all the school administration. My mother taught the infants class; she wasn't fond of babies but loved children once they became "interesting" and I think she found infants the most challenging and endearing age group. Two other ladies taught the older children and I believe they were both at the school for almost as many years as my mother. The school building was typical of those days. Red brick, square, with two large rooms each running the length of the building. The two large rooms were interconnecting and each room was split into two to give three classrooms and a staff room. The staff room was properly partitioned from the adjoining classroom by walls and a door, but the other two classrooms were simply divided by a curtain.

Teaching cannot have been easy in those conditions as each class would surely have distracted the other but maybe discipline was better then. Each of the two large rooms had the inevitable stove –

130

huge black creatures which belched smoke and fumes and had to be fed regularly with coke to give some warmth. A familiar sight in winter was rows of wet shoes drying on top of the stove and socks draped from the surrounding guards. On really cold days the frozen milk had to be placed near the fire to be thawed out ready for drinking at morning "playtime".

At one corner of the building was a tall bell tower, accessible from inside the classroom, and in early years the bell was rung morning and afternoon by one of the older boys to summon the pupils to school. In later years both the bell and the tower were found to be unsafe and a handbell was used instead.

The school had two entrances, one for juniors and one for infants and as was the practice in those days, when the bell was rung pupils formed into lines and filed quietly into school to begin lessons.

The toilets were in a separate block across the playground and their popularity depended on the weather. In summer it was very pleasant to be excused from class and wander in the sunshine for a few minutes, but in winter it was a different story and you had to be pretty desperate to run across the playground to the unheated cubicles and expose your nether regions to the chill winds.

The toilets were not connected to the main sewer and consisted of two rows of cubicles back to back, one for girls and one for boys. The seat was simply a plank of wood with a hole in it. About six feet beneath the cubicles was a pit running the whole length of the toilet block, and at regular intervals destructible peat was put into the pit. Every so often some unfortunate person, the caretaker possibly, had to descend into the pit to clean it out.

On one occasion a small boy – at least it was always assumed to be a boy, although the culprit was never found – climbed down into the pit and amused himself by poking people's bottoms! Outraged pupils reported this to my mother who, although seeing the funny side of it, had to question the whole school and threaten dire consequences should it happen again. She warned the other teachers not to look at her as she was admonishing the pupils otherwise she would burst out laughing. She said she could imagine the delight with which the offender carried out his prank – not everyone's idea of fun though!

I visited my mother's school as often as possible but particularly on special occasions such as sports day or at Christmas. Sports day was held in a field at the back of the school. It didn't belong to the school and probably had to be cleared of animals before it could be used. There were all the usual races including egg and spoon, three-legged and wheelbarrow, as well as the serious 100 yards, hurdles etc. I remember the weather as always being good on sports day but that's probably not true. It was, however, always a fun day with many of the parents attending and competing, lots of noise and hustle and bustle, bunting and prizes for the winners.

Christmas parties were wonderful and even when I was at grammar school I would try to attend them. They started at 1.30 pm and ended about 4 pm. Great quantities of sandwiches, cake, jelly and tinned cream were prepared. I'm not sure who did this, as far as I was concerned it just appeared. Each carrying their own named plate and cup brought from home, the children would walk along the village street to the hall where school dinners were served and, dressed in their best party clothes, demolish in minutes what had previously taken hours to prepare. After the food it was back to the school for games. As the games progressed and the children became more and more excited, the noise level rose until a whistle had to be blown to restore some semblance of order to the proceedings. At four o'clock the party finished and each child was given a paper bag containing an orange, a balloon and some sweets before being collected by their parents or shepherded onto the school buses. Tidying up afterwards took some time but I never minded as the party had been such fun and even the troublesome children had been good for a few hours.

Also at Christmas there was the school concert. This usually entailed a few short appearances by individual children or small groups reciting poetry, dancing, singing or playing an instrument and was followed by "The Play" which had to involve the whole school. This was no mean feat as some children simply cannot sing or act, but no one could be left out for fear of favouritism.

Whenever possible my father would be roped in to play the piano and my mother would produce and direct the play. As with all school performances but particularly with small children, there were forgotten words, wrong entrances and shyness, but generally a good time was had by all and parents were very proud of their offspring.

As with Miss Read's "Fairacre", the village had a small post office and general stores, a pub and a church and certainly in the 1940s and 1950s most people grew up in the village, married a local boy or girl and settled in the village to bring up their own children. With better means of transport and communication I imagine life in the village is now very different.

On a recent trip we visited Hilmarton to look at the school. Remarkably it still looks the same from the outside and the village itself seems little changed apart from some new houses. I know that teaching methods have changed and I'm sure the school has been modernised – particularly the toilets – but I still think of it as "Mum's School" and have very fond memories of her days there.'

THE WORLD OF WORK

ON THE LAND

Farming has changed so much over the last 50 or so years. Before the Second World War we were still working with horses, and the labour intensive farming year followed the same peaceful round it had done for decades. These are memories of farming as it was, and of some of the men on whose backs the work was carried – the farm labourers, and the old drovers of the Plain.

FARMING IN THE EARLY 1900s

'My father farmed land on the Pembroke Estate at Barford St Martin. He employed about twelve workers. Six carters arrived at 6 am to feed the ten horses. They then went home for breakfast in their cottages close to the farm, returning to start work from 7 am until 5 pm six days a week. There were three shepherds who looked after about 600 sheep. There were no fences on the downs, so they had to be up there with their dogs to prevent the sheep from straying. The lambing pens were on the hill. They were made of hurdles covered in straw. Lambing of these pedigree Hampshire Downs took place in December and January, and was a very cold experience at night in winter. The shepherd's hut was warm inside, which made it seem all the colder when you went out. Three general labourers were employed around the farm as well as a groom gardener. The carters with their horses did all the work which is now mechanised – ploughing, sowing, harrowing, rolling and harvesting.

There were two dairies, one with 20 cows looked after by a dairyman and his wife, who lived in Arnold's Cottage. The other with 40 cows was in Dairy Road at the far end of the village. Here there were two dairymen. The water meadows were properly irrigated and the cows were put out to grass there on 20th March each year, my father's birthday.

Ploughing was hard work for men and horses – usually with a single plough with two horses. On the very heavy land this did not go deep enough, so after the first ploughing the men with the steam plough were engaged to go deeper. This consisted of two steam traction engines, one at either end of the field. A six-furrow plough was attached with a hawser. The engines then pulled it up and down the field.

On the Tuesday before Christmas my father took me as a treat to

Ready to start the milking at Highgate Farm, Wootton Bassett in 1913. Each man is similarly equipped with a hat, smock, three-legged stool and milking pail.

Salisbury Market. We went by pony and trap to The Red Lion where the ostler stabled the pony and looked after the trap. He would have it all harnessed up for the time we wanted to return.

Just after the war my father bought his first car, a Talbot Darracq. He took driving lessons from the chauffeur at Hurdcott. He practised in the yard. The first time he wanted to stop he did not reach for the handbrake outside on the running board, but shouted "Whoa there". The chauffeur had to run to get hold of the brake to prevent the car from running into the big walnut tree! The car had acetylene headlights and oil side and rear lights.'

THE DROVERS

'The following account of the life of the drovers was written down in the 1970s by a popular local raconteur, Mr R H Wilson, whose family persuaded him to share his memories of the turn of the century.

"Of all walks of life, or if you prefer it, of all 'life's walks' those

135

of the drovers from the beginning of the century until the First World War were very different to those of the other farm workers – varying between complete loneliness during the day's journey along the Downland sheep walks when they would probably not meet a soul, and the convivial get-together when they put in for the night.

During those first years of the 20th century, when I was more or less a full time drover myself, we rarely had less than six of our own men on the road, and many freelancers, at one and the same time. I was never allowed to take part in the long treks, some of which are hardly credible in these times and would certainly be impossible.

On one occasion my father sold a big drove of cattle to the Duke of Marlborough, and they had to be delivered to Blenheim. All the regular drovers were on other journeys, and it was decided that the foreman at our farm at Shrivenham should take them. He had a large family and his wage was twelve shillings a week; he was given 13 shillings and sevenpence for one night's lodgings, as the journey would take two days, and for his railway fare home from Woodstock. He slept rough, in a yard with his cattle, thus saving on his lodgings, reached Blenheim about four o'clock the next day, looked at the money, and said to himself, 'My youngsters can do with this', and he and his dog walked the 30 odd miles home during the night, arriving in time to start work at six o'clock. This same foreman had an opportunity of earning many times that sum by way of perks later on.

My father had been given the contract to supply beef cattle to the troops engaged on vast Army manoeuvres and based on Churn Downs, near Ilsley. All these cattle had to be prime quality and I think had to be delivered daily during the fortnight that the exercise lasted. My father arranged for a butcher friend to do the slaughtering at the camp, and on the first day the Quartermaster told our foreman to bring a horse and cart with him on future deliveries and that he could have all the bullocks' heads. He found a ready market for these luxuries at a shilling a time in the villages en route. I do not know how many cattle were involved, but I do know that the fortnight's contract netted a profit of £2,000.

The average freelance drovers were little more than nomads, always sleeping rough, but a cheerful, civil and gay lot of good fellows. They all had good dogs – dual-purpose – being capable of controlling a difficult drove of sheep or cattle, and at night, silently piloting a hare or two through a gateway or gap in a hedge that had been previously netted. They were almost without exception experienced poachers, and when not actively engaged in their craft, were 'nocturnal'.

Our farm is situated on the Ridgeway, the oldest public highway in Britain, a 30 ft wide grass track, and was used by many thousands of sheep on their way to Ilsley sheep fairs. Our head drover, Bert Swatton, once had twelve droves in view at the same time, slowly gliding along this most beautiful part of Wiltshire.

There were ample buildings and yards actually on the Ridgeway to accommodate the sheep and cattle, and an ever-open 'doss down' at the farm, a half mile down below, in the village. This was a cosy loose-box, containing bundles of dry, clean straw for their beds, and frequently the first thing we saw, on peeping out of the window in the morning, would be two or three men and their dogs – waiting for a free breakfast and anxious to be gone as early as possible to resume their journeys.

A worthy Master Drover was Fred Lawton – based on London, who for nearly 50 years met our weekly consignment of sheep and cattle and walked them from the station to the market, between the hours of 2 am and 4 am, this being the only time they were allowed to use the London streets, and they were always penned and in the right lots when my father arrived in the market at 5 am.

I expect it would be safe to say that 'Wilson's drovers' have traversed every road and sheep walk in the South and South West of England since the late 1700s – until lorries drove them out of business.

My great great grandfather lived at Longcot, near Faringdon in Berkshire, and had the contract to supply beef cattle to the Fleet when lying at both Southampton and Portsmouth. These cattle would have to travel by road, they were slaughtered on the quay, salted and put straight on board. And great great grandfather was paid on the spot in gold, which he carried in saddle bags on his horse.

Highwaymen were still in business, but as he was usually accompanied by two or three mounted drovers he was not worried unduly; but on one occasion after taking cattle to Portsmouth he was delayed, and was returning alone and failed to reach his usual lodgings near Winchester before dark, and a ruffian jumped out of a ditch and grabbed the saddle bags. My tough old forbear was always prepared for such a situation, but preferred to arm himself with a short heavy stick, which he felt could be more quickly brought into action than a more lethal pistol. He gave the thug a terrific crack with the stick, which broke his arm so completely that he saw it fall. This was followed by an equally violent wallop on the head and he jogged gently on in to Winchester." '

'My life on a farm in the 1920s was very different to life today. I remember my father starting his day at haymaking times at daybreak. He would take the horses and mowing machine and go to the fields and start cutting the mowing grass while the dew was still on it so that it would have long days to dry.

At 6.30 am he would bring the cows in from the fields for milking which was all done by hand. He would then bring the milk in pails to the milk house where it had to be put through the separator and cooler, and then into churns to be ready for the waggon to take it to Staverton dairy. Then all the milk house implements had to be washed and the whole place scrubbed through. Milk was also sold at two pennies a pint to people in the hamlet.

My father would then come in for a cooked breakfast which my mother had prepared. However, first there was the stove to light after removing the ashes from the previous day, as apart from a little paraffin oil stove for Father's first cup of tea it was the only cooking stove.

Breakfast consisted of rashers of bacon cut from a side of half a pig which had been reared on the farm and now hung in the larder, and the eggs from the hens and ducks which were all on the farm. They

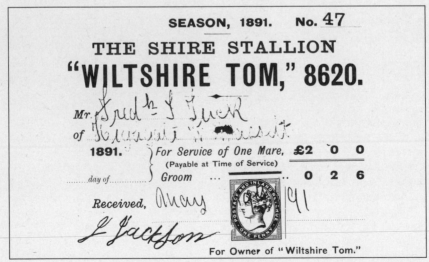

Shire stallions such as Wiltshire Tom were a common sight on the roads right up to the Second World War, being led by their grooms from farm to farm. Oddly enough, the grooms were often small men, but they were true horsemen and controlled their huge charges with ease.

were fed on corn and maize; it was my job to feed the hens and collect the eggs. In the spring it was lovely to watch the hens with the small fluffy chickens.

Potatoes, which were food for the pigs, were boiled with the skins on in a boiler. My earliest memory is being given a little hoe and pretending to help my father hoe mangolds which were grown for cattle food.

Haymaking was a very hard job with long hours as it was all done by hand and horses. Everyone in the family helped with raking the hay in heaps, then the men would put it on the waggons with hay forks.

Meals were taken to the hay fields in baskets. They consisted of loaves of bread, hunks of cheese, slices of cold boiled bacon, raw and pickled onions, with cold tea, cider and home-made lemonade to wash it down.

Butter was made once a week. The cream from the separated milk was put in a butter churn and one had to turn the handle. It seemed like hours until the cream finally turned to butter.'

'My cousin was born and brought up on a mixed farm of 520 acres situated on the hill slopes to the north overlooking Box. He is the fourth generation of a family of tenant farmers who now owns the farm himself. His great grandfather moved to Box from Saltford with a team of horses to work on the railway and the Box tunnel during the time of Brunel.

During his boyhood his father had eleven men working on the farm and eight horses were used for hauling. Extra help was employed at haymaking and harvest time.

He remembers hay being cut by scythes, although later on a mower was used. The men worked as a team and turned the hay to help it to dry out, each man taking a swathe. A horse was used with a mechanical sweep to bring the hay to the rick which was built in the corner of the field.

Corn was cut by a binder pulled by two horses. The horse nearest to the growing corn wore a muzzle to prevent his having a feed while he worked! The sheaves cut by the binder were stacked in stooks of about six or eight sheaves each and were left to dry, depending on the weather. Oats took the longest to dry and were left out for three Sundays at least. When the sheaves were sufficiently dry they were hauled to the rickyard, made into ricks and thatched to keep out the rain. During the winter the threshing drum came in and ricks were dismantled, the sheaves being put through the drum to separate the corn from the straw.

We remember many happy times in the harvest field, having tea which had been brought out by the farmer's wife for everyone. Everything was much more leisurely in those days and there were no tractors before the Second World War. The farmer relied solely on horses and other machinery.

On my cousin's farm there were 36 shorthorn cows, each with her own name, milked twice a day at 6 am and 4 pm. The men milked by hand and sat on three-legged stools with a bucket between their knees. The milk was then poured into a vat and allowed to flow slowly over a ribbed metal cooling vessel, which had cold water flowing through the middle of it so that the milk could be cooled quickly. It was then collected into a 17 gallon churn for transport to Box station and London.

Farm workers started work at 7 am if they had no horses to look after, but the carter started at 5.30 am in order to feed and water the horses before the other men arrived in the morning. In the summer he had to fetch the horses in from the field. The farm worker's wages were about £2 a week and 21 hours overtime was worth 14 shillings!'

FARMING DURING THE SECOND WORLD WAR

'I joined the Land Army at the end of 1939 when we were being called up to aid the war effort. The farm was quite near my home so I was able to go home each night. My father was called up in September so mother was relieved as I was the eldest of eight children. It was a mixed farm consisting of dairy, sheep, pigs, chicken, beef cattle and corn. We would start milking at 5.30 am. The cows were marvellous – such gentle creatures. They would await their turn patiently to go into their allotted place in the milking parlour without any trouble. We'd milk approximately 60-70 cows twice daily.

Of course during the year there'd be seasonal work. January to March were the severe months both for us and the beasts. Much of the work then revolved around the farm year. Cattle had to be fed and cleaned. Hay taken from the rick, root crops from the clamp and cake from the store. On fine days there'd be fields to be ploughed, also sowing the spring corn. We still used horses plus spicked-wheeled tractors. Much of the machinery and equipment was checked and repaired, harrows, reapers, binders and threshers overhauled. Fences and hedges were mended and hurdles repaired ready for lambing soon to begin. During these months also we'd thrash last year's grain, feeding the thresher from the top of the round corn ricks. Often we'd find a mouse in our boots or up a trouser leg. The combine harvester wasn't used until nearly the end of the war.

140

Spring and early summer were the most exciting seasons, with young lambs, new calves, baby chicks, piglets etc and the new shades of green adorning the hedgerows, trees and meadows. The shepherd lived in a caravan near his flock during the lambing season and we'd take home the orphans and rear them on bottles. This is also the time of thinning and hoeing, plus rolling fields of young corn shoots. In early June or when the grass was fit, haymaking would begin. The grass was cut, tossed and turned until it was dry enough to be gathered. Then it would be pitched onto horse-drawn waggons and taken on the long haul to the rickyard where the ricks would be built and then thatched with straw. On a fine day we'd work until dusk. During the war double summer time was introduced so often it would be 10 pm before we'd finish.

Shearing the sheep would also take place in July and early August. A gang of shearers – during the war two men – would travel from farm to farm.

Harvesting the wheat, barley and oats would start in August. The binder would toss the cut and bound sheaves onto the ground and they'd be stacked into stooks until dry. These would eventually be collected and taken to the farmyard and made into circular ricks and generally thrashed after Christmas. This was the period of rabbit stews. They were killed whilst hopefully scuttling for safety from the cornfields. We missed the harvest suppers as they were suspended during the war but always managed to celebrate with a pint of cider. In the late autumn the fields would again be prepared for the following seasons, ploughed and sown with winter corn.

It was hard work, compensated for by the many new friends we made from all walks of life and the humorous stories we can still tell of our time on the farm.'

MANOR FARM IN THE LATE 1940s

'We arrived in Wiltshire at Manor Farm, Berwick St James at Michaelmas, 29th September 1944. Our home was thatched with three downstairs rooms, two with kitchen ranges, one with a fireplace, and I had a water hand pump over the stone sink. There were three bedrooms, with a door at the top and bottom of the stairs to stop the draught. Electricity had been brought to the village in 1938 and every house had two light plugs and a socket so electric wires were looped from one room to another and one had to resort to candles and lamps also.

The population at that time was below 200 and apart from one man who was a radio and electric assistant and many older couples, the remainder of the men worked on our farm and the neighbouring

Druids Lodge Estate as carpenters, jockeys or blacksmiths. The larger houses were tiled and the smaller houses were thatched or with slates. They were built of flint and stone, some brick and some chalk, called mud walls. Most houses had their own well and those who did not collected water from the well house in the centre of the village where it was hand pumped from a borehole.

Some houses had quite valuable pieces of furniture handed down to them, and there were always pictures and photos and a mantelpiece full of pretty china. Many of the beds were hair and feather beds home-made from saving duck and chicken feathers.

The farm, of 1,500 acres was then some arable, growing wheat, oats, barley and swedes, mangolds and turnips for cattle and sheep. There was a milking herd of about 75 shorthorns, which were milked by hand until we installed an alfa laval bucket-milking machine when we came. These were looked after by the cowman and his son. The cowman had worked on the farm since he left school at the age of eleven and continued until he retired at 70.

The 300 Hampshire Down sheep were looked after by a shepherd as a hurdle flock where there were no fences and a pen of hurdles had to be moved every day. At lambing time a pen was made and he spent his nights for a while in the shepherd's hut in an armchair, where there was a coal stove for warming lambs and boiling a kettle.

There were two carters and five shire horses. The carters brought in the horses at 5.30 am to feed then went to breakfast and were back to harness up and be ready at seven o'clock to do the land work. They returned at 3.30 pm to feed the horses and unharness, groom and inspect their feet and turn them out to the field again before going home.

The blacksmith worked all day in the blacksmith's shop where there were hand-blown bellows for the fire, shoeing everyone's horses and repairing machinery including putting the metal band on the outside of the wooden spoked waggon and cart wheels.

The total work force for the farm in 1945 was 14 men and one woman. There was always something to do. In 1945 and 1946 the corn was cut by tender and stooked and when fit was then built into ricks which were threshed in the winter months. The corn was put in two cut sacks – how many would know how to carry or stack those today.

The harvest of 1945 we had Italian prisoners of war who were very lazy. In 1946 there were German prisoners of war from a camp on the Druids Lodge Estate. These caught rabbits as the corn was cut, skinned them and asked me to cook them, so each day they had a saucepan of rabbit and a saucepan of potatoes and a can of tea. Rabbit pie or fried rabbit was a common meal in all houses. Our first combine harvester was a Minneapolis Moline which came in boxes from America under a lease/lend government agreement and was put together on the farm. My husband and his tool box was with it most of the time for break downs. At the end of harvest it was collected, as also was a neighbour's, and no payment was made.

There were some water meadows which were "drowned" in February, that is by a series of hatches the water from the river ran in ditches across the meadows until they were lowered in water. This was to protect the grass from frost and when drained again would grow quickly.

A part of the farm, as also a neighbour's, had been used for Army tank training and this was handed back rather churned up after the war. The Druids Estate also kept a number of racehorses and had a gallop for many miles around the farm. There were regular shoots of pheasants and partridge and hare coursing at the end of the season.

The market in Salisbury was used for sale of cattle, sheep, pigs and any livestock. Before the present market site, Wooley and Wallis had their sale yard in Castle Street, Jefferies in Brown Street and Knapmans in New Canal. The Corn Exchange was on the site of the present library, where you took your samples of corn for sale.'

THE LABOURERS

'"Sidney Arthur Bodman, salt of the earth," was how the speaker at Sidney's golden wedding anniversary described him. To all who knew him it was a most apt compliment. He was the ninth son of 14 children born to a farmer who in those Victorian times would have been described as a "gentleman farmer".

To illustrate his character we must go back to the 1930s when Sid was in his mid forties and himself father of ten children and so, by necessity, no stranger to hard work. Sid's appetite for work was not only born of necessity however, he happily thrived on it. Sid had himself been a farmer but by cruel misfortune, which is another story, had lost his farm and was working for a local farmer at Sutton Benger. It was a stiflingly hot day that found him clearing weeds and debris from a meadow pond, aided by his teenage son Bob, who also worked for the farmer. They had made an early start and had toiled non stop for some four hours, when young Bob said to his father, "Dad, I'm bushed, I'll have to take a break."

Sid worked on, making no comment. Barely two minutes had elapsed when the farmer appeared. Spotting the lad seated he stormed, "On your feet, boy! I don't pay you to idle your time." The farmer walked on and young Bob rose wearily and said to Sid, "That was hard of him wasn't it, Dad?" Sid, without looking or stopping, replied, "Well, he was right wasn't he son?"

The following years found Sid working as a gardener to a local gentleman. One day, while hoeing a row of vegetables he was approached by the gentleman who was holding in his hands a pair of nearly new boots. Showing Sid first the uppers and then turning them over to display the soles, he said, "Tell me, Sidney, what size boots do you wear?"

Sid paused for a moment, no doubt mindful of his five growing sons. "Sevens, eights, nines and tens, sir," replied Sidney Arthur Bodman. Salt of the earth.'

'Our house, the White House, was miles from anywhere, over towards Baydon Hole Farm. We lived out there and my uncle Tom used to live next door. I'm 78 years of age now, my sister Phyllis is 71 and brother Len 73. My father was head carter, looked after horses and worked on the land, for Mr Baylis. He worked for him for 19 years.

My mother, she used to look after chickens, and go out in the field picking up stones all day – what you call stone-picking. So that the binders, when they cut the corn, they didn't go over any heavy stones. Mostly the women used to do it, paid about five shillings a week or something like that. Very little money.

And she used to take in a lodger, Jackie Brilling I think his name was. He used to work on the land as well. And after he'd done a day's work he used to sit by the fire every night polishing his garden fork. He used to polish it. Well, that's the way they used to go on. The handles of the forks they used to use, during the harvest where they used to pitch corn up, the handles of the forks and the grips, they used to shine, really shine!

They used to wear corduroy trousers, they used to pull 'em up then they used to strap them round there. And puttees – no wellingtons in those days! No, no – boots and puttees. There were always clothes around the stove, a high stove with a rack around. You'd be surprised to see the shape of different things around the stove.

If it was wet, if the weather was really, really bad, Dad used to say, "Oh I'll take you to school in the old dung cart." And he used to wrap us up in West of England sacks and bring us up to school, up here in the village. West of England sacks were used to put wheat in, which would weigh, full up, two and a half hundredweight. The farmer used to hire them from the West of England Sack Hiring Company. On a wet day, when it was too wet to get in the field with the horses, you'd have a sack needle and you'd sit in the barn all day

144

long mending these sacks where the rats made holes in them, and all that. Used to patch them up. We used to come home from school and help. In the summertime, when they were busy harvesting, Mother used to say, "Get off down that barn and patch some of those sacks up," and away we had to go! We never used to get nothing for it, no.

During my school days I was a bit of a lad but I'd treat my teachers with respect. I wasn't all that bright in education, but I still got through life. When I was 14 I left school and went to work on the land. The first day at work, the old farmer said to me, "Take those two horses and go out in the field and start ploughing the field." I didn't know a little thing what I was going to do. I didn't know how to even hitch the horse on. But I persevered and I found a way to do it.

At age of 14 I lost my father. I had a fight through life to try and help my mother survive. I was earning seven and sixpence a week at the time but I give my mother seven shillings and I kept the sixpence myself. I could buy a packet of Woodbines for a penny, which was five Woodbines in a packet. Then I used to live with one of my aunties and me and my brother used to have to wash in the old village tank where the horses used to water before we're allowed to go into bed. We had a very, very hard life.

When I became 16 the farmer I worked for, Mr Spackman, said he was going to get a tractor. So he said to me, "You can drive the tractor." Well, the first day I went straight through the hedge and out the other side. I had no idea how to drive a tractor or anything else. But I learned as I went along. I never give up on anything. If I says I do a thing I do a thing and I persevere and persevere and I drove that tractor.

By then my money went up to ten shillings a week. So my mother said to me, she says, "You give me nine shillings," she said, "and you can have a shilling." In those days I thought a shilling was a great lot of money.'

THE MACHINES

'The family firm was R & J Reeves of Bratton, making drills and ploughs for nearly 200 years from the 1780s to 1970. My grandfather Henry Reeves was a clever engineer and later the firm was well known as manufacturers of hay and straw stacking elevators. At first it was under patent from a Mr Andrews, whose wooden machine opened by a kind of scissor movement of steel chains. Then Henry had a brilliant idea – using the chains to open the trough straight into a folded-in-half position, by horse gear at first, then later engine power (Lister). This Advance Elevator had a timber frame; later Henry designed a steel frame elevator which was gradually raised till the top of the rick had been built.

Sadly, when the hay baler was invented it became difficult to sell the steel elevators on which the men had worked during the winter, including the foundry where the castings were made, so R & J Reeves & Son Ltd closed down in 1970.'

'My father in law William Osbourne worked for his uncle Bill Cowley of Allington, who leased steam rollers. They were almost the first men to steam roll the roads in this area. When William had saved sufficient money he bought a steam engine for himself, paying hundreds not thousands, and having to go to Northampton to fetch it. He drove it back to Luckington on iron wheels and threshing drum, calling at water hydrants on the way.

He had threshing customers within a six mile radius of Luckington. He had to get up at six o'clock to get sufficient steam pressure to enable him to start work at eight o'clock. The hire of the machinery was £3 a day, coal sixpence a hundredweight, and some farmers had difficulty in paying.

Lady Douglas, the late Duke of Beaufort's sister, who lived at Claremont (a large house in the village) liked a ride on the engine and downed her pint of cider with the rest of the men.

It was tradition for the men of the village to follow the threshing drum to find work, this carried on until the war when land girls took over.'

IN SERVICE

With the 'big house' demanding both indoor and outdoor staff, and even the most modest of middle class families employing at least one servant, before the Second World War going into service was commonly the only option available to young girls leaving school. It could be a good life, and it certainly gave opportunites for travel beyond the confines of one's town or village, but it was hard work for little pay.

FOURTH HOUSEMAID AT THE PARK

'The year was 1929 and I was longing to go to work; for I did not appreciate looking after my younger sisters. So when my Guide captain visited Mother asking if she would consider me coming to work at her home at the Park, I was ready and willing. For already I was familiar with the staff areas as us Guides worried either the cook, head housemaid or one of the ladies maids to help us through our various badges. Even so, the size of the house was quite a shock and I was often lost at first. In those days the house was lots bigger than now – as the Second Baron had the various wings removed and made to its original state.

I was engaged as a fourth housemaid – by the housekeeper who wanted to know if I was C of E and did I like dogs? My wages would be £16 per year with ten shillings laundry money per month. I would be entitled to one half day each week with every other Sunday from lunchtime until 2 pm sharp. She promised as I had come in March, no doubt I would get one week's holiday later, after the other girls had theirs, they were entitled to 17 days. The housekeeper was responsible for me – but the head housemaid instructed me in my duties until I got used to the work. The family consisted of her Ladyship who had three sons and the daughter, who was familiar being my Guide captain. The Colonel had died a little before my arrival, but the Lady was hostess to her father in law who was a widower, and came down from the London house quite often at weekends with his valet and Fifi the pekinese. He was the First Baron.

The staff as well as the housemaids consisted firstly of the butler, a most awe inspiring man to one so young – but I soon got used

147

to him. He told me he had been Groom of the Chambers to Lord Lonsdale and had worked in very large establishments. I didn't enquire whatever that meant or whatever his duties would have been! There was a first and second footman, hall boy and odd job man. The latter seemed to be forever scrubbing passages – cleaning windows, and looking after the boilers, but how he secretly drank! We all expected he would end up in the lake, for he always rode his bicycle home, no matter in what state he was. The kitchen staff had a chef, cook, kitchen maid and scullery maid; they did their own cleaning and did not join us for any meals. Then too there were the two ladies maids, who with the butler and housekeeper had meals in the latter's room. Us girls breakfasted and had tea in our own sitting room, but joined the men for lunch and dinner in the servants hall.

We were very fond of a dear old house carpenter who was more than a friend; when we had an accident which fortunately was not often, he repaired so cleverly. The electricity was not mains supply, the electrician lived in the village and he it was who saw to the changing of bulbs and fuses. During spring-cleaning he would dismantle the chandeliers and wash all the fiddling small pieces and reassemble with such patience. How they glittered afterwards!

Outside I gradually got to know some of the staff – there were many estate workers. The home farm of course supplied the Jersey milk, cream and butter for our needs. There were many gardeners and groundsmen, the former bringing in the plants and flowers in abundance. The grapes, peaches, nectarines were really luscious. I can still imagine the aroma of those grapes.

The Bothy housed the single gardeners, who had their cooking and cleaning done by a woman from the village.

The laundry was run by a man and wife with two laundry maids. They were kept very busy, as the London house sent theirs in huge hampers by rail.

I had almost forgotten the chauffeurs, there were three, one to drive the Park bus, also two grooms, as the Lady and her daughter rode to hounds. There were also racehorses at Sparsholt, near Wantage. I remember Polyphonto, a great favourite with us all. When the trainer came to see the Lady, the jockey Eph Smith or sometimes Steve Donoghue would be in the pantry, giving the men a tip!

After I had got down to the work it came quite natural, and I even took pleasure in what I was doing. I cleaned entrance halls through the front and the flower room, when the gardeners had finished making a mess, and the housekeeper's room before breakfast, which was also my job to get laid and carried in by 8 am. So it was often up by 6 am to get finished on time.

Then the rest of the day was cleaning our sitting room and the various staff bedrooms, bathrooms and landings. When the third left I was promoted, and my duties were some steel grates and brasses. I cleaned the smoking room which had two grey parrots, one in each window – what a mess they made! – the billiards room and front hall. Upstairs it was bathrooms, dressing rooms, the bachelor wing and some stairs. Usually a room was turned out each day or we prepared rooms for visitors.

Arriving as I did at spring-cleaning time, I was soon initiated into climbing very high steps and swinging the turk's head, which I found very painful round the shoulders, neck and arms at first, for we often had three extension rods which meant great care in controlling the wretched thing. The house carpenter and odd-job man took up all the carpets, which were beaten outside by the estate workers.

There were miles of floors to be scrubbed or polished as well as all the paint to wash, tapestries to be brushed down and ornaments washed, not to mention furniture and beds to be beaten and brushed. All the polished furniture was then washed and leathered in vinegar water before polishing with beeswax and turpentine. Not for us the silicone easy polishes. I had many blisters cutting up the blocks of beeswax before adding the turps and setting it in a bowl of hot water to melt.

Of course whilst all this upheaval was going on, for about two and a half months the people went abroad – they had a place in Spain. When they returned it was the weekends full of visitors, then everyone was in the London house during the season, for more jollifications in the week. There would then be a lull in the proceedings with not quite so many weekends, and holidays for us would start, after which the family adjourned to Scotland for a few weeks and, on their return, hunting and cubbing parties would begin, with shooting usually at weekends. So we met lots of society people, some quite well known, and royalty now and then.

When the first Baron died the Lady decided to get a place of her own, as her elder son wished to make vast alterations to the house. So we were all moved to a house at Shrivenham, which is now the Royal Military College of Science. There we had a wonderful nine months, with a smaller house and not nearly so much to do. The Lady had bought a house in Gloucestershire and, as there was so much decorating to be done, we had 15 weeks holiday on board wages, until we were able to get moved in. It was Jubilee year, I remember. We had wonderful party invitations to our former homes and the intended one. Then, too, I was able to see the Jubilee

Trooping of the Colour, that was really something special for this country girl.

So eventually we settled in the Park in Gloucester and soon grew to love our new home. The daughter had married and often visited with her children, so too had the second son, with his three children. Life was not so hectic and I was courting the footman, so my friend and I often accompanied him shooting rabbits or rooks. The Lady, ever thoughtful for her staff, gave her permission as she thought we would otherwise leave through boredom! She hated changes and was always sorry to see any of us leave. No one really wanted to, it was generally to get married, or the men left to better themselves.

By now I had had another promotion which meant I was looking after visiting ladies who came without maids. I loved that part of my work, for I had long admired nice clothes and jewels. I was cleaning the library, dining room, sitting room, etc, and handling more lovely things, through the front as well as the visitors' bedrooms.

Eventually war clouds were looming and the staff gradually heard the call of duty – I left with many regrets to live with my parents and do my part in the war effort. The Lady corresponded for a long time hoping I would return to join her putting her house in order – but as I was married and had a son by that time it was impossible.

It was a busy life while it lasted – we met interesting people and I have fond memories of those days long past.'

AT THE MANOR HOUSE

'When I left school in the late 1930s I went to work as a housemaid in a big manor house near the village of Bathford. The staff consisted of a butler, head housemaid, under housemaid, cook and kitchen maid. Times were very hard; we had to get up by candlelight at six o'clock and clean out the fire grates and light the oil lamps to clean up the rooms – quite a chore in the winter months. We had breakfast, then went to the dining room for prayers each morning. The rest of the day we worked hard. During the little time we had to ourselves in the evenings we had to learn a hymn to say to our lady on Sunday evenings. We had one half day a week and every other Sunday afternoon. Sunday mornings we were taken to the village church where we had to sit behind our lady of the manor. Our salary to start was £16 a year.'

MOVING AROUND

'When I went out to work first I was sent to service as all girls were in them days, aged 14. I went to Nunney Court (Somerset) as under

For many girls, going into service was the only work available when they left school. Joyce Helps, aged 14, was taken on as a housemaid near Bathford in 1937.

housemaid. That meant cleaning out grates, lighting fires in the morning, blackleading grates – the brass was all done with Brasso – and dusting. When you think how you worked, what a fool you were. I mean, girls wouldn't come down to that now. We had lamps and candles. The butler did the silver and they had someone in to do the washing – I didn't have to help with that. Then I went to the vicarage at St John's church in Frome. I was house parlourmaid and used to have to do the waiting on table in a black dress and a white apron and hat. Between Nunney and the Randolphs, I was up at Worley in Essex at Mr Heseltine's grandmother's for years. Oh, he's just like his grandmother. I can see her now, an old lady sat up in bed. I was parlourmaid there and they had six servants. They used to have beautiful balls, all the ladies in their beautiful clothes, and I used to help with the suppers. They had grand food and we more or less ate the same.'

SERVICE WITH A SMILE

'I lived in Winterbourne Monkton and left school in 1934, going straight into service as a kitchen maid. I wore a blue gingham dress, white bibbed apron, mob cap and ward shoes, all of which were much too big. I was only four ft ten inches tall. It was a good thing that kitchen maids were not allowed above stairs.

All day was spent scrubbing, the floors and tables and even the

151

legs. I had to pump water and scrub the brown stone sink. Mind you, that sink was useful. I stood in it to kiss my boyfriend through the bars on the window. Followers were not allowed.

The kitchen range was the bane of my life; it had to be blackleaded and rubbed with emery paper and polished until it gleamed. I longed for my Mum, and often cried, but I knew that if I went home my Mum would make me go back.

Later on, I became a housemaid. The house was large, so we were all kept very busy. I still had three fires to contend with. When I was 17 I took over the parlourmaid's job, as she was leaving to be married.

I had to be washed and changed into a black dress, lace cuffs and collars, frilly apron and cap threaded with black velvet ribbon by 10.30 am, ready to answer the door to callers. The household consisted of one elderly lady who entertained a lot, and held at-home days. She always had visitors and early morning trays were taken to each room, also hot water in brass cans.

There was always a lot of work to do, laying the table, which was a work of art, serving the meals and standing in the room throughout the meals. Then there were all the other things which went to keep the household running smoothly.

Madeira wine and cake were served in the morning room on at-home days. Everything that was used in the dining room, drawing room or morning room was washed up by me in my pantry. None of the best china or silver ever went into the kitchen.

I enjoyed my work (though not at first). We were taught service with a smile, how to behave correctly and in a civil manner. The rest of the staff became part of my family.

We were allowed one half day a week, and Cook always gave me a large basin of dripping and a ham bone to take home to my Mum. My wages were 28 shillings a month, and we had to sign the wages book. On Sundays we all attended church, sitting in the family pew. The work was hard, the hours were long, but I have never regretted going into service.'

THE PARLOURMAID AND THE CHAUFFEUR

'I was 14 the first week in December 1930, and started work the second week in December as house parlourmaid. There was a cook-general, and I waited at table, did the bedrooms and answered the door, cleaned the silver etc. My day started at 6.30 am when I laid the table for breakfast at 8.30. While the family had breakfast I made the beds and started the upstairs work, then cleared the tables etc and helped Cook wash up. Then I cleaned the dining room and laid the table for lunch, and finished off upstairs. After waiting at table for lunch, Cook and I had our lunch then I changed from my mob cap, black stockings, flat-heeled shoes and large white apron into the afternoon uniform of brown dress with coffee-coloured cap and lace-trimmed apron. This had to be done by 2.30. I served afternoon tea on silver trays, and waited at table for the evening meal. The day ended at ten, but I had to ask if I could go to bed, and if there were guests I had to wait until they were gone home.

After about four months Cook left to get married and I was asked to do it all. I agreed on condition that there was no waiting at table. I had only learnt cooking at school, but my mother had been cook-general for titled people, and she gave me tips. The job was quite stressful, but I got used to it. I had two half days off a week, and I earned £25 a year and my keep. I was lucky though, treated as one of the family, and they took me to Wales when they went to their holiday cottage. This was a break, I still had to work, but I had some time in the afternoons to walk on the beach, and I had another week's holiday as well.

When we were at home, in Chippenham, the house was full of dogs. They had kennels and bred Bedlington terriers, but they also kept a lot of rabbits. They took me to Crufts several times and I was lucky to be treated so well. When they had a change of financial circumstances they gave me a month's notice, sold the big house and moved to the cottage in Wales. They took the chauffeur with them.'

'I worked in the brickyard, in Chippenham, and used to collect the bread from the bakery of Oscar Hunt on my way home. My friend worked at the big house and he suggested I apply for the post of gardener and odd-job man there. I had to stoke the coke-fired central heating boiler, and the fire which heated the greenhouse. There was gardening and I fed the dogs in the kennels and looked after the rabbits. One night the rabbits all died and we were taking them out in wheelbarrows.

I had to keep the car clean and well polished, and one day I started the engine. Marjorie, the daughter of the house, came round the corner and caught me. She asked if I was interested in cars and when I said "Yes" she offered to teach me to drive. She gave me a lesson every day for nearly a week, then she said I could drive, and the following weekend I drove them to London. After that I drove the car most of the time, taking the lady to visit Lady Coventry at Monkton House, Lady Cooper, and to Crufts. When they sold up I went to Wales with them. The week before Christmas I took them to Malvern, and then I came home to Chippenham, to my mother until I had to go to Malvern to take them back to Wales. Of course, there were not many cars about in Chippenham in those days. My day started at 8 am and I got 35 shillings a week and my keep. Out of this I bought a boat – 18 footer at £1 a foot. I stayed in Wales for five years, then came back to work as a tiler and plasterer and I helped to build Yewstock Crescent. Later I worked at Westinghouse but it affected my health, so I left and went to work on the ambulances until my retirement.'

AT THE VICARAGE

'I left school at 14 and was kept home to help with two younger sisters. When my youngest sister left school I was found a job with a vicar and his wife at Swindon.

The church and vicarage was in the centre of the town. The vicarage was huge with stained glass windows in the kitchen so you couldn't see what was going on in the street. The fair came several times a year and I had great pleasure watching from my bedroom. The church has been pulled down now and shops built in its place.

The vicar employed an elderly lady to do the cooking on a huge polished kitchen range and the steel fire-irons and fender looked lovely. I had to be downstairs by seven o'clock or I was told off. I had to clean the range and light the fire, sweep the dining room and sitting room with a dustpan and brush and dust, then lay the breakfast table. By then the cook had the breakfast ready . . . scrambled eggs or kedgeree and toast and tea. By 8.30 I was starving and ready for my breakfast!

There was plenty to do during the day, kitchen lino to polish and there was no electricity.

I had to wear a uniform, striped cotton dress, apron and cap for work, black dress for afternoons and always black stockings.

We had to attend church three times on Sundays and I only had a weekend off once a month. Then I went by train to the nearest railway station and was taken home by the horse and cart that had carried the farmers' milk to the station.

The water in the house had to be pumped upstairs to the toilet and bath. The servants weren't allowed to use the bath but had to heat up cans of hot water and sit in a hip-bath. Being tall my feet always hung outside!

After two years we moved to a small village, still no electricity, still coping with lamps. I was in the church choir and was at several pretty weddings. I wasn't there long because I had to cycle if I wanted to go home, not nice on dark nights.

I then got a job with the village doctor in my home village. What a difference, three lovely children and a nice family to work with. I

154

did the cleaning and some cooking with the doctor's wife and took the children out. The house had a sort of carbide gas so there were no lamps. We cooked on a big oil stove with oven. We always had a hot midday meal and just sandwiches and cocoa for supper, so I was able to go out.

The doctor had a busy life, surgery every morning and evening. He did his own dispensing and also extracted teeth. One day the chair broke and an old lady patient fell over, luckily unhurt but minus the tooth!

I had to answer the telephone if the family were out and to be sure to get the message right!

After a couple of years the doctor and his family and I moved to the Isle of Wight. We stayed in a hotel until we got the huge house ready. From my bedroom I could see the ships anchored at Cowes and made many friends and could visit them often.

By this time my sister was working in Bristol and helped to get me a job with a couple who lived in a super flat on the Downs, the smartest part of Bristol, quite close to the Mayor's House. Very often the Mayor passed, dressed in his robes, going to a special do.

My duties at this house were to keep the place clean with the help of the caretaker's wife, a jolly little lady. I had a large bedsitting room and the flat was full of super antique furniture, lovely china and glass. They entertained a lot. The boss was a wine shipper and all the famous wine and spirit people came to meals. I waited at table after preparing the dishes. Champagne was drunk and I was always offered a glass.

They were very generous to me and it was good to meet my sister. We used to cycle home on Sunday, 20 miles and return by bus and leave our bikes for Father to take back.

I stayed there until I was married in 1937 and was presented with a cheque for the wedding breakfast and a lovely clock which is still in good working order.'

'I suffered from homesickness in my first household when I was 14, the vicarage at Charlton All Saints. I remember being shown by the senior maid how to throw open the windows and knock the dust off hundreds and hundreds of books in my master's library. My mistress was given to being late for church services and I remember the tense moments at supper when the Canon would look down the table, shake his head and say mournfully, "Late again, Emily?"

My second job was as head cook to a wealthy racehorse trainer at Downton. Here there were numerous other staff kept in house and garden and I was responsible for training the younger maids. Expeditions to Salisbury from Downton were infrequent all-day affairs with a long journey by slow motor bus and an inevitable visit to a shop called the Maypole, which sold all kinds of country provisions and was situated on the corner near St Thomas's church.'

THE GREAT WESTERN RAILWAY

Swindon's industrial prosperity was created by the coming of the Great Western Railway works to the town in the 19th century. In many ways, the 'Works' *was* the town and was a close knit community of workers and their families.

THE GREAT WESTERN WORKS

'The original railway workshops at Swindon were not like the great modern ones of today, but built and run in a very different way. The family were taken by horse and cart to the little railway village, which I think exists today, but was very primitive then with no water indoors or electricity, only pumps in backyards and lamps or candles at night.

The railway looked after the men, who worked for long hours. Most of the big trains were built there as it was one of the first railways in the country.

One man looked after the horses which pulled the carts taking equipment from one depot to another. These animals were housed in stables alongside the works so it meant being at work early – 5 am – to feed, water and get the harnesses on them ready for work at 7 am each day.

They sometimes had to act as a ganger – the man who goes along the railway line to tap the line with a hammer to listen for faults on the line and report it back to the depot for repairs to be made. You had to turn your hand to anything you were asked to do then, or you were out of a job.'

'Harry Mundy was born on 8th June 1905 at Upper Stratton. His father was a keen musician and he taught both his sons to play brass instruments, encouraging them to become accomplished bandsmen. Harry started work in 1919 as a general labourer and had a number of jobs whilst playing the euphonium in his spare time. He and his brother joined Cricklade Town Band in 1924 and would cycle over for practice.

He joined the rail works in 1930 working in the yards and thanks to his association with the GWR Band was soon promoted for working in the X Shop and so to learning the trade. The X Shop made crossovers for the rails, junctions and points and this work from drawings was learnt by watching a more experienced man. Work was allocated by the chargeman who issued the drawings but very large jobs had their drawings on roller blinds for easy reference. The standards were very high and only a tolerance of a third of an inch was allowed.

In 1935 Harry married and moved to Cricklade and so went to work on the local train. In 1939 he was exempt from military service as he was an experienced machine drill operator and the X Shop manufactured bomb casings during the war years. Swindon luckily escaped the bombings but a few stray planes were brought down in the area. Very large crossovers needed wooden beams two feet wide and 10 inches deep bolted together. The driller had to be very precise to keep the hole straight for the bolt and this was done by eye and

The Great Western Railway was more than just an employer, it touched every aspect of its employees' lives. The GWR Band is pictured here displaying the 'Daily Mirror' cup they won in 1927.

checked with a broom handle! Harry made a + square for this purpose to ensure the drill didn't deviate up or down, left or right. Innovative ideas were not often accepted as every job was copied exactly from older men but this simple idea was accepted and used.

In 1963 a new X Shop was built on the now Great Western Way and a new washroom included. Until then the men had a special circular washbasin with individual taps made of stainless steel. The new X Shop was needed to make bigger switching gear and had three clocks in it so the men could all see the time rather than depend on the chargeman's watch.

As Beeching closed down many rail lines, work had to be competitive but Swindon was loath to change or reduce the price of work and so more and more work went to Derby and the works closed in March 1986.

Harry retired in 1970 and finally stopped playing with Cricklade Band in 1976. His son and two grandsons are keen bandsmen and Harry's love of music lifted him from labourer to factoryman and enriched his life, as it still does today.'

'When the Railway made Swindon an important centre it must have attracted workers from far and near. My maternal grandparents came from Wales and my paternal grandparents from Bradford and Trowbridge. As a child nearly everyone we knew worked in the factory or offices. The Co-operative Society was quite a big employer – no supermarkets then – and we had Garrards Engineering Works, a shirt factory, a laundry and Wills Tobacco factory. Boys followed their father's trade and there was always someone to put a good word in, and ambitious people often made sure they attended the right church or chapel.

Four of my uncles worked in the offices and three, including my father, in the works. My two brothers followed him but my elder brother was bright and was in the Drawing Office and moved away later, though still working for the Great Western Railway. Dad worked in the Brass Shop as a chargeman and when I started work gave me a brass trivet and two heavy brass paperweights. The office staff were able to join a pension scheme at some time or other but when Dad finished work at 65 there was only the Old Age Pension of ten shillings a week and club money.

My mother used to tell me of the days when men started work at six and came home to breakfast. The hooter used to sound – I can remember it at dinnertime, and of course Saturday morning was part of the working week – hours were long then. I was lucky enough to have a grammar school education but most children started work at 14. At 16 after three months work at Garrards I was taken on as

158

a "Lady Clerk" in the GW offices. First I worked briefly in the Mileage Office and then for two years in a smaller office as a shorthand typist in the CME's Department. We got our big rise at 18 years to 30 shillings a week and I then earned enough to pay Mother for my keep and the rest covered my expenses. Of course working for the railway we had cheap travel and the yearly office outing was by train – I can remember going to the Gower Coast once and the meals served to us from the tiny kitchen were excellent.

Though my family was by no means well off we always had an annual holiday, by train of course and usually in Cornwall. The factory closed down for a week in July – Trip week, but the holiday was unpaid so it was really like a lock out. Our luggage was sent on ahead in a big tin trunk and we had rooms and attendance at our destination where of course we often met other Swindon people. Trains ran at all hours of the night which added to the excitement. Not everyone could afford holidays though. Some went just for a day and others not at all.

The workers' needs were catered for well. The Medical Fund building at the bottom of Milton Road housed Turkish baths, doctors and dentists. "A tooth in the head is worth two on a plate," is a notice I recall in the waiting room. There were also two swimming baths – small and large. The latter was boarded over in the winter and dances and other events held there. I have heard my father say, though, that men worked on with hernias and other complaints rather than seek advice, because of course reports of these things could filter back. Many employees lived in the houses built and owned by the railway. There was also the GW hospital and the Mechanics Institute which at one time housed a library and billiard tables. The Playhouse Theatre was later established in this building just opposite the main entrance to the works where the men clocked in. There was a Drill Hall in the nearby pleasant park, where my sister went for gym classes. The event of the year as far as we children were concerned was the GWR Fete held in the park – I can still see the flaring gas jets when darkness fell, the brandy snaps and the exciting rides, not to mention the slab of Fete cake we all received made by the Co-op. In the evening when dark fell there was a magnificent firework display.

At that time the Great Western Railway shaped most of our lives. Swindon was an ordinary place, full of ordinary people. The total population before the Second World War equalled that of those living in Toothill now. Wherever you went you met people you knew and who knew you. The works and offices were a hive of activity and it's a vastly different Swindon we visit these days. Looking back it was a very nice place to grow up in.'

159

'I came to live in Swindon in 1948. I used to take my daughter to school and in conversation with other mums was amazed when they said that their husbands worked "inside".

I could not remember hearing about there being a prison in Swindon and of course there is not. I discovered that working "inside" meant that their husbands worked in the Railway works.'

WORKING ON THE RAILWAY

'Ever since I can remember I wanted to be an engine driver and follow in my father's footsteps. I remember going to the Milk Bank and climbing the hoarding outside the signalbox opposite the fish and chip shop to watch the trains pass through the station. On occasions I would spot my father on the station pilot, and with my twin brother we would be able to ride on the footplate around the station, much to the envy of my school friends.

In December 1940 I attended an interview conducted by Mr A M Duck, Chief Foreman at the Swindon Running Shed, in his beautifully carpeted office. After the short formality I was sent to Park House, and told that if I was medically fit I could start as a cleaner. This occurred in February 1941. Our duties included cleaning engines, especially on prestige trains like the 9 am Swindon to Paddington and the 9.40 pm train to Leicester and return to Swindon, worked by a Swindon crew. This train, as it travelled on the Great Central line had an engine, usually 29xx class, which was always kept in tip-top condition. Cleaning oil was used on the engine and tender, the copper and brass polished with brick dust.

On night duty 10 pm to 6 am we went out "calling" drivers and firemen who were on duty on early shift, knocking at their doors approximately one hour before they had to report for duty.

Shortly after, on my 17th birthday, I was appointed a fireman and transferred to Old Oak Common. My mother was worried about my being in London, as the Germans were bombing nightly – luckily for me, the majority of bombs fell around East London, but I had to ring Swindon each morning to let my family know I was still well. After only six weeks I was sent back to Swindon where I stayed until I was made redundant.

At this time (1941) 1,000 men worked at the Running Shed, of whom 750 were drivers and firemen. As I grew older I passed through different "links", each link consisting of around twelve weekly jobs, and as I progressed I passed into the top jobs, ie passenger work, until I reached the top link. When I reached this link I was fireman to Driver Walter Hurley and on 16 May 1957 we were chosen to work the Royal train when Princess Margaret came to Swindon to open the new hospital. We drove the train back to Paddington, leaving Swindon at 16.07 and arriving in London at 17.28. We had been advised to dress suitably!

We reported for duty at 15.50; the engine was No 6014 immaculate in green and black, the copper, brass and side rods shining in the afternoon sun. Princess Margaret arrived at the station and joined the train promptly, and we left Swindon with Mr Charlie Pullen, the Headquarters Inspector on the footplate, which was usual on a Royal train. We were told to wash our hands on the approach to Paddington station as the Princess might wish to be introduced to us, but as we stopped at the marker on Platform 8 so that the red carpet would be in the correct position, the Princess, after being greeted by the stationmaster resplendent in top hat and morning coat, proceeded to the car awaiting her. My driver and I were disappointed we were not presented, but two weeks later Walter Hurley and myself received a letter from the Loco Superintendent thanking us for the special effort we had made, and enclosing £1 for the driver and ten shillings for me.

In 1959, I went to Park House again to sit my examination to pass as a driver. I passed, becoming a driver after 19 years apprenticeship.

By this time diesels had started to appear, but I spent many happy years driving steam engines until they were eventually withdrawn, and with their withdrawal much of the magic and romance died.

Swindon men worked trains between Paddington, Swansea, Taunton, Banbury, Weymouth, Longbridge, Southampton and Cheltenham over the M&SW. I also worked trains from Purton, Highworth and Cirencester bringing workmen into Swindon. I have many memories of running into Paddington when passengers would come up to the engine and enquire how the trip went – they would love to be allowed on the footplate.

During the war we would work ammunition and government stores trains to Southampton and other docks for the use of our forces abroad; also ambulance trains with injured members of the Allied Forces returning for treatment – sometimes we would be stopped and told to proceed slowly as an operation had to be performed. There were many long hours on duty.

The standard of safety on the GWR was the highest of any of the railway companies and was achieved by strict discipline impressed upon men from the first day worked. This discipline resulted in very few accidents, and one involving passengers was rare indeed.

Only once did I cause any damage. I worked a train of fertilizer to Melksham and, whilst pushing the train into Melksham Yard, the wheels on the Hymak engine slipped and eventually hit the blocks at the end of the yard. About four box vans became derailed and the doors broke open. The sacks of fertilizer fell out of the vans, spreading quite a large amount on the ground. I eventually had to see an inspector to explain what had happened and I was told to be more careful in future. Although not in the good books of the powers that be, I was highly praised by the local Allotment Society which had been informed of the incident and allowed to collect the fertilizer free of charge.

In 1980, aged 55, clutching a Teasmade, happy memories of 40 years' service, many many miles on the clock, my redundancy notice in my pocket, I left the railway like many before me with a touch of regret, but sure in the knowledge that it truly had been God's Wonderful Railway.'

THE STONE QUARRIES

Lovely cream coloured Bath stone has long been one of Wiltshire's most famous products, the quarrying giving work to generations of local men. The work was hard and dangerous, with little attention paid to safety for the quarrymen.

HARD AND DANGEROUS

'My husband's family lived in Atworth and at least three generations of them worked in the quarries. Pictures we have show large blocks of stone taken from the quarry being carried in trolleys along a railway to the sites where they were stacked ready to be collected by men with horses and carts for the building sites around the area. There were no electric saws in those days but all the stone was cut with huge crosscut saws used by two men, one at each side, pushing and pulling together and keeping up the rhythm as they sawed.

Life was very hard for the men who worked there, as some had to walk many miles before they even got to the quarry. They would often arrive soaking wet having trudged through muddy fields or along country roads in all weathers – there were no buses then. The hours on site were very long and since most men could not get home for meals they had to take bread and cheese or some such food to eat.

Quarrying was a very dangerous job and many men lost their lives using the crude and heavy machinery. There was no protective clothing – most men were from poor families and clothes had to be worn until they were threadbare.'

'Box village is situated within the Bath stone quarrying area and many villagers come from families whose men worked underground or in jobs such as masons, carters, blacksmiths etc above ground. My stonemason friend Fred, now in his seventies, told me tales of his father, one of seven children of a quarryman.

Fred's father had to leave school at the age of eleven to earn money and his first job was delivering milk, but he was exceptionally intelligent and attracted the attention of someone in the Bath Stone firms who took him on as a "messenger" at two shillings and sixpence a week. His duties were to sweep and tidy the yard and carry water to the stone face, where it was used to wash out the stone dust during stone cutting. He continued to educate himself in his spare time and was one of the lucky ones at the quarry who could read and write. In their work breaks the quarrymen sat on the ground and listened to anyone who could read to them; Fred's father was sometimes called upon to read and explain any "hard words".

Eventually he progressed to become overseer of four quarries in the Corsham area – Spring Quarry, Hawthorn Park, Monks Park and Park Lane near Weston. He carried out his duties by riding round the area on his bicycle – he never got his hands dirty and always had a fresh clean stiff collar every day. In the summer he wore a straw boater. Fred remembers parties of professional men – architects, builders, engineers etc – coming to Corsham by train and being met by coach and taken to various sites to be addressed by his father and shown round the workings. Afterwards he was always warmly congratulated and a hat passed round, donations usually amounting to sixpence from each visitor, and the total collected, probably about £1, was sufficient to kit out Fred and his brother with a new suit each. Later when the Bath Stone firms became the Bath and Portland Stone firms, Fred's father became known by the nickname "Mr Bath and Portland". His earnings in 1939 amounted to £4 a week. His son, a deputy foreman, earned one shilling and sevenpence halfpenny an hour, and labourers one shilling and a penny an hour.

Fred remembers how the stone was extracted before the introduction of mechanical cutters. He can explain how picks of varying length handles were used to take off the narrow top layer immediately below the quarry roof. The pick handles were made of hickory, a wood which is immensely strong, but bendable. Beneath the ceiling level saws of various lengths were used. Quarrymen were paid on piece rates based on extraction per square yard, two square yards being an average day's work for seven shillings and sixpence.

Horses were used underground to haul the stone on trolleys to the bottom of the shaft, and also above ground for stacking in the yards. From Spring Quarry there was a low, narrow underground passage which led to a forge where the horses were taken to be shod. Parts of this passage were so low that the boy "messenger" riding along with a horse would have to crouch low on the horse's back, carrying his little benzolene lamp. When Fred was young all lighting below ground was from these small lamps, about four inches in diameter, with the wick protruding from the centre. There was no fear of a naked flame, as in a coal mine.

As a schoolboy, Fred remembers how, in 1930, arrangements were made to pipe water from Rudloe to Neston and gangs of navvies were employed to dig out the trench. After school Fred and his brother were allowed, having had their tea, to go out and spend a few hours watching this operation. In winter they had to be back home by 6 pm after warming themselves at the night watchman's brazier, and in summer they stayed out until 9 pm. The whole of this digging was completed by pick and shovel – hard work in all weathers. The men wore old pieces of sacks to protect them from the rain.

Bath stone is famous worldwide and was exported in large quantities. Sometimes local skills were also taken beyond Wiltshire. Fred, after his four years' apprenticeship as a stonemason, worked for various firms and travelled to places as far apart as Liverpool Street station, London (where his work can be seen), and Jamaica, where he stayed for 14 months working on a church.

Safety at work was left very much to the discretion of the quarrymen, who judged when to stop extracting at a particular area of a quarry – timber props were used and columns of uncut stone were left as pillars to support the roof.'

OTHER WAYS WE MADE
A LIVING

**These are just a few memories of some of the countless other ways
we made a living in the past, from flax production to saw mills,
glove making to the village blacksmith and wheelwright.**

A THRIVING HAMLET

'Ludwell is within the parish of Donhead St Mary in the south of
Wiltshire, close to the Dorset border. In the early part of this century
it was a thriving hamlet with many industries and people came from
the surrounding villages to work there. There were three general
stores, two of which had bakeries attached to them, a butcher's
shop, a tailor's shop, a local builder, a harnessmaker, two public
houses, several dairy farms and a watercress farm and in the
neighbouring hamlet of Birdbush there was a flourishing waggon
works and a threshing tackle business.

The butcher's shop was originally in the yard of The Grove Arms
public house, and my father ran both. In 1904 he moved to the
present butcher's shop which he had built for £90 and it was in the
house adjoining it that I was born in 1909. Father killed all his own
meat in the slaughterhouse. He bought sheep and pigs locally from
the farmers and pig-keepers. He attended markets in Sturminster
Newton and Gillingham to buy bullocks which would be brought to
Ludwell on the hoof by a couple of drovers and their dogs.

If he bought cattle at Salisbury Market they would come back by
train to Semley station and would be fetched from there. On a
Saturday morning it was my job to walk across the footpath to the
village of Charlton to deliver joints of meat to various houses. I had
a special little basket to carry the meat but I could have only been
six or seven years old at the time.

The tailor's shop was run by Tom Gatehouse who did all the
cutting and fitting. He employed four men who worked on the
ground floor, sitting cross-legged on the bench which was raised
about two feet off the floor, where they made all the jackets by hand.
There was always a stove going to heat the pressing irons which
were of various shapes and weights. On the upper floor there were
four or five women employed and it was their job to make all the

trousers. I could buy a jacket and waistcoat in hard wearing tweed and a pair of corduroy breeches all made to fit me for £5.

The harnessmaker was Nehemiah (Puffer) Tatchell and he employed two men. They worked long hours from 8 am until 8 pm, but Saturday was a half day when they finished at 4 pm. They made the harness for all the horses on the farms and for the carriage horses at the big houses. They also repaired all the horse collars and heavy pads.

Five men were employed on the watercress beds and they all lived locally. The spring that supplies the beds rises in Ludwell and is channelled into the beds. They cut the watercress by hand and it used to be put into big wicker hampers, that were called flats. These were taken by horse and van to Semley station and sent by rail to Birmingham, Bristol, London and Manchester.

The waggon works at Birdbush of H Harrington and Sons employed about ten men and made agricultural waggons and carts. The works were carried out on both sides of the main road and waggons would be pushed from one side of the road to the other.

At the top of Brook Hill lived Samuel Laws who operated a threshing tackle business. He owned about four or five sets of tackle consisting of a steam engine, the threshing machine, an elevator, a living van and sometimes a straw tyer. When they were travelling between farms with all this equipment, the driver would look after the engine and the man who fed the sheaves into the threshing machine would also be up in the engine acting as steersman. At the back of the outfit rode the man who cut the sheaves and he had a rope attached to the steersman's arm and if anything wanted to pass them he would pull the rope so that they could pull in somewhere. In the summer the threshing tackle would return to Brook Hill to be overhauled ready for the next winter but the steam engines would go round to the big estates to provide power for sawmills to cut up timber.'

STONE AND GLOVES

'The stone quarries provided most of the employment at one time for the people of Neston, apart from farming and being in service. People came from all around to work in the mines. Before mechanisation stone was hauled to the surface by carthorses. I believe the quarries were all in production up to the beginning of the Second World War. Monks Park Quarry is now the only one open.

Villagers were also employed in the glove factory. Men were employed doing the tanning, and the skins were pegged out to dry. The gloves were machine stitched by the women, and were lined by outworkers. I was an outworker when I first married in 1930 and I earned about ten shillings a week, which was good going.'

THE SAW MILLS

'Broughton Gifford Saw Mills was founded by my grandfather, Henry John Harding over 70 years ago. At that time, horses were used to transport the large tree trunks to the mill; two horses were needed to pull the largest trees and as many as eight of these strong animals were kept busy hauling timber quite long distances back to the mill. Two men felled the trees and three or four were responsible for their safe delivery to the yard.

As time went on, transport improved, and a tractor was purchased. This early model had wooden wheels with iron rims, the latter being attached by workmen in the mill forge. It was quite a sight to see the huge trees being brought along the village street, causing a certain amount of excitement in this then very peaceful setting.

Some of the wood was made into boxes, which went from Holt station by train to Wales, for use in the tin mines. Coffin boards were cut and assembled for the convenience of people in the locality. My grandfather sometimes headed the cortège to the church, resplendent in full funeral attire and wearing his elegant top hat! Later, this part of the business was taken over by another firm.

As time went on the transportation of timber improved; large tractors taking the place of horses. The huge crane which removed the necessity for manual lifting provided a very good landmark for the village.

There would be at least 200 tree trunks piled in the yard at a time and a small railway was installed to carry boards from A to B. As a child I longed to ride on this, but was, of course, not allowed to.

My grandfather employed about 16 men in the saw mill yard. The people of the village bought their logs from this source, collecting them in assorted containers, including wheelbarrows, old prams and those four-wheeled trucks so beloved of small boys.

The enormous quantity of sawdust was carried by chute onto a large heap at the rear of the mill, much of this was sold to a Trowbridge firm for the smoking of hams!

During the firm's history there were a number of fires, some in the aforementioned sawdust pile and two in the actual mill building, but all were successfully extinguished with the help of the Fire Brigade.

It is an interesting fact that all the oak used inside the *Queen Mary* was supplied by the Broughton Gifford saw mills; this magnificent liner can be seen at Long Beach, California, USA. Oak was also supplied for the *QE2*. This grand wood also went to a London firm for export to France, for use as veneer in the furniture trade.

My uncle, Mr Fred Harding, a son of Henry John, often travelled 60 miles a day looking for oak trees to keep the mill in production; so many trees had died through Dutch Elm disease that business looked precarious when the mill finally closed around 1983. It was a great loss to the village, having provided employment for men, and logs for warmth, for a great number of years. Villagers were sad to see it close.'

THE BLACKSMITH AND THE CARPENTER

'For many years my father was the Luckington village blacksmith or farrier, as they are now called. He had his yard and forge where he shod most of the horses, ponies, carthorses, and hunters for the local farmers and gentry. The horse shoes were all made by hand – not mass produced as they are today. The iron he used came up from Bristol and each horse had its own individual size of shoes. The fire to heat up the iron and shoes was kept going by hand bellows. As the shoes were hammered out on the anvil and then cooled in a water trough, the horse would be tied up nearby ready to be fitted.

Across the other side of the yard was a carpenter's shop. Not only was Mr Sherborne making doors, windows etc, but he was also the village undertaker. Each coffin was hand-made and polished to a very high standard. Quite often a farmer would take in a cart wheel which needed repairing, so the carpenter did whatever wooden repairs he could, then the wheel would be taken over the other side of the yard to the blacksmith's forge and the wheel would have a new iron ring put completely around. This was called bonding. There was also a very large whetstone where choppers, axes and any other agricultural tools could be sharpened.

Today most farriers are mobile – with their vans, ready made shoes, car phones etc, but the smell of horse hoof as a hot shoe is fitted is still wonderful to me and brings back so many memories. To see a huge 17 hands hunter patiently waiting to have a set of new shoes fitted is something never to be forgotten.'

'I was born in a very small village where my father was a blacksmith. My vivid memories of that time are of my father, a rather small man, putting shoes on very large horses, shires, percherons and others, which at that time did most of the work on the farms. The horses towered over my father and to a small girl were very frightening. Another memory of the blacksmith's forge is of how the iron tyres or bands were put onto the wooden cartwheels of that time. A circular fire was made in the forecourt of the smithy. This was made of "faggots" of wood, which were bundles of sticks, large and small, which were cut in the local copses. The circular iron band was heated in this fire, and then when red hot was put onto the wheel which was laid flat on an iron platform and bolted down. The very hot iron burned itself onto the wooden wheel rim, and was immediately cooled with cold water being poured onto it, shrinking the iron onto the wheel. I was only allowed to watch this operation through an upstairs window. How different those carts and large horses were from the enormous tractors and machinery used on farms today.'

FLAX

'Many country folk will remember the glorious sight of fields covered with a cloth of blue blossom, carried on long slender stems undulating in the breeze like a restless sea.

These same slender stems also evoke memories of many hours work, often in a dusty filthy atmosphere, transforming them into a vital component of the Second World War effort.

Flax stems contain long, strong fibres which when processed are converted into linen thread. Nylon was unknown at this time, except perhaps as stockings brought by the American Forces!

The flax was harvested by pulling it up to obtain the longest possible fibres, then threshed to obtain seed both for replanting and to produce linseed oil. Because of the toughness of the outer casing on each stem, the crop was then returned to the field and laid out to allow the dew, rain etc to soften it, a process knows as "rotting".

When adjudged fit, it was then taken back to the mill where machines were used to remove that outer casing, exposing the golden fibres but generating clouds of dust to be endured by the workers. No masks or extractor fans were available. The urgency of the requirement demanded that the operations continued 24 hours a day.

Coming from the machines, the fibres passed to the "dressers" whose job it was to remove any extraneous matter and to straighten them by hand for further handling. By then the fibres had become as fine as blonde hair and just as difficult to handle.

The product was then made up into hanks for onward transmission to spinning and weaving mills to become linen thread and eventually parachute lines, webbing equipment etc.

The whole process is probably by now a lost art, in its original form.'

THE TANNERY

'My mother lived in West Harnham. Her father had a small tannery business in a field at the side of the lane that went up to the chalk pit. Prior to the First World War, most of his business was curing the skins of sheep for parchment for government departments. They went out of business during the war, as it was a luxury product.'

THE POST OFFICE

'It was in October 1914, just after the start of the First World War, that at the age of 15½ I joined the main Chippenham post office as a clerk. The post office at that time was situated at 50 Market Place. The second floor of this building housed the telegraph office. Here telegrams were passed to and from other countrywide telegraph offices, all communications being in morse code. My job was to take telegrams from sub post offices and individual telephone subscribers and pass them to the telegraphists for transmission. I similarly passed on the messages received by the telegraphists. The weekly starting salary for this job was 15 shillings.

In 1920, I transferred to the telephone division of the post office, and was shortly promoted to Officer in Charge of the Chippenham exchange, which occupied the two end cottages of Providence Terrace, then part of Froghamshire. There was one manual switchboard, operated by four girls, and serving the 150 subcribers. The switchboard occupied the upper floors of the cottages and the engineers were on the ground floor. Chippenham exchange remained a manual system until 1936 when the present automatic exchange opposite the railway station was opened. I continued as supervisor until I retired in 1959, when I was awarded the Imperial Service Medal. This was a royal award for long service, but the custom has now discontinued. At the time of my retirement the number of subscribers had increased to 2,000.

Life was not all work however, and in 1927 at a cost of 27 guineas, together with four friends I enjoyed a Mediterranean cruise. In 1936 I also cruised to the northern capitals of Norway, Sweden and Denmark. In Stockholm, one of my travelling companions contacted the telephone exchange and we were given a conducted tour of the exchange by a supervisor and one of the directors, who passed a greeting to the Bristol exchange.'

170

THE IRONWORKS

'Iron ore was discovered at the Hane near Westbury in 1841 while the railway line was being cut, and mining continued there until the smelting works closed down in 1923.

My father still remembers the fiery glow in the sky at night made by the furnaces at the ironworks. My great uncle was the driver of a small train which carried iron from the mine holes to the smelters via a bridge under Frogmore Road. Little did we know in later years when we took the cows through the bridge under the road and over the railway line that this was the route to the mineholes many years before.'

WILTON CARPETS

'My grandfather worked in the Wilton carpet factory. Sometimes certain dyes of wool ran out and the workers were laid off without pay. To keep the family, my grandfather swept chimneys, walking miles a day to go to a chimney.'

BASKETS AND LACE

'My mother was born in April 1899, the twelfth child of a family of 15 children. They lived most of their childhood days on Moot Farm, Downton. Their father was the dairyman, William Hatcher.

The older children helped to look after the younger ones, and with the housework. It was probably a hard life, but a happy one, according to Mother. She remembered how one sister found it difficult, one day, to cook on the open range – to keep the large cooking pot simmering, the large pudding in a cloth on one side, while on the other side boiling the meat and vegetables. Only on Sundays did they have both, usually they had one or the other.

To supplement their income, her mother helped with the hand milking in the dairy, early in the morning before the children were awake and again in the afternoon.

She also made gloves, while the younger children played around her feet, Mother recalled. The older girls were also taught to make gloves, as well as to sew and make their own clothes, embroider, knit and cook.

In June 1924 Mother married Eric Eastman, who was the son of the Downton basket maker of Iron Bridge, The Borough, Downton. The terraced house near the bridge was then in three: the basket shop and work-shop; the middle house, where the newly weds lived, one

Albert Eastman was carrying on a 300 year old tradition as basket maker at Downton up until the 1950s.

room up and one room down; and the house at the end where Eric's parents lived.

It was while living here that Mother learnt to make lace, I understand, as Father was away a lot working as a plumber on building projects.

I believe Mother made lace for the old Downton lace industry for many years, probably up until the Second World War. I remember her making lace at Alderbury where we lived then, before that war. She didn't have time afterwards. I have found some pieces of bobbin lace she made, and also a very lovely lace trimmed blouse or camisole, with lace insertions, of three large circles, around a machine made white-work filet motif, all delicately hand hemstitched on. The lace is a simple diamond Torchon design.

The other hobby of hers was to help in the basket shop, serving and mending the cane bottom seats of chairs. There had been Eastman's basket makers in Downton for around 300 years, I am told, on the site opposite the Downton Tannery. At the beginning of the First World War the basket making industry was in trouble, sales went down and the sons that were working there in the family business left, some to go into war work or into the forces. I believe my Grandad (Albert Eastman) ran a carrier's business during this time.

There was an Eastman's basket shop, selling their baskets, chairs and sofas, originally in the High Street, Downton. After the war, Grandad gave up the carrier's business and bought his own basket making business at the Iron Bridge, Downton, re-employing his three brothers, and two of their sons, later on. They sold baskets all over the world for many years. Grandad made baskets right up to the 1950s that I know of, and enjoyed every minute of it. He was also a well known fisherman on the river Avon, catching a very large fish, a pike, which he had stuffed and put into a glass case. This always took pride of place on the shelf in his shop, and later in a special place in the house. He was also a "Drowner", cutting the weeds up and down the river Avon from his home area.

About 1934-5 my parents left Downton and went to live in Alderbury, on the edge of Longford Estate, where father was the plumber and water engineer. During the war, Father was in the Home Guard, and Mother helped with the machine milking in the dairy at the bottom of the garden. Later on, at the end of the war, Mother knitted two-ply garments for the Stonehenge knitting industry, for about twelve shillings and sixpence for long sleeves. I remember they were very intricate patterns.'

THE WATERCRESS BEDS

'My husband worked all his life on the watercress beds at Coombe Bissett. These were seasonally repaired and planted by sprinkling plants on the surface of the water with a pronged fork. Later the cress was harvested – in months with an R in them – and he would push the bundles up the track in an old wheelbarrow to where it would be collected by a taxi-cab and taken to Salisbury market.'

EELS AT THE POWER STATION

'In 1947 as a young bride I came to Downton, near Salisbury, where my new husband worked at the smallest power station in the Southern Division. It was also the most attractive, being housed in an old grist mill. We lived in part of the old mill, our garden surrounded by water. The station had a Brush diesel, also an Armfield water turbine, this supplied most of Downton's needs including a large tannery opposite.

My husband carried out the duties of electrician cum turbine driver, switchboard attendant, diesel plant operator, station superintendent, and eel trapper. This latter job was carried out in a building specially designed for the purpose. October was the best month for large catches, a good catch for one night being around 200. The record for one night was 740, the largest eel caught at Downton being 4lb 3oz. The eels were placed in a tank let in the floor of a store room through which a constant stream of water flowed, and when a sufficient number had been caught they were packed into wateright boxes and sent off by rail from Downton to London, the condition of their acceptance being they must be alive on arrival. At this time they were an average price of two shillings and ninepence per lb; this produced a reasonable revenue which was off-set against the running cost of the power station. In 1956 during the September quarter, the whole of the running expenses of the station, including oil, maintenance and wages, were £37, the revenue from the sales of eels was £43.

Eels were caught at Downton power station in the late 1940s and sold to London fishmongers. The duties of eel trapper were included with more mundane pursuits such as station superintendent!

My husband worked at the power station for over 40 years. It was closed down in 1973, the machinery dismantled and the building made into private dwellings.'

A POLICEMAN'S LOT

'In 1927 a friend said, "Why don't you join the Police Force? You're tall enough." I was six feet tall. I applied, was accepted and afer five months' training at Devizes, was sent to Swindon where I spent the next three years.

It was part of the duty of the police on night duty at that time to also attend the Swindon Town home football matches, to sit around the perimeter of the pitch and be on standby for any disturbance – there was no pay or charge for this duty! Only two police officers were employed officially, these patrolled the ground – the charge to the football club for this was twelve shillings and sixpence and was kept by the Wiltshire County Council.

From Swindon I moved to Charlton, near Malmesbury. The police house was an old cottage without electricity, gas, telephone or water! (The latter was delivered daily in a water cart.) The County paid £4 per annum for this cottage – the charge included rent and rates. There was one pub in the village, The Horse and Groom – it was kept by three old maids who wore long black skirts, white aprons and mob caps. One did the outside work, one served and one cleaned.

I left Charlton in 1935 and moved to Holt – what luxury – a modern house. My beat included several villages and duties in Bradford on Avon. All travel was made either on foot or bicycle. Duties, night and day, were called point duties. I had to be at a given destination, usually a telephone kiosk, where I could be contacted at a given time – no mobile radios in those days!

Police were also called upon to be present at post mortems and at farms where cattle infected with foot and mouth disease or anthrax were disposed of by burying in lime or burning, and to administer the strict precautions required to contain the outbreak.

When war broke out it was my duty to place evacuees in local households – most were Jewish and I recall that the now famous Vidal Sassoon, his mother and brother were one of the families to be settled in.

We also helped with policing at events such as Ascot races, County shows and of course great Royal occasions. I was on duty at the funeral of George VI – we spent several days in barracks at Windsor and at the funeral procession we lined the streets.

In 1955 I moved to Trowbridge where I drove a police car – a nice

175

wind-down to my retirement in 1957. I enjoyed my life as a police constable and have no regrets at my choice of profession.'

LEATHER WORKING

'James I was king in the early 17th century when Thomas Beaven commenced the business of woolstapling, fellmongering and leather dressing in Holt.

In the olden days before the advent of mechanised transport, it must have been a delightful sight to see teams of white mules and horses drawing waggon loads of wool from all over Wiltshire and the Duke of Beaufort's estate at Badminton to Beaven's woolstapling premises at Holt. Sheepskins were regularly collected by horse and cart from slaughterhouses all over the county and surrounding district, which on arrival at the fellmonger's yard created a fisherman's paradise for live bait!

The fellmonger treated the skins on the flesh side with sodium sulphide. This would penetrate overnight to allow the wool to literally fall off next day. There are 13 different sorts of wool on a sheep's back. After treatment and purifying, the woolstapler would grade before transfer to the cloth mills. The pelt would then be pickled using the old method of liming etc until the 1920s when the introduction of tumbling and spirits of salt changed the timing of production. Skins entering the yard on Monday were out on Friday as crust oil leathers. Previous to this, it was in January and out September. No waste was allowed as all skins were trimmed of tails, heads and various other bits, which were collected by the glue manufacturers.

Around 1870 the pelt was split into two. The grain side was tanned for skivers, the lining being dressed for wash leathers and gloves. The glove department developed with agricultural and housemaid gloves, later with a high class production. In 1951 Beaven's entered the clothing industry with coloured suedes and pebble grain, which were in high demand on the continent, where the jackets were made and re-exported to be sold at Harrods!

A considerable amount of experimenting was done to improve the absorption of water by the crust oil leather (chamois) and no smears. There is no doubt whatsoever the 1960s proved that J & T Beaven Ltd were producing the best in the world.

J & T Beaven Ltd are now a subsidiary of the Pittard (Yeovil) Group and are still producing crust oil leathers and skivers.'

WAR & PEACE

THE GREAT WAR 1914-18

The First World War brought the end of a way of life for many in Wiltshire, as the men marched away and the Army took over acres of land at the very heart of the county. The cutting of the regimental crests in the Downs in South Wiltshire was only one of the more tangible legacies of this period of upheaval. Casualties of the war were many, of course – and it wasn't only the men who came back from the war with problems, as the story of 'General' shows.

THE END OF AN IDYLL

'My father had been a journeyman baker when the chance of becoming his own master occurred at a bakery with a public house attached in Imber on Salisbury Plain. I was born in 1907 and was three weeks old when we moved – it became home for the next ten years.

Imber was a paradise for children, and in spite of few books and no cinemas we were never bored as so many exciting things went on outside. It was purely agricultural – flocks of sheep grazed and the acres of corn stretched out for miles.

During the early summer we roamed far and wide over the Plain without restriction, in search of peewit eggs and mushrooms. The cry of peewits, the lark song, the sight of the harebells, the excited jump of a hare on the short springy turf – all this encapsulated the essence of Salisbury Plain for me.

In 1914 this idyllic existence stopped. War was declared and Imber became the centre of military operations that soon sounded its death knell. Khaki uniforms were everywhere and sounds of gunfire shattered the peace. We could no longer wander the village – large areas were out of bounds. I considered myself fortunate to have been at Imber whilst it was so peaceful, like a time capsule for the 1800s to 1900s.

Nobody now lives at Imber – it is a deserted village and is open about once a year for people to visit. It is in the middle of an army training ground.'

'As a schoolgirl I still remember when our army were on manoeuvres they seemed to be marching along the road at Brinkworth in their thousands, then came the cavalry on their lovely black horses and lastly the horse-drawn gun carriages. They were on their way to Charlton Park, where they stayed for several days.

Later the war started and a lot of our young lads were called up, and some of the young women took over the men's work on the farms and some went to the factories to make munitions. It was a very busy time for everyone.'

'YOUR DADDY'S GOING TO BE A SOLDIER'

'The first thing I can remember is when I was four. My Dad was out forking the flower beds and the lady opposite from The Bath Arms came across to go into the post office which my mother ran for the village of Horningsham. She said to me, "Your Daddy's going to be a soldier tomorrow." That was in 1915.

We grew our own vegetables. When Dad went to war I can remember we had four or five fowls and Mother thought she'd kill one of them as we were short of meat; they were old and weren't laying any eggs. She didn't know how to kill it but she managed to get hold of it, knocked it on the head, knocked it stupid with a stick and then chopped its head off on the chopping block and it ran around the garden. We laughed to see this fowl running around without a head. We used to hurry home from school − my brother Henry was two years younger than me − finding all the acorns and beechnuts we could take home and crush between two bricks to feed the fowls.

One day, a Saturday, Mother made a stew and she'd thickened it and we had it all on our plates and were sat down to eat our dinner. "Hark, what's that?" And there were the bagpipes. We'd never seen or heard tell of the bagpipes. We went out and there were the soldiers marching all down the hill from Maiden Bradley. There was a camp at Sutton Veny for Australians and New Zealanders and so many of them died over there, they've got a plot for them. They used to march from Sutton Veny nearly up to Maiden Bradley, down the road right into Horningsham and back to Sutton Veny. When we went in Mother put all the stew back and warmed it up again.

We had an open fire with an oven each side and two things which swung out to put the saucepans on. Mother didn't bake bread because she had a full time job with the post office and the telephone. She had to be on call full time − she didn't know what it was like to have a night's sleep − because there was a hospital for wounded soldiers at Longleat and she had to be on call when a new batch was coming in.

Dad was badly gassed. He was with the Somerset Light Infantry on the limber with the horses, like the gun carriages they use at the

179

Tournament. The transport in front of him was hit and the one behind, but he was in the middle and escaped.

After the war, Dad went and worked a little while at the nurseries at Longleat; they used to grow seeds and plant all their own trees on the estate and they had a marvellous greenhouse and gardens. Then Dad stayed home and helped Mum with the post office and telegrams and then he took a postman's route on foot. He used to go down Broadslade, down to Longleat and to County Cottage. I've heard Mum say that he was never the same after he came out of the war.'

'WE'LL SOON BE HOME AGAIN'

'When the war broke out my two brothers were farmers at Wingfield but both volunteered for the war and just left my mother and me to look after everything. "Well," they said, "it won't be long, we shall soon be home again." My oldest brother was already training once a year in the Royal Wiltshire Yeomanry so of course he went first, then my younger brother followed. Well, Mother and I managed. I did the milking of course, but we made no more butter or cheese and sold our milk to the WU Dairies. We also gave up pigs, just kept cows, horses and chickens and by jove it was hard work as the years went by. My oldest brother was badly gassed and poisoned but used to get leave as he was in France but my younger brother went out to India and the Persian Gulf where he had part of his foot blown off and he did not get home till 1919.'

LIFE GOES ON

'I was born in 1908, four years after my brother, and we lived in Tetbury next to my grandfather who lived at The Fox Inn. The pubs opened at six o'clock in the morning and the workers went in for their pint on the way to work. Grandfather had a parrot and customers taught it to say "whoa". It would shout this as the horse and cart started up the steep hill, which of course caused chaos!

In 1914 the war started and we moved to Sherston in Wiltshire. My father took over the carrier business from an uncle who had gone into the Navy. The business consisted of two horses and a high trap, also a kind of cart.

We had to work hard; my brother and I collected eggs, rabbits and chickens from the local farms. I loved driving the horse round the lanes in the high trap. On reaching home the eggs had to be washed and packed, the insides taken from the rabbits and the chickens plucked. These my father took to Bristol, 20 miles away. It took nearly a day to get there and he delivered them to the shops.

He had a depot in Bristol and he collected goods from firms and brought them back to Sherston and other villages. All the local shops relied on my father. There were only basic foods like flour, sugar, fats. We fed well at home but there was no rationing, so food became scarce. Fish was awful, it was either salted or pickled. But my father knew lots of people who gave or sold him things.

In 1915 our headmaster was called up and we had quite a few changes. Our new lady headteacher was always wielding the cane.

Our special treat was when Father took us on the lorry to a pantomime in Bristol where we met several actresses and they gave us boxes of chocolates. We usually only had a few sweets as our halfpenny each week didn't buy much.

At the end of the war I remember my cousin came home gassed. He later went to work for Sir George Holford at Westonbirt House as his coachman, driving round the arboretum Sundays, planting trees with Sir George.

By the end of the war Father bought a motor lorry and sold the horses and carts. Petrol was delivered to the house in two-gallon cans.

The cinema came to Sherston in a huge tent in the pub yard. A big traction engine drove the apparatus and the lighting was by torches. We sat on forms and saw silent films, while an old man played the piano. Sadly the tent caught fire, eventually, and we no longer had pictures.'

'A Cycle Corps was billeted in Bratton village for some time and the chapel was opened for them on Saturday evenings; our pastor, Rev Charles Hobbs, and the vicar both stood at the door to welcome them.

Reeves Works had the first car in the village, an ancient Humber. On a trial run with Jo Stiles, formerly a carter and now trained as a driver, it tried to get "up street" but stuck and had to be helped by a Works water cart passing by! Reeves also had the prototype of the first army tank in the yard for repair after a breakdown. When done it was taken up the Castle for tests. My mother was one of several who tried to go up and watch but was turned back by sentries.'

'I think my first conscious memory in childhood was of standing in my cot and looking at the bedroom window and seeing a travelling rug stretched across it. This I later learned was because there was a war on and there were fears of Zeppelin raids – even in quiet old Devizes.'

CASUALTIES OF WAR

'When my father, born 1889, left school he joined the family firm of wheelwrights and undertakers, but he wanted to see something of the world so he "put his age on" and joined the army where he saw service in this country, Africa and India. He went to war in 1914 and was blinded in November the same year. He joined St Dunstan's, the fifth blinded person to enter. He was taught to make coconut fibre doormats. They were so well made someone told him it was just as well he did not have to rely on income from the mats to keep the family – they just never wore out.'

'During an evening service at Wishford the sister of one of the lads killed wept the whole time. I think of it every time I sing "Oh God our help in ages past".'

'GENERAL'

'Of all the creatures on the farm, I should imagine that General, the big white carthorse, had the most character. General had been in the Great War and in the mud and horror of France had pulled a gun carrier. Shipped back to Blighty, shell-shocked and blind in one eye, he had been put up for sale at a local horse auction for ex-war horses and there he had the great fortune to be bought by Dad. I don't think that there were many bidders for the General, who had the reputation for being savage. Now, Dad understood and loved horses and from then on the old warrior was in good hands. General was quite placid until it thundered or he heard a gunshot, then the poor thing thought he was once more back at the Front and he'd bolt across fields or over hedges, taking whatever implements he happened to be hitched to with him. Whenever the clouds gathered and the sultry air foretold a thunderstorm, Dad would walk General up and down and talk to him until he became calm.

Sometimes he was used to draw the large trap. I think Dad was always at the reins then, just in case of trouble. On one occasion we were going to Calne, all the family aboard. Rain started as we neared Quemerford and an unsuspecting pedestrian raised her umbrella as General trotted up the hill. I suppose he must have caught a glimpse of this out of the corner of his good eye and he bolted. Down London Road, New Road and across the Strand he galloped; Dad stood up in his seat and clutched the reins and the rest of us cowered in our seats. The steep incline of High Street lowered the pace somewhat but we didn't come to a halt until we were on the Hilmarton Road.

After many years of hard work, General was retired and supposed to spend the rest of his life in leisure, cropping the short grass of the Home Field. Years later however, the elevator got stuck in the gateway between the Long Ground and More Mead. It had been a very wet summer and this was the last straw. Bonny and Trooper couldn't shift the heavy machinery and it was imperative that the next rick should be started before the next deluge. "Old Gen could move it," said Dad. In spite of family opposition the old horse was led out and harnessed to the elevator and, despite his age, he pulled the heavy implement clear with ease and with what the onlookers felt was great pride.

General died just before the last war started. No one was quite sure how old he was but he certainly had an adventurous life.'

THE CUTTING OF THE BADGES

'Ten miles west of Salisbury, on the A30 London to Exeter road, lies the village of Fovant, which many servicemen of the 1914-18 war visited, first as a training camp, and latterly as the Demobilisation

The Army Christmas Pudding Fund was a scheme to ensure that the men at the Front would receive some festive cheer in 1916. Children were encouraged to give their sixpences — a great deal of money to a child in those days.

Centre through which so many passed on their way back to civilian life.

With the outbreak of war in August 1914 and the need to find accommodation for the new army, the authorities took over many thousands of acres of agricultural land for training camps, amongst these being Fovant.

Two rifle ranges were laid out with the downs forming a natural background, and good farming land became a network of huts, parade grounds and metalled road. There were general stores, tea-rooms, power and pumping stations, and a picture palace, and a single track railway line linked up the camp with the main line at Dinton. Compton Chamberlayne to the east and Sutton Mandeville to the west soon had their quota of camps, and many thousands of men from regular and territorial regiments, and troops from Australia, carried out training here before going into action on the Western Front.

It was not until the early 1920s that the last troops departed; today apart from the occasional irregular surfaces in the fields that were once so level, one sign only remains to show that this was not always a purely agricultural district – the Badges.

The idea of cutting their regimental badge in the chalk hillside originated in 1916 from The London Rifle Brigade. Volunteers were called upon to do the work in their off duty hours, and their efforts proved so successful that other units soon followed their example and by the end of the war the hillside showed a fair picture of what units had been stationed in the district.

Work was carried out from 4 am to 7 am, and was hard labour on the very steep slope, the first job being to mark out the badges to scale. Then followed the removal of the turf, and filling the cavities with chalk. It is recorded that the Sixth City of London Regiment badge took three months to complete. Sadly not all badges received this kind of attention and those that were laid out with chalk on the surface of the downs did not survive.

With the departure of the troops the badges soon became overgrown with weeds and grass, and with the outbreak of war in 1939 any maintenance work had to cease, the authorities wishing the badges to be camouflaged as being a potential landmark for enemy aircraft. Nature soon provided this camouflage, sheep and cattle grazing on the hillside also did much damage, and by the end of the war it seemed that the badges had gone for good.

After the war, enquiries were made by various regiments as to the possibility of restoring their badges, but their efforts at first met with little success. Eventually, however, members of the Fovant Home Guard Old Comrades Association agreed to restore the badges of the

184

London regiments, and work commenced on Sunday 12th June 1949. Early in 1950, members of the Association decided to cut their own badge, that of the Wiltshire Regiment, soon followed by that of The Wiltshire Yeomanry. The funding for this work came from donations made by the regimental associations and a fund from the Australian Government. By 1953 nine of the original badges had been restored, which together with the two Wiltshire badges and the Royal Signals Badges added in 1970, make up the twelve badges to be seen today.

In 1963, due to reduced membership the Fovant Home Guard Old Comrades Associaton became The Fovant Badges Society, which continues today, with its aims "To maintain and to preserve the Badges on the Downs in South Wiltshire". We have members who remember as children the forming of the camps, the building of the railway, the trips by rail (threepence return Dinton-Fovant) to see films at the garrison cinema, and also boxing bouts by the soldiers. One remembers, as a child, dressed in her purple velvet frock, sitting on an Australian soldier's knee in the Tipperary Tea Rooms; another's grandfather supplied milk to the camps, and he remembers visiting the hospital at Fovant.'

THE SECOND WORLD WAR
1939-45

When war came again 20 years later, Wiltshire became used to the sight of soldiers and prisoners of war – and those dreaded telegrams, though happily some were not bad news. Bombs fell on the county, we struggled with rationing and make do and mend, and generally we tried to get on with our lives for those six long years. Some people came to Wiltshire for the first time during the war, finding country life very different to what they had been used to in the city.

DODGING THE BOMBS

'In the spring of 1941, one night while I was on Home Guard duties

I heard a loud bang. A German aircraft had dropped three bombs in an effort to extinguish the local searchlight battery. The first landed near an isolated farm near Sound Bottom, north of the village of Mildenhall. The second fell on downland adjacent to Manton Down Racing Stables. The third bomb exploded right in the middle of the Marlborough-Broad Hinton road, about 300 yards the Marlborough side of Rockley.

An unusual feature was that all the rubble was blown out sideways. A man who lived in Wootton Bassett was driving a small Austin Riley car and drove straight into the crater. He was rescued and taken to Savernake Hospital, where he recovered in a week or so. It took many loads of stone to repair the crater.'

'It was 1941, and August on our farm near Chippenham. We had been harvesting that day and a long trailer of sacked up wheat had been left on the field at the end of the day. At about half past eleven we heard the approach of an enemy aircraft and suddenly realised we were being bombed. There were fires starting in the fields all round the farm and a number of large bombs had exploded. I suddenly found myself blown from my seat across to the door of the room and saying to my family, "How did I get here?" But I was alright and soon recovered.

We all bravely went outside and found there seemed to be fires everywhere. We rather pathetically tried to put some out with buckets of water, but it was hopeless. It wasn't until the next morning that we discovered the trailer of wheat was completely burned out – we couldn't somehow believe it. There were a number of bomb craters about 20 ft deep and 20 ft wide in some of the fields. Fortunately, no one was injured and there had been no structural damage.

The following day, the Germans broadcast that Hullavington aerodrome had been heavily bombed and almost completely destroyed. We lived about a mile away and we never heard of any damage at the aerodrome, so perhaps the German observer thought our farm and land was the aerodrome.'

'Having left school in 1942 I worked in Marks & Spencer, Swindon. We were asked to do our bit for the war effort. My effort was to be a firefighter – I was 17. I went for one session of training and put out a small fire using a chair as a shield and a hose. On Wednesday afternoons when the store was closed, I would sit on the roof of Marks & Spencer with a stirrup pump, a bucket of sand and a tin hat waiting for the Germans to drop their bombs. I really believed I would be able to stop the store burning down. My bit to help the war!'

SOLDIERS

'Life before the war in the quiet hamlet of Wingfield was carefree, even though the villagers had to work very hard on the five farms that made up the main part of the village. Workers used to spend many hours in the hayfields during the hot summer months, and hedging and ditching in the autumn-winter, there always seemed plenty to do.

Then we were plunged into disruption by the war and the Army who had been billeted in the manor house (Wingfield House, which had been owned by Sir Vincent Cailard and taken over by his son, when he died). Our homes were requisitioned by the Army and two soldiers were billeted with each family; the owner of the house had to give up one room, ie bedroom or sitting room for this purpose, while the main regiment was in the big house. The officers were in a farmer's house or in the lodge attached to the manor house (which was a gardener's cottage). In 1939 the Royal Staffordshire Artillery Regiment came and all their gun carriages were placed along the grass verges, underneath the avenues of trees, for camouflage reasons. We young maidens got very friendly with the lads cleaning their guns, it was all very exciting for us.

The lodge itself was a very important place, as all the officers and chiefs of staff visited it regularly. The villagers welcomed the intrusion, as they were able to exchange eggs, milk, chicken, rabbits etc with the cooks for dried fruit (especially as it was nearly Christmas), margarine, suet and sometimes sugar, so on the whole we all did very well, especially as goods were rationed then. It was a very sad time when they went to embark for France in 1940, as we had made many good friends, and some kept in touch after the war. One girl married one lad and he lived in our village until 1960, until he died.

The next regiment that came was the Searchlight Battery from Wales. This was a bit more dangerous for us, as we were in the direct line for the German bombers to get to Bath and Bristol. We had a few stray bombs dropped across the village but all missed the target.

There are many happy and sad memories, especially after they left, as on D-Day a great many wounded soldiers of all nationalities and regiments were brought to Wingfield House, before being repatriated to their own units to be nursed back to health. This house was a Red Cross hospital in the First World War, so it had a lot of memories for the very old villagers.'

'Just before the outbreak of war my husband and I went to live in the village of Netheravon, he as the police constable. As many

187

people will know, it is not easy to be accepted as a newcomer in a village and being a local PC makes it more difficult still. However, by good fortune I was asked to join the WI. In those days they were mostly young married women, for few women worked at that time. So I soon made friends among the members, especially as I could play the piano, teach country dancing and was keen on drama, all of which I put to good use.

Then came the war, and worst of all the tragedy of Dunkirk. There was an army camp as well as an RAF camp just outside the village, and many soldiers were brought to Netheravon straight from the beaches. Some had uniforms soaked in sea-water, some were even without proper footwear and they started to wander about the village with nowhere to go other than a public house, there being no cafe.

So the WI fomed a special committee from members who had time to spare to see what we could do for them. First we wanted a place where they could meet. Just behind the village street was an old brewery which had not been used for many years, and we went to see the owner who said we could certainly use it. Now it was husbands to the rescue. They helped us clean the old place up and whitewashed all the walls. Then we approached the Food Ministry and got permits for tea, margarine, cooking fat and a little sugar, all of which were rationed. We were able to buy potatoes, eggs and milk locally. We begged and borrowed cooking utensils, teapots, oil stoves and cookers, small tables, trestle tables and chairs and benches. In an incredibly short time we were ready for business. We had a roster of ladies who would make tea, cook, wait at table and wash up. I was put in charge of the till. We opened every evening except Sunday from 6.30 pm to 10 pm.

The soldiers were delighted. It was somewhere to sit and talk away from camp. We charged only enough to cover expenses, for egg and toast, beans on toast, egg and chips and sometimes egg, beans and chips! The old brewery was soon a hive of activity. The local priest-in-charge (our vicar had gone to war as a chaplain) came in as a sort of accountant. Every night I carried home the takings and on Saturday mornings he came to check the takings, bills and receipts. Then we bagged up the money which he banked for us. All the money was ploughed back again for food and drink for the troops and we kept going as long as we were needed.

What a happy band of workers we were in what was a very difficult time of life for most people. How different from today. Who would now dare to carry a bag of money home every night by way of an unlit farm track? My only fear was the "wump, wump" sound of German planes flying overhead on their way to bomb Midlands towns and cities.'

'In 1940 I was expecting my first baby and we were living at what is now Oakhangar Barn near Fovant village hall. Soldiers had come back from Dunkirk and some were camped out on two pieces of land nearby, some near what is now the Youth Club and others in front of our cottage.

It was so hot that summer that they would stand in the river to keep cool. They used to hang mirrors on trees to shave. When the nurse came in to me they'd ask, "Anything happening yet?" and she'd call back, "Not yet!"

Chris was born on 1st July and the midwife opened the window and called down, "We've got a beautiful baby boy in here" and they cheered. I suppose many of them were family men and they got interested knowing there was a baby expected.

One young soldier asked to come along when I went for a walk pushing my new baby in the pram. He missed his family. He came from Sidcup in Kent. Later we had a card from his mother saying that he went back out to the war and never came back. I won't forget

Pam Hillier's home was 'open house' for the American servicemen stationed in Devizes, who came for tea or coffee and a chat. Many local children enjoyed the company of their new 'uncles' — and the sweets they usually produced!

the summer that Chris was born.

I remember when Granny Coombes decided to bake cakes for the soldiers. She made two or three batches and took them out. "Anyone want a cake while they're still warm?" she asked. They certainly did – those cakes went like – like hot cakes!'

'There were American servicemen at Fugglestone, and at Christmas the GI Father Christmas would be available to the local children in Wilton, who were delighted to visit. Young Hugh was four years old and loved it, but one year old Tom would only cry.

Every evening the GIs would hold their "taps" ceremony – the lowering of the Stars and Stripes for the day while the bugler played taps.

I helped at the canteen in Wilton House, buttering buns alongside the Dowager Lady Pembroke, and served tea and sandwiches to the troops.'

PRISONERS OF WAR

'I lived in Carlton Terrace, Devizes, opposite the then police station. I remember sitting on a wall watching the Italian POWs coming off the train and then being marched from the station up to the barracks. They looked poverty stricken – brown overalls with black patches. They were well looked after as POWs and many never went back after the war.'

'During the war we had Italian and then German prisoners to work on the farm at Burbage. The Italians soon destroyed our idea of the proper demeanour of a conquered people. They soon became Alec, Cookie and Bruno to us all. Alec was a tailor by trade and did all sorts of tailoring jobs for us but he soon became an accomplished tractor driver, careering round the fields with gay abandon and christening his tractor "my Spitfire". Bruno had a passion for babies and endeared himself to the village mums by dashing up to the prams with cries of "Oh, the beautiful bambino" and embracing mum as well as baby, which added colour and excitement to our drab village street usually rattling with tanks.

When Italy surrendered and the Italians went home we were all a little sad and the children cried when they knew they would not see Alec and his "Spitfire" any more. He promised he would return, "but next time," he vowed, "I will bring my scissors." Alas, when he wrote years later we had no job to offer him with or without his scissors.

After this cheerful interlude in wartime life the replacing Germans struck a sombre note. We prepared to be aloof and were somewhat apprehensive. After years of aeroplanes buzzing overhead which might, and sometimes did, drop bombs on us, no ice cream, and toys and sweets in short supply all because of the Germans, the children naturally viewed their arrival with some alarm. I well remember my four year old, after long and silent inspection, running up full of relief, "Come and see the Germans, Mum, they're alright."

Indeed they were. The three Germans lived in a tumbledown cottage which would never be passed for habitation today and "did" for themselves. They were not allowed to shop so I had to do their shopping for them, which often became a bit complicated with language difficulties. These German prisoners were tremendous workers and their physical strength was a great asset when most farm labour was supplied by old men and land girls. If Alec's "Spitfire" lost some of its dash, perhaps it gained in efficiency.'

RATIONS, CONCERTS AND HOSTELS

'I helped my husband run a general store at Brinkworth, selling a wide range of goods. I was up by half past six in the morning and was often still doing the books at midnight. The shop was open until nine o'clock, so it was a long day.

During the war there was a lot to do as rations had to be ordered, weighed and measured each week. The supplies of rationed food were ordered with a permit from the Food Office in Malmesbury depending on the registration for different commodities. All the coupons had to be sent to the Food Office at the end of the month. When soldiers came home on leave or were billeted nearby there were no rations for them so we sometimes went without ourselves. Sides of bacon did not take into account the bones, so it was impossible to fulfil all the orders, and sometimes hams were sent instead of the bacon to rasher! Farmers were given permits from the Food Office during haymaking for their workers, and they might need up to four pounds of cheese.'

'From the local paper in 1942 – "Under the direction of Mr R Brinkworth the Home Guard, Cadets and Rangers, assisted by friends, gave a concert in the Rifle Range at Sherston on Tuesday evening, in aid of the Red Cross which will benefit by some £22.

The show was a revelation of the real entertainment value that can be provided by local talent, who improvised their costumes. High spots were a cowboy thriller by the Cadets, 'The Chad Valley Bank

Robbery' written by cadet George Stevens, and the comic songs of Don Neal.

Mr J Wilson presided and in a short interval thanked those who had taken part and commended the work of the Red Cross to the audience." '

'The war brought great changes to Neston. The Bristol Aircraft Company and the Birmingham Small Arms took over the mines at Neston as they provided underground shelter for the factories. A new road was built joining the Bradford Road and Westwells to provide easy access to the factories. This is now known as Westwell Road. Huts were put up to provide hostels and accommodaton for workmen and their families – there were 14 sites in all around Neston, including some for displaced persons from Poland, Estonia, Latvia, Lithuania etc. A cinema was built for the use of both factory workers and their families and villagers; we paid sixpence to go in. It was also used for all sorts of social events. A hospital was built, and a school for the displaced children, as they couldn't speak any English.'

'At the outbreak of war I decided to leave school before I needed to, so I started work at Hilmarton Post Office and General Stores and knew all about rationing from the start! We used to have a large jug of golden syrup on top of the stove and have to pour the ration of syrup into jars that the customers had to provide. The large slabs of cooking fat were weighed in portions according to the size of the family, two ounces each per week. Suet and other very scarce foods were saved up and then shared out on the country round, next time it would be the village folks' turn. Sometimes it would cause a customer to say, "Where is my suet etc?" until we explained it was their turn next! For some reason we always seemed to have lots of cakes, also cigarettes, and often on some Saturdays the shop would be full of customers after these. Some customers had their groceries delivered in a large basket in the village, which I carried round.

Sometimes I cycled to the country places to collect orders and at times went on a round with my boss to deliver them, ending up having tea with the family at the last farm.

The daily papers were dropped in bulk at the Stores for customers to collect. I used to deliver these to my neighbours and to the Searchlight Battery on my way home. On cycling to work in the mornings I had the job of posting the soldiers' mail, someone would watch for me coming down the road and stand at the gate with a pile of envelopes.

I met lots of people other than the locals, such as the RAF families who were billeted in the village, and was actually in the shop when a bus load of evacuee adults arrived. It was sad as they came in for their rations and were asking each other who and where they had been with and to! One of them was upset as she wanted to go to the same place as another member of her family. They settled in, and there was one family in particular who included mother, father, son and wife, daughter and husband and a young nephew and their two single teenagers, a son and daughter! I often wonder what happened to all the people we got to know so well. Working in the shop you heard all their troubles.

Once an army convoy stopped in the village for two days. We were very busy then, for they came in for whatever we were allowed to sell them which was not rationed and I remember we had two or three large wooden crates of broken biscuits. Needless to say, these were soon sold out.

The Searchlight Battery was named *"Yer Tiz"* on the gate of the field they were in. At Christmas my father said, "Ask two or three of those chaps if they would like to come." They were very pleased and three came on the Christmas night to tea. After that it snowballed as one original would bring another fresh one and in the end for the year they were there most of them had been to our house and some made it "home from home". To this day my mother hears from some at Christmas, and their wives.

Living right out in the wilds we thought we were safe from the bombs, but in the early hours one morning one dropped in line with our house just opposite in a field. Luckily it missed us and exploded underground, but there was quite a large crater left.

At 10 pm one winter's night a loud knock came on our door. It was an army Captain wanting to commandeer the use of our house, as two planes had crashed in the next field to ours. Two crew died so the soldiers had to guard everything until the RAF took over the next day.'

THOSE TELEGRAMS

'I came – with my parents – to Donhead in 1938 when my father retired from teaching, and the county seemed to accept us with open arms. After life in a big town the warm friendliness here was so refreshing. Complete strangers greeted one in the lanes and we soon got used to replying in like manner. I remember on a pitch-black night in war time seeing the glow from cigarette ends as I heard men's footsteps approaching and then hearing friendly voices greeting me by name, so reassuring.

There was a small one-man post office on the main road and we had many telegrams in those days as we had no telephone. There was a smart telegraph boy but, if he was not available, the postmaster used to ask any passing motorist to deliver them. My mother had terrible memories of telegrams during the First World War so – seeing her face – a kindly stranger reassured her by saying as he handed over the envelope, "It's all right, just to say they can't come till next weekend."

During part of the war I worked in a guest house in Tisbury and there was great excitement when two "spies" were arrested. A lady living in a big house on the outskirts of the town had let a wing of it to the local Officers Mess. She was called on one day by two nuns asking for alms. She went away to get her purse and, on returning, spotted the two nuns peering through the curtain that divided her sitting room from the Officers Mess. She pretended ignorance but her suspicions were aroused still more as they departed by a sight of the heavy men's boots which were sticking out from under the nuns' robes. She reported this and two men masquerading as nuns were later arrested!'

'Several years after the war, on visiting Madame Tussaud's for the first time, I realised that I had seen a waxwork tableau before.

My father was on an aircraft carrier that accompanied convoys across the Atlantic and had been away for some months, so my mother had taken my sister, brother and me to stay with his parents for Christmas in 1943.

We spent the afternoon of Christmas Eve visiting several people in the village delivering presents. As we returned we were in an excitable mood, thinking about next morning and the parcels that had surreptitiously been given to our mother that afternoon.

There was a bicycle leaning against the wall and as we turned into the gate I saw my grandparents standing on the top step with a yellow envelope somehow suspended between them and the telegraph boy. In a strange voice my grandmother called my mother to open the telegram.

Suddenly everything changed. There was great excitement. My father's ship had docked and he would come next morning to a station 15 miles away. As there were no buses and no petrol for private cars, we had to find a taxi for Christmas morning. I remember nothing more about that Christmas except happiness.'

FRUIT AND PIGS!

'My mother originally belonged to the Britford WI and used to ride her bicycle to the Britford village hall each month. Then they started up a WI at Nunton, meeting at the parish room.

During the war they used to gather at Nunton Farmhouse to do canning of fruit and vegetables with a canning machine that was turned by hand a set number of times to seal the silver-coloured cans; these were then put in a net and plunged into boiling water in an old copper that was situated in our boilerhouse at the back of the house.

The WI also met at Nunton to do basketmaking with cane. I actually made a basket. The Italian prisoners of war that helped on the farm (they came from a camp at Wilton) also made baskets from the willow trees in the meadows and sold them for cigarettes. I remember that the one I made, and one made by the Italians, we used for collecting eggs right up till 1970 at my farm at Britford.

The WI ran a competition to see who could grow the most potatoes from two tubers. My mother and father grew plants from each "eye" of the tubers in pots, and then planted them out, and I believe grew over half a hundredweight from them! I am sure many didn't believe it was genuine.

There was also a "Pig Club" during the war, run by my father and Miss Stevenson (the present Lord Radnor's great aunt) who lived at Bodenham House. Many people (at least 20) kept a pig in their garden and were allowed a ration of meal sufficient to keep half a pig, the rest of its feed to come from household and garden waste. When the pigs were fat, they were slaughtered, I believe, at Downton Bacon Factory, and half the pig went to the national food ration and the owner could keep the other half back for their own use. Also, if you kept bees you were allowed a special sugar ration to help keep the bees alive during the winter. This was to help the fruit crops to be heavier, as the production of fruit was so important owing to the almost total lack of oranges and bananas from abroad. I can remember my mother taking the local schoolchildren on walks gathering rose hips, again for the national effort to produce Vitamin C in the form of rosehip syrup.

Lastly, I can vividly remember the visits of the American doctors and nurses from the hospital at the top of the hill; they used to come to see the sheep having their lambs in the spring. They often had supper with us, and liked nothing better than my father's draught cider from our apple orchards (where the council houses now stand), with crusty bread, cheddar cheese and raw onions. Many of the younger ladies in the village took full advantage of the presence of the young Americans, who had plenty of money – and nylons! No names, no pack drill!'

195

'My husband and I were both born in London. We lived there until a few years after we married. We started our married life in a flat in Dulwich in 1935. Just before the war my mother-in-law married, for the second time. He was a Somerset man, and they eventually moved from their London house to a cottage in Wiltshire. Through them, in 1941, we were lucky enough to be able to rent a cottage in the same village – about ten minutes drive from Longleat Estate. The rent was twelve shillings and sixpence a week. In relation to London prices this seemed very reasonable but to the local people who rented their cottages for amounts like two shillings it seemed exorbitant!

The cottage had been empty for some time, after having a succession of tenants and it was in a dreadful condition. It took me three weeks cleaning, and many tears, before I could move in with my two year old daughter. At times I despaired of ever sorting it out, but after the bombing in London the country was a haven of peace and quiet.

My husband continued to work in London for about one year, travelling down on the train at weekends. To save money he took his bike on the train (it went in the guard's van) and cycled part of the way home. He was expecting to be called up into the army at any time, but eventually he left London, and became involved in the building of the American Hospital in Longleat Park, working for the Air Ministry. He became Clerk of Works there.

The cottage consisted of kitchen, dining room and sitting room, with three bedrooms, but no running water, heating or electricity. For sanitation there was an Elsan – a chemical closet – which was in a small hut in the garden. There was half an acre of land around the cottage, with an adjoining orchard, and lovely views across the valley. At one end of the cottage was a large storage room and above, reached by an open wooden staircase, was a loft which many years before had been used as a small village school. The pupils used to pay one penny a week. I knew of three elderly men in the village who had gone to school there. The teacher used to live along the lane. He had a wooden leg and it was rumoured that he used to take his leg off and use it to threaten the children!

It was all so different from our flat in London. In the kitchen by the sink was a hand-operated pump which drew water up from the well in the corner of the orchard. My daughter used to swing up and down on the handle. In the corner was a large brick-built copper, which was used for heating the water. To do this we had to light a fire underneath. We had to do this for all our hot water for the laundry and baths. We used to bath in the kitchen in a large tin bath I was able to buy.

During the war many of our relatives came to stay to escape from the bombing and we also had several evacuees, who stayed for many months. One weekend I remember my husband arriving from London to find that the only place he could sleep was in the sitting room as the place was so crowded.

Our son was born in 1945 and he went to the village school. He was very keen on playing tennis – he used to practise for hours hitting the ball against the end wall of the cottage. The nearest tennis court was in the grounds of Longleat Estate and he wrote and asked Lord Bath if he could use it as the only other courts were seven miles away. Lord Bath granted permission and Jim spent many happy hours there. Longleat at that time was a quiet country mansion, with very few visitors – quite different to today.

I joined the Women's Institute, my husband played in the local cricket team and he joined the Home Guard. I helped at the nearest farm for a month, milking the cows by hand, morning and afternoon. The farmer was amazed how easily I managed the milking as I had never done anything like that before. We all used to join in at harvest time – family, friends, evacuees – we would help to tie the corn into stooks after it had been cut and then it was balanced in bundles of three to dry, and we would help to build the haystacks when the hayfields were mown. Life in the country was so different to the anonymous life of London and the sense of community was a joy and delight.'

'I lived on the Isle of Dogs in London and after continual bombing I brought my partially-sighted mother and my little girl of 18 months, and a line full of wet baby washing, to Christian Malford. I couldn't get on the train fast enough because the previous night I had been dug out of a blitzed air raid shelter. In 1939 my mother had been evacuated for a time to Wiltshire and after the previous night's trauma we decided where we wanted to go. Without warning we returned to the farmhouse she knew, where we were given a bed for the night. the next night we were given temporary shelter in an old cottage – sacks for curtains, apples on the floor and one iron bedstead.

The bombing eased and my mother went back to London but I stayed on for the child's sake. A slightly better cottage became vacant, but it was extremely difficult to obtain bits of furniture etc. then by chance I met Ivy at the railway halt at Christian Malford. She had two children and by some misfortune her landlady had had to ask her to leave. She had been evacuated from Hastings where her husband was a sergeant in the RAF. And there she was, crying her eyes out on the platform.

Eventually, with the help of the billeting officer and because I could offer Ivy a roof and floor space, blankets and mattresses arrived. When I first arrived I had slept on the floor wrapped in blankets. We both settled down very happily together. Ivy helped me bath the children in the copper while it was still warm after washing day. I was a trainee dressmaker, so I was able to help Ivy by making clothes for the children.

I had hoped to have my furniture moved down from London, but our house was bombed and we lost everything. Ivy and I were very poor. My husband, a full time ARP worker, was able to send me 30 shillings a week, and Ivy did better, with £3 10s 0d from her husband. Before Ivy appeared I had just survived, my budget being five shillings per week rent, five shillings for coal, and £1 for food and oil. Cooking was by a solid fuel stove. Water and toilet facilities were, of course, down the garden path. I remember cooking a suet pudding in an enamel mug as I had not yet collected all the basic kitchen utensils. I wrapped it up in paper, put it in the mug partially filled with water, but as there was no lid and steaming was difficult, at half time I turned it upside down to ensure it was cooked both ends.

There was much fun with Ivy. We bought a secondhand radio for £3 for instalments of five shillings a week, after I had earned a little extra from a sewing job. We used to enjoy Victor Sylvester, particularly when he introduced his programme with the words, "Here we are under the chandeliers, drinking champagne", while we were drinking cocoa by the light of a candle stuck in a bottle!

Eventually Ivy moved to a larger place so that we could both have our husbands to visit us. I still went on collecting household equipment. My father had promised to visit and bring the shovel and chopper from London, but the house was bombed and he was killed before this happened. We went up for his funeral and there, amidst the ruins of our house, was a hook on the wall with the shovel and chopper hanging from it, all ready for the journey.'

A WAAF AT YATESBURY

'The year 1941 was my first experience of living in Wiltshire, when as an LACW in the WAAF, I was posted to Yatesbury, that large collection of wooden huts, nestling on the Marlborough Downs under the Cherhill White Horse and looking across to Avebury. The White Horse, along with the other Wiltshire white horses, was covered with ash to prevent it being used as a landmark by enemy aircraft.

Yatesbury was No 2 Radio School, which at that time housed about 9,000 personnel, both permanent staff and trainees on the radio and radar courses. Not much of this huge area of the unit is visible today, apart from the large hangars, now used as storage warehouses by Syms Ltd of Calne, being the only viable things of the old airfield. The rest of it has been ploughed up. The old gymnasium stands in grand isolation in the fields, and is used by the farmer for his farming tools etc.

I had been trained as a cook and butcher and, along with some other women posted to Yatesbury, travelled from London Paddington to Chippenham, changing trains, dragging our heavy kit bags. These were the long canvas sack-type, white with a blue band round the middle. We crossed the platform, onto the little train to Calne – what a delightful little line this was. We were met by a male driver, with an RAF blue-painted bus, and we were soon loaded onto it, plus the kit bags (someone weighed mine on the railway scales and it weighed 80lbs). We drove out of the little town of Calne, and up the hill to the unit. As we drove in through the gates, another bus was ready to go out. A Physical Training Instructor jumped on to our bus. "Anyone who can play cricket?" No reply at first, and I said yes I did, but I did not have my sports kit easily available. "Never mind that," she said, "we have some spare." So I was bundled onto the waiting bus, setting off I knew not where. We went the way we had just come, and later I learned we were at Compton Bassett, the next unit. We had a good game, and tea, before returning to Yatesbury. It was late, and arriving at the Guard Room once again, everyone departed, taking no notice of me. I felt very lost. I did not know where my kit had gone, had no blankets, bedding, not even a bed. Fortunately the corporal on guard duty was a sensible young man; he contacted the Duty Officer, who turned the wheels, and I was fixed up with a billet and bedding. I shall never forget my arrival at Yatesbury.

I worked in various kitchens, of different sizes. The RAF kitchens were four large wings, holding up to 2,000 airmen, while the smaller ones were the officers, the sergeants, the sisters (nursing sisters), the station hospital and headquarters, all catering for much smaller numbers. When working in the large wings, as No 3 Wing, one's day was long and hard work, but very rewarding. The 24 hours were covered by three shifts of cooks and assistants, mainly women, and a few men who were not on overseas duty.

After a time of being cook and butcher, I was ill and the Medical Officer recommended I should re-muster. So I re-mustered to a

199

batwoman, as I had not attained the age of 23 and could not become a nurse as I had always wished to do. I remained at Yatesbury, but moved into a room at the end of one of the officers' huts. There were on average 20 officers to look after, up to the ranks of Squadron Leader or Wing Commander, along with some very junior ranks. My job was to keep their rooms clean and polished, polish shoes and buttons, and keep the uniforms pressed and clean of any little marks. The officers had to see to their own laundry and getting their uniforms to the cleaners. Often they gave me the job of taking them to Calne, whenever I had any time off. Also they would ask me to wash a shirt, as they wanted to meet their girlfriend or go to a dance. They did not think about it until the last minute. As soap was on ration I used to say "No clean shirt until a coupon is produced". I always had plenty of coupons that way. It was a good thing there were hot radiators, and I also used to iron them dry, at very short notice. Officers were allowed to wear soft Van Heusen collars but we had material ones. At that time there were several Chinese laundries in Commercial Road, Swindon where we took bundles of our collars to be laundered and starched and ironed nearly stiff at sixpence for six, which when worn cut one's neck and were very uncomfortable for the first day of the clean collar. I used to put soap along the edge, but they did look much smarter and we put up with the discomfort. Later we too were allowed to wear Van Heusen collars (supplied by ourselves, and which we used our precious clothing coupons for).

Soap coupons, sweet and cigarette coupons were issued monthly on pay parade and had to be signed for. As I didn't smoke, I exchanged mine with other people's sweet coupons, so I was always sought after at the end of the month when theirs were used up. We had twelve clothing coupons a year, but they didn't stretch to much.

The day as a batwoman started with getting up about 5.45 am, stacking one's bed, and then I had to go and call the Duty Batman or woman, who had slept in the main building of the Officers Mess in case of emergencies and to answer the telephone. I would make the tea for my officers; the cook had usually lit the fire and had the kettles boiling. I took the tea to my Batting Room, where cups and saucers were kept, and then called the officers with a cup of tea at 6.30 am. I collected the uniforms and shoes to clean, returning to their rooms by 7 am when I found most of them had gone to sleep again, and often their tea was cold. Brasso was supplied, also black shoe polish for the officers, but we had to buy our own.

Buttons on the tunics were held in a button stick, which prevented the Brasso getting on to the material. The morning was spent in making beds, polishing and dusting.

The afternoon was for pressing trousers and jackets, keeping them smart for parades and best wear. In the evening we took turns to be on duty in the Mess, where we answered the telephones and took messages.

One evening I was on telephone duty and Squadron Leader Wright telephoned from the Station Theatre, where he was putting on a production of Gilbert and Sullivan. He asked me to look and see if there were any poles in the Mess. I was used to his strange requests, so I set off, looking in every nook and behind the doors without finding any. On returning to the telephone, I said, "No sir, I cannot see any." The reply came, "When one comes in would you ask him to ring the Station Theatre." It was not until then did I realise I should be looking for Polish officers and not bundles of poles. After a suitable interval I went and fetched one from the ante room, where there were half a dozen reading the papers. Sqd Leader Wright never knew what I had done.

Another time I mistook the time on the alarm clock, which I should have heard as it had two loud bells on the top. I jumped out of bed, rushed round all the rooms calling the officers, and up to the kitchen to get the tea to find no one up, so I called the Duty Batman, and went to the kitchen to find no fire lit or kettle boiling. It was then that I looked at the clock − it said 5 am! I went back at the normal time, and none of the officers knew I had called them an hour and a half early, they were all fast asleep. Some officers were rather high spirited. They used to come in the front door and slide all the way down the corridor to their rooms, leaving long scars on my polished floor, the regulation brown cork lino. As they didn't take any notice of me, I used to mix their shoes up in the morning, on purpose, and used to hear, "Have you got your own shoes?" as they went from room to room. "She's done it again!"

Many officers came from other countries to learn about the radar, and radio operations. Most of them could speak a litle English. I especially remember a Dutch group, who in their off duty periods put on some excellent concerts with a male voice choir; they were Naval officers. We had Canadians who were always very generous to us batting staff. When they received food parcels from home, boxes of chocolate were always very welcome, and made to last as long as possible. I once received a pair of real nylon stockings. Our service regulation stockings were thick lisle gun metal colour. Of course I was not allowed to wear the nylons, so I sent them to my aunt.

We had one half day a week, and a 48 hour pass once a month, and seven days leave every three months. The 48 hour pass and leave had to be taken off the unit. I often went to a Youth Hostel for the 48 hours. At that time Marlborough Youth Hostel was in the old town mill, until about 1945 when it was closed, I think because the top floor was unsafe.

When I was 23, I was at last old enough to become a nurse. But it did not happen straight away, I had to really fight for it, and at every turn I was told I was a good batwoman and they didn't want to lose me. I was thinking more of a career if I left the service. Eventually I got the Medical Officer and the CO on my side, and I was allowed to re-muster to Medical Orderly.

I started my training at the station hospital, still at Yatesbury. There were wards for airmen and airwomen, giving the total 200 beds. Most of the cases were routine operations of appendicitis, and other emergency operations, along with broken bones and injuries, as we were not a unit with bombers or fighter aircraft. Our aircraft were for training, Lysanders and Proctors. The medical cases were such things as pneumonias and bronchitis.

The unit was in a very bleak position, and whilst there we suffered a series of very severe winters. We used to get snowed in and nothing could get up the hill, before the hill was lowered and widened on the Cherhill side and realigned on the Beckhampton side. One year, I think about 1943, we had snow, deep snow for about six weeks, and everything was frozen hard. That year it was so cold that to have extra warmth people were going to bed in their greatcoats. I complained to the CO and the WAAF were issued with another blanket. We were not allowed to use the water for baths, as a lot of the pipes froze.

As a cook I slept in a long hut in headquarters, and these huts had five beds down the centre. The newcomers had these beds, as no one liked the middle, and as soon as a vacant one came on the side, the next one in turn moved to the side beds. At this time the beds were very heavy, and the lower part pushed in under the top half. When pulled out for sleeping there was a ridge, just about where one's hips rested. Once a week was "domestic night" when the whole unit stayed in and cleaned, polished, sometimes a kit inspection. It was usually at least 8.30 pm before the Duty Officer was finished inspecting, so it was too late to go out, apart from to go to the NAAFI, YMCA or Maccalm Club, which was on the unit.

At Christmas there was a tradition that the bands would lead a column of airmen and women through the huts. If you were not up and ready to join on to the crocodile, the bed was picked up and deposited firmly outside, whatever the weather. This was great fun, and we ended in front of the station hospital where the bands played carols, and we all sang to the patients, after which we all departed to our own wings and dining room for breakfast. During the war very few went home, so we all joined in any celebrations. I really do not know where the traditional fayre came from. The puddings and mincemeat were made on the unit, apples and carrots helped the dried fruit out. Nothing seemed to be short, as the menu had a full plate, turkey, stuffing, bread sauce – in fact the lot, and the big puddings were brought in flaming. Officers waited on our ranks for Christmas dinner. Nuts, cigarettes and a bottle of beer appeared, crackers and paper hats. The dining room was decorated with greenery, and the tree had decorations, usually made by the "girls". After the war, Christmas was not so good, the spirit had gone, although the food was the same with plenty to eat, but only a handful of personnel, and their holiday was at New Year.

We all had to be in camp by 10 pm. There was a guard on the gate, and one was challenged with "Who goes there". If one didn't reply quickly, one was likely to receive a bullet, or bayonet charge. At one time we had to give the password, woe betide those who forgot. Everyone had to show their identity card, which had their photograph on it. We also wore round our necks identity discs, and had to wear them at all times. One was red, and one green, with our number on. One could not be destroyed by fire, the other could not be destroyed by water. Of course our respirator and steel helmet were carried at all times, until the risk of air raids was past.

Once a week we had gas drill, and had to wear our respirators for the day (apart from the patients in the hospital who had such things as pneumonia). It was very hot in the cookhouse. Personnel who wore spectacles had a special pair of glasses which were flat and fitted in the mask. Both the glasses and the inside of the glass panel had to be smeared with anti-dim, to stop them from steaming up. Sometimes we used to have to go into a hut, where a little of the gas was released. For this one had to don one's gas cape, a long oiled material coat which covered us all over and down to our feet. It had a hood and a pouch at the back for the backpack. When inside the little hut we had to lift the mask and sniff the gas, so that we would know the smell if we were ever in an attack. Mustard gas was very long lasting and the area was fenced off for a long time until it was no longer toxic. We then had to go through the Decontamination Centre next door, which had three sections. First we removed the contaminated clothing, then went into the middle room where we cleansed ourselves, and into the third room to dress in clean clothing. There was an ointment which we rubbed on exposed areas of skin, to prevent the mustard gas from burning our skin. One night a week we had to sleep in the respirator, which was very uncomfortable, so we used to lay them on the pillow and as we heard the steps of the Inspecting Officer coming along the wooden corridor on went the mask and everyone was "fast asleep", but when she was safely away in the next hut, off they came again.

We had a number of things we could do when off duty. Besides having a cinema, for which we paid fourpence, there were military bands, dance bands, and some small group who played musical instruments for concerts and ENSA shows. We had a Gilbert and Sullivan Opera Group, as well as another which put on plays. We had a station theatre which was a large hangar, fitted up with a stage, lights and so on. About once a month we were allowed to buy such things as embroidery kits which came from "Penelope", packed especially for the Forces, Air Force coloured knitting wool which was very good quality, and occasionally, we could have an allocation of parachute silk for making underwear. There were night classes also, run by the Education Department. Outside of the unit was the White Horse Cafe, halfway down the A4, towards the village of Cherhill. It was a sort of transport cafe, where one could get a meal, and many an evening on the way back from Calne we went in for a cup of tea. There was a Forces canteen in Calne, open all day and in the evenings. There was a library on the unit, and one in Calne, opposite the town hall, which we could use. In Silver Street the Methodist church had a Forces canteen, and many an airman or woman was invited to the homes of the people of Calne, making friendships which lasted many years after. We had bounds which we could not go beyond without a pass, which were Marlborough, Chippenham, Devizes, Swindon.

On VE Day, the message was announced on the tannoy to say that the war had ended, and we were all called on parade. Most of the unit was given the rest of the day off. During the afternoon the airmen built a huge bonfire. They didn't stop at rubbish, but chairs and items of furniture went on it. They even burnt a Proctor plane. Everyone on the unit had to pay five shillings out of their pay to replace the items, and we had a severe dressing down from the Commanding Officer.'

WAR WORK

With the men called up into the services, women took on the hitherto male preserves of heavy industry and showed their worth. Others helped where they could, perhaps by going into the fields to give a hand with the flax harvest. Everyone did their bit for the war effort.

LIFE IN MARLBOROUGH

'The outbreak of war was just a couple of months away when in my late teens I decided to give up my dead end job and learn a trade. I was fond of sewing and chose soft furnishing, an apprentice being required at an old established and reputable furnishing firm which occupied large premises in Marlborough's wide High Street. They were also funeral directors, the coffins all hand-made on the premises by the skilled cabinet makers, who donned top hats to act as bearers at the funerals.

On my first day I got a shock on returning from lunch to find a coffin, fortunately empty, on trestles in the middle of the small workroom. I found this was waiting to be lined by the elderly upholsterer in charge of soft furnishings. However, I soon got acclimatised to this side of the business although the packets marked "shrouds" on shelves outside our workroom didn't exactly cheer one up, and the little white coffins for the infants for which I sewed tiny pillows were rather poignant. My wages were 15 shillings for a five and a half day week, which was five shillings more than the other apprentice who started with me. I was told to keep this secret as it was a favour to my aunt who had been my employer's children's much loved nanny, and had worked for years in the soft furnishing department after they got older, so I had a hard act to follow.

I'm glad to say I didn't let my aunt down. the first day or two was taken up with getting used to the heavy old fashioned treadle machines which would persist in going backwards. No electric machines in that shop. My fellow apprentice soon threw in the towel but I persevered and in a short time I began to get on very well with the work, which was very varied; curtains, hand sewn pelmets, loose covers, bedspreads and cushions, all made to a very high standard. There was also a lot of heavy mundane work, mattress and pillowcases, coconut matting to bind, then so popular on the stone and brick floors of the houses, and carpet sewing. Plain Wilton carpet then favoured by the gentry mostly came in 27 inch wide strips, and these had all to be sewn together by hand to make a carpet, with strong thread and a carpet needle, in a large loft especially for the purpose. This sounds a rotten job, and it took hours with no wireless and no company to relieve the boredom, but funnily enough I quite liked it, though it no doubt contributed to the lumps on my fingers today. Often sewing jobs had to be undertaken in some of the large houses in and around Marlborough and this made an interesting break from the workroom. As the war progressed most of the employees went into the services or war work, and when the old upholsterer retired I took over his work of cutting out the soft furnishings, often in very large houses, skilled work which is highly paid today. By then I was getting 30 shillings a week and was 21 years old.

Soon however, Mr Ernest Bevin decided it was time I did my bit for the war effort in spite of pleas from my elderly employer, and along with several girls from my home town I was directed to Swindon to start a course designed to train us in basic engineering in eight weeks. Swindon was only eleven miles away but as we were to work shifts we had to find lodgings in a town already bulging with war workers. My sister was working outside the town at the Stirling Bomber Factory and we found digs at Rodbourne Cheney, but this meant rising at 5.30 am to reach the centre of Swindon by 7 am on foot to catch the works buses as there were no early buses from the outskirts. How we hated that engineering course. In a little warren of back streets now all swept away, the workshop was like a sunless black cavern, its walls lined with benches and tools presided over by our instructor, a dour humourless man who obviously wasn't enjoying his war job for he never smiled. Most of the girls were from the Swindon area and there was plenty of wartime camaraderie but those two months spent endlessly filing two small pieces of metal, the object being to fit them into each other, still remains to this day an unpleasant interlude. I made a lasting friend of the girl on the bench next to me, the young wife of a Marine overseas, evacuated from Portsmouth to Marlborough. She had a very devil-may-care attitude towards the course, and took no interest in what she was doing. I did try my best, and gained some grudging praise from the instructor at the end of the course. Not bad for a girl was how he rated my efforts.

At last we were considered ready to be let loose on the world of engineering and instead of going to a factory were sent to an Air Ministry Maintenance Unit, high on the bleak Wiltshire downs at

These four young farm workers from Donhead – Harry, John, David and Albert – gave their free time to do their bit for their country in the local Home Guard.

Wroughton aerodrome a few miles from Swindon. We were the first women ever sent to work on the aircraft and it was obvious nobody wanted us and didn't know what to do with us. There were no facilities for women, or rest rooms, although these would come later, along with a welfare officer as many more women replaced the men, mostly becoming very highly skilled. A shock awaited us as we entered the canteen. The rough facilities and the unpleasant odour that always pervaded the place appalled us. I was still quite fastidious and was particularly affronted by the jam jars on the tables acting as salt cellars. I think I only ever visited it once more in my three years on the site and that was to a Workers Playtime concert.

On hearing how low our wages were to be we were all very worried that we wouldn't have enough to pay for our lodgings and we gathered in the pub in the village near the aerodrome to discuss it. After a couple of glasses of cider and full of dutch courage we decided to go back to Swindon Labour Exchange en masse to protest. Our little mutiny soon fizzled out, as we got short shrift there, being threatened with dire consequences if we didn't go where we were directed.

My heart sank when I saw the huge hangars where we were to work. As a girl I always felt the cold, and although it was then summertime, we were told how bitter it was in the winter and I wondered if I would be able to stick it. We were each put to work with a skilled fitter. I think we were more of a hindrance to them at first, but they were mostly young men and took it in good part. I remember the urns of cocoa wheeled into the hangars at break time. The joke was that although it was drinkable, in no way did it resemble cocoa, but we were glad enough of it. After a few weeks in dungarees and turban I had the chance of doing clerical work in one of the offices, and thinking of the long winter ahead I jumped at it, eventually holding quite a responsible position in one of the main offices and given civil servant status. My first boss had been one of the handful of survivors of the crash of the airship R101 in France before the war, his scarred hands telling the tale.

Gradually the whole production line at the aerodrome concentrated on building the great wooden-horse gliders. Later on a June night in 1944 coming home from a dance I was to see the sky over Marlborough filled with an armada of these gliders steadily making their way to the coast. A sight I've never forgotten, as with the dawn of D Day. My future husband was also to fly to Arnhem only to be taken prisoner.

There hadn't been much enemy activity in the skies over our part of Wiltshire. In 1942 together with my sister, I had very good digs in Ferndale Road, Swindon and one misty August morning we were making our way up Regent Street to catch our buses to work, around 7 am. Suddenly out of the clouds a lone enemy raider appeared and began to strafe the street at rooftop level. Terrified we huddled against a shop front, and I remember hearing a whine that I thought was bullets. He soon flew out of sight and shaken we continued our walk to the buses, not a very good start to the day.

Our landlady's husband was a french polisher in the Great Western Railway works near the house. All the woodwork in their spotless home was french polished and he had even attempted to give the Morrison table shelter in the living room a polished top. One night that same month the sirens went and, always tired, my sister and I had reluctantly got up at our landlady's insistence to join her under the table. Suddenly there was a terrific noise and everything went dark. We were terrified but unhurt. After a while I ventured out from under the table and could see the kitchen was demolished, the apple tree from the garden through its roof. The irony was that I had trod carefully down the garden path the night before so as not to dislodge the ripening apples from its low hanging branches. As I climbed the stairs in search of a candle I could see the night sky through the roof, but I didn't tell my landlady as she was very proud of her new home. As the time went by we grew desperate to use the toilet, now demolished along with the kitchen. My landlady solved our predicament by lifting down the large glass bowl which covered the ceiling light. We couldn't help seeing the funny side of this and started to laugh in spite of everything.

A desolate scene met our eyes the next morning. Several people had been killed and there was a large gap in the row of houses, just a few doors away from our house, which itself was not habitable. A large crater behind the houses showed where the bomb meant for the railway works had fallen. This frightening experience and narrow escape brought home to me what it must have been like to have been bombed night after night in the big cities.

Eventually bus services improved and for the last part of my war work I travelled daily from my home in Marlborough, leaving at 6.30 am in the blackout and getting home about 7 pm. It was imperative to turn up for work, only a doctor's certificate excused any absence. Sometimes in bad weather the bus couldn't quite reach the aerodrome and I have trudged the last part of the journey on foot through the snowdrifts. In the good weather I would sometimes cycle across the downs to my work from Marlborough, instead of taking the roundabout bus service. This was only five miles as the crow flies but the lonely high track led through an army training ground. Skull and crossbone signs warned off intruders, but as the manoeuvres didn't start very early and usually finished before we came home a colleague and I used to chance it. How different one feels about these risks when young, I wouldn't dream of doing it today.

At last the war ended and, my mother falling ill, I was granted my early release to nurse her. I left with no regrets but 50 years later I still remember with affection the many friends I made and the laughs we shared together in those far off eventful days.'

PULLING FLAX

'Women were needed to help out on the land and about eight women and girls were employed on our local farm at Upavon, doing various jobs. A favourite job was weeding in fields of corn or flax. The flax fields were a pretty sight, like carpets of blue, When the flax was harvested it went to the local flax factory for processing into linseed oil etc. It was all very hard work and we suffered from stiff backs due to all the bending. The sun always seemed to be shining and we developed lovely tans. One particular day we had stopped for our break and were enjoying a rest by the stream when we realised we had company. A group of American soldiers were camping in the next field and they shared their rations with us. Amongst these were sachets of instant coffee – something we had never seen before – and we went home that day anxious to try out our new drink.'

THE COLOUR OF THEIR SKIN!

'Most people in Wilton during those days had skin stained orange from working with flares, green from camouflage paint or white from the whiting works ... "by the colour of their skin you shall know where they work!".'

IN THE GWR WORKSHOP

'I first came to Wiltshire during the war, but I was familiar with the area, always having relatives living in Wiltshire and visiting them quite often. It was 1941 and most people were getting used to moving from one place to another. I had been doing war work in London so was transferred and found myself in a GWR workshop making 25lb shells for a gun that soon became outdated.

No provision had been made for women in the workshops, so I found myself with 30 other women in 'O' shop, which the men considered the best shop in the works. It made the precision tools for the making of engines etc. We were a great novelty to the remaining men who were either too old, or with some disability making them unfit for the services.

Our first job was to trim the tops of the quite heavy shells and put them onto a belt, which was not a moving one, but merely rollers. This was very hard on our hands as we had no gloves, so we asked the foreman for gloves and he promised them, several times we were promised them. During our first week all the girls had joined the NUR so after asking continually, we all stopped work, much to the men in the shop's dismay. The said we would not get the gloves, but we did, having stopped work only one afternoon.

It was the other men in the shop who taught us the job, which after the shells was much more interesting. Being women, the management had to provide us with a rest room; most of the men had their lunch beside their lathes, if they didn't go out. They were very envious of our rest room, but we told them they would have it after the war. They said never! And as far as I know they never did. It was turned into a gauge room when the women had gone.

It had been an interesting job, and had given us an insight into the conditions some men worked in.

I came on the bus from Wanborough which meant we had to rely on the bus to get us there on time. But 'O' shop was a long way from the main gate so we had to walk through "miles" of workshops until we arrived at 'O' shop and clocked on. Most mornings we lost our first half hour's pay. We worked three eight-hour shifts, and it was on nights I saw the man I shall always remember, who showed me how the iron bolts that keep the railway lines in place are made.

The furnace which heats the iron is kept in all the year round, going out once to be cleaned. He had a long ladle which was dipped into the red hot molten iron, and then, telling us to keep back, he poured it into square-shaped moulds, hundreds of them. It was in the open at night and quite a sight, but a hot very dirty job. In fact I never go on the railway without thinking of him.

Working alongside men showed us we could do the work, given the training, which surprised us, and that a mixture of people, old, young, Londoners and from all parts, could work together in harmony.

I was four years in the "Western" (Great Western Railway in Swindon) and became shop steward in the National Union of Railwaymen.'

THE LAND ARMY

Working on the land was one of the options open to young women called up to serve their country, and many girls happily opted for the open air life. It could be something of a shock to a city-bred system, but they were doing essential work and soon came to adjust to the long hours and the hardships.

DOWN FROM YORKSHIRE

'We came to Pewsey station from Yorkshire, to Fifield, on 30th March 1941. The daffodils were poking through the snow, I loved that. There was a chain all round the farm garden which later on was taken to make into tanks. It was a beautiful diamond-shaped chain across stone posts and that was my first impression of the farm.

A lot of people didn't like us because we were here and their boys were not. Except one old lady who used to see us walking to work. She used to come out and say, "Good marnin' to 'ee, bless 'ee." It was a long time before we knew what she was saying.

There were eight or ten of us. I lived in lodgings but Coombe Farm House was a Land Army hostel and housed 32. We worked very hard but they looked after us very well.

I learned to milk and it was horrible, I can't stand the smell of it and it was hand-milking. I went to the boss and said, "Look, if you want a girl to do your milking you'd better get one and let me go home", which of course I wasn't allowed to do as I'd signed on. We just didn't want to go in the ATS or into factories, we'd rather go on the land and you had to do something when you got to be 21. So rather than wait and be sent into something you didn't want, we became land girls.

I learned to drive in about 20 minutes, after I'd complained about milking. Every farmer had a student; someone whose father was paying for him to learn. He sent me into the field with the student (and this tractor) who said, "Sit here, you do this and you do that, and this is the throttle . . . now, you do it." Anyway the tractor went. He got off, stuck a stick in the field and said, "Now reverse the tractor and go backwards round that." So I did. He said, "Well done, you can drive, that's good enough," took me back to the farm and the farmer sent me on an errand to a place four miles north of Pewsey. I managed but when I came to come home I'd forgotten how to start it. The other man came to my aid and I did get home, but it was a long journey.

We had rations given to us every fortnight. Of course, everyone had ration books but farm workers were fed extra well. Our landlady could get twice the ration that others had and we earned two guineas a week but we had to give her one guinea. We learned to smoke and learned how to tell the weather. There was an old, old man who used to stand still and say, "By four o'clock this afternoon it'll be raining" and we learned to recognise the signs ourselves.

We started at seven in the morning and worked until dusk. In the summertime, of course, we had to work very late.

We could go dancing in Fittleton, Netheravon or Enford and on Sunday afternoons to Marlborough to tea dances. There was always plenty of transport. The American army were wonderful to us, they sent us transport but wherever you went you had wardens from the hostel to come with you, you were well watched.

We were always together, at least, four of us; when the local people began to know us, then they grew to like us and we got to like Wiltshire. At first we didn't, we thought it was a dreadful place, nothing like Yorkshire. Mind you, when I was coming here an old man told me, "People are like the land they live on, it is lovely and rich here and its people are industrious." In Wiltshire the people are "mean" because their soil is mean and stony, they are very careful. Places like Cornwall have craggy people like their land. Everywhere I've gone, I've remembered that. That first summer we were here, it was beautiful; Wiltshire took on lovely colours, all gold and white and brown and green. The farmers chopped up the hedges to make the fields bigger. We went into a field on a Monday morning and it took until late Friday night to finish reaping the harvest. But there were all these chequered colours, and blue too because they grew a lot of flax. In Devizes they had a flax factory. I got to know it because I had an ID bracelet and it got lost in one of the sheaves. The girls who were working in this factory found it and my boss took me there to retrieve it.

Sometimes we were taken in covered lorries to Warminster to dance in a lovely place with a black band at one end and a white band at the other and no stops in between, one played after the other. We used to see real plays by ENSA at Larkhill, with actors who have been famous and some we still see on TV. It only cost threepence. Mind you, we walked there. We used to go to the cinema at Airfield Camp (Netheravon), they used to show at least two different films each week.

Buses ran every 20 minutes although they were slower; it cost sixpence to go to Amesbury and a shilling to Salisbury. The roads were thick with tanks and all the ground at Beecher's Barn and the fields were covered in tents because there were so many Americans; at Airfield Camp we used to count the planes flying out and back as we worked on the land. One day I was having a ride in a tank when Mr Churchill arrived to review the troops; I was in the front row keeping low. Then of course they had the dogs up there and we were scared of them, trained alsations. I'm still scared of them although they were beautiful animals.

Of course, the tractors didn't have hoods. You sat out in the weather getting soaking wet and stayed out until you'd finished the job. I don't remember any waterproofs or ever getting a cold either. When my landlady was dying I cared for her. She was like a mother to me. We had candles to light us to bed and paraffin lamps were fixed up everywhere. No running water, you had to pump it up or get it from the well and then heat it in the copper.

You couldn't get home when you'd like to, you had to go home between haymaking and harvesting; you could go home either at Christmas or New Year. I went home for New Year and I waited at the station in London. All the trains were full of soldiers and they piled in and piled out, and none of us could get in. I waited for hours, until midnight when everyone in the station started to sing and then I cried and cried. When I came back it was the only time that Netheravon was bombed and I am sure they followed that train. Only incendiary bombs mind you but one fell down a chimney in Mill Road and chopped off Mr Chubb's toe. That was the family who owned Stonehenge and then presented it to the nation.

213

I remember one old man called "carter", no one knew his name. They taught him to drive a tractor and he was thrilled to bits and his wife was so proud. He drove up to the farm and had to go round a circular drive past a flower bed. He spoke to the boss, touched his hat and got back on the tractor; then he drove right over the garden. He was standing up shouting "Whoa, whoa . . . ". There were a lot of people there and we'd been so proud to see he could drive.'

WE GOT USED TO IT

'I came to Wiltshire in 1942 as a Land Army girl. I had previously worked in a bank in London and my only knowledge of the countryside had been the annual Girl Guide camp, usually in Sussex.

I was sent to a training centre at Lockeridge, near Marlborough. There were eight trainees and a warden and we lived in a converted railway carriage. We did a month's training on the farms owned by Mr Swanton. We learned to milk cows, to drive a tractor and to help with the harvest. Most of us had never milked a cow before and our hands ached terribly at first but we got used to it.

My first job was at a farm near Malmesbury where I worked for an elderly farmer, helping him with the milking and general farm work. From there I moved to a farm at Cricklade, here they had a milking machine so we only had to strip out the cows after the machine had done the hard work. The last farm that I worked at was at Ludwell in the south of the county. Here I delivered the milk around the villages and as I eventually married the farmer's son I am still here now and our son carries on the farming.'

A CHILD'S WAR

Children soon came to regard war as almost a normal way of life and accepted the restrictions and hardships with resignation. Some children, from the heavily bombed cities, came to the peace of rural Wiltshire as evacuees. Many found kindness and lifelong friends, but a few were sadly unhappy in their temporary new life.

KEEPING US BUSY

'One of our war efforts at Greathouse was to catch white butterflies, which did a lot of damage then before pesticides. We were armed with old tennis racquets and allowed to go all over the gardens and grounds (keeping to the paths of course in the kitchen garden). There was a double row of lavender bushes across the kitchen garden and some lovely buddleia bushes in the herbaceous border. We were paid for the number caught. My grandfather used to sit by the lavender bush in our back yard and added to our collection by swiping them with his cap.

On Saturday mornings we were called by a loud "Ya-hoo-hoo" from Mrs Garnett in the drive, and went with her to the potting shed with our jars of Cabbage White butterflies (plus a few others which had been caught by mistake, had their colours rubbed off, and mixed well with the white ones). Once in the dim potting shed we had to count out the butterflies in front of Mrs Garnett. The number would be noted then we took them into the greenhouses, dug a small hole, and buried them. After covering them over and slashing the ground well so they couldn't be used again we went up to the library where the numbers and date were entered officially with the current rate of pay. We were paid a halfpenny each butterfly at the beginning of the season. This gradually dropped to sixpence per 100 at the height of the season. We were also paid to keep the patch of Lower Common clear of litter. The wages were paid periodically in National Savings stamps. Although it was only pence for each task it mounted up, and in later years I was glad to cash in my Savings Certificates.

We all helped pick strawberries, blackcurrants (singly to allow the others to ripen), raspberries, loganberries, and gooseberries. We were forbidden to eat one until we were told we may. One day the green gooseberries were too tempting, Mrs Garnett was the other side of the thick bush, and I succumbed to temptation. A voice quickly said, "Bet! Are you eating a gooseberry?" "No! Ma'am," I replied as I quickly swallowed the fruit. I can still feel the pain as it stuck for hours afterwards.

The estate had two Guernsey cows, for the cream. We had separated milk in the morning which Dad brought down as he came home for breakfast at 8.30 am. When he was called up for army service we collected it. In the afternoon we had it more or less straight from the cow. Mum used to pour the quart of milk into a large bowl to leave overnight. Next day we would skim off the thick yellow cream and whisk it into butter. It was quite a few years before Mum could afford the outright purchase of a small butter churn. This was a pity as we could have saved a lot overall from the number of whisks we bought and broke.

Mrs Garnett thought a lot of her cows and liked to keep us gainfully occupied. She had the idea that wild parsley was good for the cows and often took us with her to pick the tall stems to feed the cows. It may have been a wheeze to get us cutting down the herbage around the edge of the orchard when there was a shortage of staff in wartime. We were even encouraged to go and hold the parsley out to the cows, Chestnut and Cody, across an electric fence unsupervised. One hot day when we were feeding them, Chestnut found the flies a nuisance and tossed her head catching my brother's cheek with her horn. For a long time he had three dimples instead of his usual two.'

'While attending Gorse Hill Girls School during the war we did our bit by Digging for Victory. Each class had a small piece of land to cultivate and grow vegetables – this was part of a sports ground belonging to the Gas Works Club in Gipsy Lane. We learnt all about double digging and if a horse went by we were out with bucket and shovel for the manure. We were all very proud of our efforts. We bought the fruits of our labour or sold them for money for seed.

Another help for the war effort was a collection box which Mum and I took round door to door each Monday to help swell the funds for the Red Cross. Several Mums and my girl friends used to make brooches out of curtain rings – this was done by buttonhole stitching around the ring then weaving to fill the centre and then embroidering flowers, etc in the centre which looked quite pretty. We also made needlecases, baby's bibs, pincushions and many other handy things which we sold. Kept us all out of mischief too.'

MY NEW BICYCLE

'I was twelve when my family moved to Westbury and Dad decided that my sister and I needed bicycles.

It was 1941 and wartime shortages meant that many things and especially bicycles were hard to come by, so our names went down on a waiting list at Macey's, the local bicycle shop in Edward Street. We hadn't long to wait before a message came that *one* bicycle had arrived and Dad would have it. As the older, my sister was given this with its gleaming chrome-plated handlebars and wheels.

How I envied her, but I was allowed to ride it sometimes and in return to clean it! Often when I was shining the chrome I looked forward to polishing my very own bicycle soon.

At last! Mr Macey had another model which he had put aside for us. I could hardly wait for Dad to take me to collect my very own bike. But what a disappointment! I almost cried when I saw it. Where were the shiny wheels and handlebars? They were painted a dull black because of wartime austerity.

Still it was a bicycle and my very own. How I cherished it and cleaned it lovingly and how it repaid me by being a veritable Hercules over many, many years, long after my sister's less sturdy model had become rusty and useless.'

THE LITTLE RED INDIAN

'Americans were stationed at Langley Burrell, The Firs in Chippenham, and at Draycot Cerne, in the Park. Soldiers used to go on marches past our front garden. When we heard marching boots approaching my brother used to don an American Indian outfit he had been given and go out to play on the front lawn. When he was spotted the soldiers used to be told to have a break on the wide verge outside. Because we never asked for gum we were usually given some. We hated hearing children call out, "Give us some gum, chum!"

My uncle, who ran a cycle shop in Chippenham, felt sorry for one American soldier and invited him to visit his home. As my aunt and uncle frequently cycled out to see us, Robert Bailey was loaned a bike to come with them. He was so homesick. I remember my uncle saying that one day when they were out on bikes there was a grass snake. Immediately Robert Bailey was off the bike and killing it. The only snakes around his home in the USA were poisonous and he was taking no chances.'

BOARDING AT SALISBURY

'At the beginning of the war I lived in Kent, not far from London. When the Nazi armies overran France in May 1940 and bombing and invasion seemed imminent, my mother and I went down to Salisbury. Mrs Christie-Miller had made Clarendon House available to a school of children evacuated from Portsmouth Dockyard. My uncle was headmaster. I was to become a pupil.

My mother and I arrived at Salisbury station in the early afternoon. My uncle was there to meet us. I had not been to Salisbury before. The streets looked bleak and unfamiliar. There were few men about. The occasional army lorry passed, but there were no cars. Sandbags stood at important doorways. Some shop windows had criss-crossed tape to prevent glass flying if a bomb fell. I looked up at the cathedral spire without interest: no one told me that it was the tallest in England. More promising was a shop called "The Magnet Stores". Did it really sell magnets?

There was no time to find out, for we had to board a bus. We were soon out in the countryside and were dropped bag and baggage at the gates of the great estate. A waggon was waiting to take us on. We were to stay with the Lambards, the estate gamekeeper. Keeper's Cottage was delightful. I had never seen so perfect a little house: whitewashed, thatch-roofed and hollyhocked, nestling in the woods. In the garden lived ten retrievers, a kennel and running-line to each. We had no dogs at home. I was captivated and spent hours in their company. Life was good.

After a month we moved up to the great house itself. My mother was to look after a girls' boarding house. I became a boarder and was billeted in the pre-war servants' quarters.

Evacuees did not go home during the school holidays. 1940 was a hot summer and one afternoon it was announced that the whole school was to go on a picnic two miles away on the wooded chalk downs. Buckets of water, tin mugs and hampers of thick National Bread and margarine and a scrape-of-Marmite-if-you-were-lucky sandwiches, all were carried through the lovely countryside. While the food was distributed we sat in rows upon the springy turf among the wild and scented flowers. There came a sound of aircraft approaching rapidly. We looked up. These aircraft bore no friendly RAF roundels, but the black crosses of the Luftwaffe. We fled into the woods as the guns opened up. The danger passed as quickly as it had come. We came out of hiding and we finished our picnic.

In November 1940 the bombing got worse. At night we heard the distant rumble of guns. The glow of Portsmouth burning lit the southern horizon. For me, it was frightening. For the other boys in my dormitory it was terrifying: their families lived close by the dockyard. One morning just before dawn we lay in bed, not daring to sleep. An aircraft flew low. Its engine sound was not British. A whine. A crash. An explosion. The building shook. Windows rattled.

218

Bits of plaster fell about us. We tried to hide our terror. "You OK?" "That was a b . . . . . near one." "They're aiming for us, I know that." "Don't put the light on, you stupid b . . . . .! There's a blackout!" In the cold light of day we inspected the crater: six feet deep and 15 feet across − a circular hole in the ground with a neat bank of soil around it. It was only 300 yards from our dormitory.

The next night another non-British aircraft flew low. A whine. An eternity of waiting time. Were they really aiming for us? Would they hit us? We were now experienced connoisseurs of bombing and knew what to expect. At last, the crash. The building still stood. We had survived to live another day.

The third night. Beneath a bed there was a metal hook which swung like a pendulum − tick-tock, tick-tock. I was absolutely sure that it was a German time bomb.

Christmas 1940 and no enemy bombers flew over the school that night. We thought the Luftwaffe was celebrating Christmas too. The teachers had done their best to decorate the common room and the dining room, but it was a poor show: paper decorations couldn't be got at any price. Breakfast was the usual lumpy porridge, two slices of grey National Bread and margarine and a mug of tea. Then the long walk to the village church at Alderbury. It was drizzling with rain and the sermon was dull. We looked forward to Christmas dinner: a fragment of chicken (or was it rabbit?), inedible stuffing, mashed potatoes and sprouts − how many found their way out in the pockets of the boys? Food was so scarce that you were punished if you did not eat up everything on your plate. Pudding and a thin custard followed. There were no nuts or crackers or tangerines in wartime. Nor were there any parents: they couldn't visit the school because there were no trains or buses on that day, and the children couldn't go home because it was too dangerous.

After dinner we moved to the school room. There was a Christmas tree with lots of presents sent by loving mums and dads. When these were distributed it was found that little eight year old Diana had received nothing, absolutely nothing at all. She was in tears: no presents, no mum and far from home. In haste my mother wrapped up some of my sweets and readdressed them to Diana. I didn't like Diana much, but I didn't like to see her crying on Christmas Day. I lost my sweets, but at least I had my mum.'

'WE DON'T WANT YOU'

'Flo, then aged eleven, remembers leaving her home in Wormwood Scrubs, London on 1st September 1939 and travelling from Paddington with her two younger sisters, all tagged and labelled, with gas masks. Each child had rations – a tin of corned beef, a bar of chocolate, a tin of Nestlé milk and a tin of water biscuits – to be handed over to their evacuation hostesses but, says Flo, "we never saw any of it." On arrival at Devizes they were greeted by a line of schoolchildren who called out, "We don't want you. Go home."

They were then taken to St James's School where they were selected by those offering billets. Eventually, she and her two sisters went to a remote gamekeeper's cottage. Later on, after having been joined by their mother and the rest of their family, nine of them finished up occupying a two-bedroomed cottage in Corsham, with no running water and an outside toilet. Her elder brother joined the army at the age of 17 in order to give them more room. In 1945 there was no return to London, and Flo and her remaining brother continue to occupy the council house in Box which the family were allocated when it was first built.'

'My sister and I were evacuated from London to Wiltshire in 1939. We stayed together, and our first home (if you can call it that) was with a farm labourer and his wife. They resented us very much, and we had to sleep on boxes out in the washhouse with the dogs. We were fed there too, pigs' trotters, no green vegetables or fruit. I remember drinking lots of water in the evening to try to fill my stomach – we were hungry all the time.

When we grew out of our dresses we had to wear sacks with holes cut out for head and arms. There was no warmth in them and the rough edges made us very sore, as you may imagine.

Finally my sister contracted pneumonia and some people realised the conditions in which we were living. The vicar found another home for us. There at least we had better food, though we had ours in the kitchen, not with the rest of the family. We had dresses too, but there was a lot of cold and hard work to be done after school every day and at weekends. However, when we were taken back to London to live in an older sister's flat (our parents were killed in the Blitz) we were very neglected and unhappy, and finally we were allowed to return to Wiltshire; we were glad to come, in spite of the hard work and discipline still put upon us.

We both married Wiltshire men and brought up our families here.'

'In the autumn of 1940 I was evacuated from London to Chippenham. The Wanstead High School shared a school building with local children, but the two schools were kept entirely separate, each having its own classes and teachers. The Wanstead pupils went to school on Saturdays, when they had full use of the laboratories etc and had Mondays free, when the Chippenham students had the run of the place.

All evacuees went to a little church hall, I believe it was on the London Road, one day a week. Each school year went a different day, thus helping to ease the congestion in the main school. Trying to accommodate two schools in one building must have been a nightmare, but we seemed to manage. It was always freezing in the church hall in winter, as it was heated by only one small combustion stove. We used to stoke it up, and sit as close as possible, keeping our outdoor coats on all day.

The Wanstead High School imposed a curfew on all their children, but as my billet parents went to whist drives several evenings a week, I had to stay out of the house until they came home. As I dare not be seen out of doors after curfew, I used to sit in the shed in the garden until they returned. After a year at this house, I was "rescued" by another couple who lived further along the road and knew I was unhappy. I then stayed with them and they were extremely kind to me. I loved the countryside, and I remember gathering cowslips and primroses along the railway embankments. Fate brought my husband, family and me back to Wiltshire to live nearly 20 years ago and now I wouldn't wish to live anywhere else.'

IT WASN'T ALL BAD

'My first introduction to Wiltshire was at the age of eight and a half years, as a wartime evacuee from bomb-threatened London. A very kindly middle aged couple with one daughter, living in the village of Broughton Gifford welcomed me into their home. I found life in the country very different indeed from London, very basic in fact, mod cons being non-existent in those days.

Our lavatory was about 100 yards from the house, down a very dark and muddy path; being a town child this scared me to death, and I would never go down there at night on my own. Saturday morning was weekly bath time; as this was in front of the kitchen fire it was a happy time. I was given a pretty little bedroom in which was a very large brass bedstead. I cannot remember ever being cold in that gorgeous bed, even in the most severe weather when water froze in the water jug, and frost patterned the windows.

There were only three electric lights and one power point in the house at that time, so we lit our candles to go upstairs; on one occasion I used a torch instead and unfortunately happened to let it shine out of the window just as our special constable was cycling by. He told me off in no uncertain terms for showing a light to the enemy.

I attended the village school and made many friends. It was the custom that on the first fine day in early summer we pupils were taken on a nature walk over the fields to the canal at Whaddon. We children thought it a great adventure, especially when one year my best friend fell into the canal while fishing for tadpoles!

I often walk through the village remembering the folk of my childhood, and think of the fields in which we played. They are now covered with houses! When the war ended I was a young teenager with many local friends and interests, and I had grown very fond of the kind family who had given me a home during those troubled years. It was my choice to stay on, and I am still here in this lovely part of Wiltshire.'

'On 1st September 1939, I along with some more pupils from my school in London was among the first of many, many evacuees sent from London to "the country" for our safety from any German bombing, bearing in mind it was just two days before the war started.

We were put on trains, with no idea where we were going and although we had left our parents behind, there seemed to be the feeling of a great adventure. We had our gas masks and in our bags the two complete changes of clothes which our parents had been told we were allowed to carry. I think the Government still thought that Hitler wouldn't send his army into Poland and that a war would be avoided and that we wouldn't be away for very long. We had our linen labels securely tied to our coats. The train stopped at Swindon – we thought, this time we have arrived, but we were not allowed to get off the train and went on to Little Somerford and changed trains for the one that went to Malmesbury. There, many people had turned out to watch our arrival. We were taken to the Territorial Army drill hall which was close by and there we were each given a carrier bag containing food. I think by this time we were all feeling bemused.

We then crossed the road to the grammar school where we were put on a bus; 18 of us were being sent to Charlton, me at nine years and two months being the youngest. The other younger children were left in Malmesbury to be billeted with families.

I can still remember coming down Holloway Hill and we were all wondering where we were going. So we arrived in Charlton, at the Scout hut that was used as a village hall. There were the Billeting Officers – being Mr Jones, the auctioneer from Malmesbury, and Mr Jackson who had an outfitters in Malmesbury High Street. We were duly sorted out. I imagine the villagers had been canvassed and chose the sex and age of the children they could take. Mr Lewis

222

Barnes, a wheelwright, and Mr Montague Farmils, a carpenter on Charlton Park Estate, had the task of delivering us to our billets (the official title) where we were going to stay. I was taken to the post office, where George Barkham was awaiting the arrival back from holiday of his housekeeper who was to become my "Auntie Doris".

What a change that must have been for us coming from a city to a village that had a school, church, pub and a shop – which really was only a room in a tiny cottage on the road out of Charlton to Malmesbury and is called Walnut Tree Cottage.

In 1940 or 1941 I was joined at the post office by my mother. Neither she nor I ever returned to London, and so what we hoped was going to be a short stay turned out to be over 50 years.'

'I originally came from Portsmouth but was evacuated to Wilton, near Salisbury, during the war. We were lodged with a widowed farm carter and his spinster sister. My mother, my older sisters Ruth and Pam, and I all shared one bedroom. Pam and I went to the Church of England school in Wilton which was about a mile from the cottage where we lived.

Italian prisoners of war were in a nearby camp and did some work on the farm. I remember sitting on the large grass area in front of the cottage, in a circle, with several of these POWs. I was told later that they were enchanted with my long fair hair. Ruth remembers them making rings from the old brass hexagonal threepenny pieces and using the coloured handles of toothbrushes to simulate jewels.

Water for all our needs at the cottage was pumped up into enamel buckets and stood in the scullery ready for use. Near the pump was the lavatory – a bucket under a wooden seat and little squares of newspaper threaded on a loop of string and hung up on a nail. This tiny building attracted swarms of flies in the summer. One night we had an air raid and came downstairs to find the floor and furniture literally covered in cockroaches. Of course they quickly disappeared at the meagre light from the oil lamp. There was a radio which was run on accumulators so we were only allowed to listen to Sunday hymns and daily news programmes to conserve battery power. These batteries were hefty things and had to be taken to the village to be recharged in the basket of our landlady's bicycle.

Evacuees were not particularly popular with local people but Pam made friends with a girl whose family enjoyed making puppets. They put on a show, "Cinderella", one night in the village hall. Pam said that night was magic for her and gave her so much pleasure. She remembers bathing in the river and coming across our carter landlord having his annual bath with soap and towel.

Such were the deprivations of wartime that Ruth was eager to act as waitress at school dinners because Cook gave helpers a more generous helping. She remembers that we were always hungry, especially for sweet things. An old lady who had befriended our mother invited us all to tea. Both Ruth and Pam remember the fairy cakes, so eagerly seized upon, only to find mould all over the bottom. Nevertheless they were eaten without harm.

All this seems rather grim but there were the lovely things that happened like watching the big lumbering carthorses cavorting and rolling over in the field at the end of their day's work. Ruth loved lying on the bank of the backwater gazing down into the beautiful clear water watching the minnows, trout, pike and dace. Rustling in the hedge and she caught sight of a snake's body sliding by. Sweet wild strawberries in the hedgerow and wild violets. As I remember the cottage it was bounded by wonderful water meadows and a river seemingly full of golden yellow kingcups.'

THE NEW ARRIVAL

'During the summer of 1940, evacuee children from London were brought to our village to escape from the German bombing. I was the youngest in my family and much in need of companions as my older sisters and brother had all left home. I hurried home from school that day eager to meet the new arrival; my mother had said she would be pleased to take one child, preferably a girl. When I got home there she was, Mary, two years younger than I. She chattered away nervously and I quickly learned she had an older sister, Gladys, who was at work, and a younger brother, George, who was seven, "Our Georgie". Mary's mother had told her she must "look after Georgie", but Georgie was placed in another village, and she was most concerned about this. My mother told her we would visit Georgie and make sure he was alright.

Looking after Mary was quite a task. Getting to school in a neighbouring village was full of obstacles. The way around the roads was three miles, but we could take a short cut across the fields. However, Mary did not like cows and often on our way to school we met the cows along the lane, wandering back to the field after milking time. On our way home we had to cross a field full of big brown and white cows with large horns! Mary was very frightened of them, so one day we made a detour through another field, but alas, we did not know that the farmer had put one solitary cow in this field. Cows are very curious creatures and will stare at one, but this one did more than that – she galloped toward us mooing loudly and tossing her head. We ran! The nearest escape was a haystack in the middle of the field with barbed wire all around. We flung

224

ourselves over the wire – the cow in hot pursuit. Dishevelled and with torn dresses we were stuck, the cow was not going to let us go, so we waited and waited, and eventually the cow sauntered over to the far side of the field. Could we make it to the gate into the road, without her seeing us? Well we did, thankfully. The cow had probably had her calf taken away and was very angry.

After this episode my father found a bicycle for Mary and we taught her to ride – well almost! One day we set off to school from our house, going down a very steep hill with sharp bends. Alas, this was too much for Mary, who just did not understand about brakes – the disaster happened. Mary was cut and bruised and the bike was almost a write-off – back to the fields again.

The school holidays brought us some relief and Mary began to enjoy herself. There were four other young girls staying in a large house nearby and together we all had good times exploring the countryside. We visited Georgie and found he was fine, but a little homesick. Eventually a new home was found for Mary and Georgie together, in the next village where we all went to school. Soon after we had a Women's Land Army lady staying with us; for her too country living was a new experience.

Then my father left his job in the country and we moved to Swindon, where he did war work in the aircraft industry. Now I was an "evacuee" getting used to life in a town. There were evacuees here too, from London, and so I soon made new friends.'

ONE LONG HAPPY SUMMER

'My parents had resisted the moves to evacuate me in the earlier parts of the war. I had spent numerous nights in a garden Anderson shelter at our home on the edge of London, where each night I lay in a bunk listening to the irregular throbbing drone of the German bombers, the staccato crash of anti-aircraft guns and then the whistle and thump of the bombs.

Later however when the V1 doodlebugs arrived it seemed somehow more risky. My mother remembered a friend whose family farmed in Wiltshire. A letter was written and shortly after I was on my way from Padddington. The train ran non-stop to Reading and then onto Newbury and stations I had never then heard of. There was Hungerford, Savernake and Patney. There was my first sight of the canal and there was that final slowing down and running through the cutting before the tunnel and out to Devizes. After a brief halt we started off again down the hill through Bromham and Rowde Halt to Seend. From there it was a walk to the house on the edge of Craysmarsh Farm where I was to spend so many happy months and in years to come many happy times. "Aunt" Amy and "Uncle" Sidney welcomed me with open arms. My parents stayed a couple of days to see me settled and then had to return home. There was a war effort and time off was at a premium.

I soon settled in to a routine and made friends. There were three Cottle brothers. I was staying with Sidney whose house was on the edge of the farm. The second brother lived in the farmhouse and had two sons. The third brother also lived in the house. I soon made a particular friend of the younger son and he, together with Uncle Sidney, started to school this little London kid in Wiltshire ways. It did not matter that I protested I lived in Surrey – to them I was a Londoner and as such knew nothing about grass, trees, fields, cows and milking, horses and hay, carts and rickyards. Of course they were right but I soon learnt and as I did there grew a deep love of everything about the countryside which has lasted all my life. For that I shall be eternally grateful.

There were other things to learn nearby. It was hot at times and that meant a swim. No pools to go to so we used the nearby canal. When I tell people that I used to swim in the bridge hole down by the Barge Inn . . . well! However, there were few boats and the canal was already in advanced decay. The occasional work boat from GWR passed. The result was crystal clear water as long as you did not disturb the mud.

My uncles had a routine for controlling all these boys on the farm because there was not only the two sons and me. There were the children of the farmhands plus friends and others. The method was simple – you were given a job. Uncle Sidney had a saying when referring to boys and work on the farm. One boy a whole boy, two boys half a boy and three boys none at all! He therefore split us up, ideally one boy with one man or at the least no more than two together. Sometimes on Friday night if it had been a busy week and you had worked hard Uncle John would give out some wages to us lads and on one occasion I remember ten shillings being given.

Life went on for me for one long happy summer but then I had to return home or miss a place in grammar school. So it was back to London and by then the V2 rockets. They were even more sudden and without warning. However we survived and as each summer came round there was only one place to go – The Farm.'

AFTER THE WAR

On VE Day, towns and villages all over Wiltshire celebrated victory in Europe and the ending of the war – though some had a more unusual experience that day than others! However, the welcome return of servicemen and women meant that there was a national housing shortage and many young couples had to face married life in a converted Nissen hut.

VE DAY

'On VE Day my brother was in the RAF. He was at Coombe Down, Bath and all were given a day off. So he and a friend hitchhiked into Bath – and the car they hailed on the way for a lift was Queen Mary's! You can imagine their surprise. She asked them where they were going and told them to get in the back – "Get in dear boys". She stopped just before the Abbey, where she was due to attend a service. When they got out there were crowds round the car and they all stood aside for them. The boys then hitched another lift or two to get them home. It was a lovely surprise to see him.'

LIVING IN NISSEN HUTS

'In 1948 we were offered a Nissen hut at the crossroads, Dinton, as somebody had moved out. These huts were originally built by the Americans during the war, and when the Americans vacated the village the huts were left standing empty for some time until they were eventually occupied by squatters. There was no heating, no lighting and no water available. The Council agreed at a later date (for a small rental charge) to modernise the huts, and consequently five inner walls were constructed to make them habitable, with two bedrooms, a kitchen with a sink and cold tap, a bathroom with zinc bath and cold tap, and an old-fashioned grate and oven, set in the centre of the hut. To complete the happy abode, there was an outside toilet.

All this work was already done by the time we moved in, but I can particularly remember on one occasion the outside toilet blew over during a very bad gale of 95 mph. That night, with only two layers of galvanised tin overhead, we really thought we were going to be carried away!

Nevertheless, we had some happy times and some sad ones during the period we lived there, between 1948 and 1953. Neighbouring children were always calling in to play, and if anyone was ill they always wanted to come in and see what was going on, even when my husband had mumps and I had a miscarriage! My one big fear had always been keeping healthy, but we managed, with the family doctor making regular visits. My daughters had the usual children's ailments, including my elder daughter developing a "touch of pneumonia" (as the doctor termed it), after both of them had chicken pox and bronchitis. He told me to try and keep the temperature between 60° and 65° – yes, in a Nissen hut with two layers of tin, and in the winter, icicles hanging from the roof! We had to keep the fire grate burning at top level and we had one electric bowl burning night and day – but we survived.

It was in 1953 that the Nissen huts were all eventually demolished, as the Council had some lovely Cornish units built for all the Nissen hut dwellers. It was with great pride that my husband and I were given the responsibility of ensuring that all the new houses were completely clean and ready for the occupants. By degrees we all moved in – a period never to be forgotten, and what news for the *Salisbury Journal* reporters, who didn't hesitate to visit the site and take pictures of us "moving in" with great joy!'

'We, that is myself, my wife and two sons, arrived to live in Cricklade during September 1947. Then, a Nissen hutted camp existed at Blakehill around the area of the Ashton Keynes crossroads one mile from Cricklade. These huts were converted to dwelling places by the then Cricklade & Wootton Bassett Rural District Council, and had two bedrooms, and a kitchen fitted with an electric cooker and storage water heater. The bathroom had a large bath and a hand basin. A medium sized square stove provided the heating for the large living room.

In all there were about 150 huts on five sites, making quite an addition to the population of Cricklade. During the following year a club was housed in one of the large communal huts used by the War Department. A guard house on one site was converted into a shop, affectionately known as "Monty's", and this saved residents a mile walk into the town. My first mistake was to call Cricklade a village – I was told it was a Town!'

HIGHDAYS &
HOLIDAYS

HOW WE ENTERTAINED OURSELVES

Entertainment tended to be home-made or a community effort in the days before television, and there cannot have been many villages which did not put on dances and whist drives, concerts and plays – all with local talent. The coming of wireless and, of course, the cinema, began to take people away from these simpler pursuits, though the cinemas too began to get fewer in number by recent years. Sports were popular, though feelings might run high amongst the spectators! Women found that the starting up of a local Women's Institute gave them an outlet for education and entertainment they had never had before.

ENTERTAINMENT WAS SIMPLE

'The village hall in Barford was much used in the early years of the century as we had to provide our own entertainments. There were always whist drives and dances. My aunt, Miss Lewis from The Green Dragon, played the piano. We also played crib and darts there. Beer was brewed in The Green Dragon which was open all day long from the very early morning.'

'Entertainment was simple in the 1920s. A sing-song round the piano. Mother was a lovely pianist. A game of whist with our friends and a game of tennis in the recreation ground at Highworth, sixpence an hour. Church on Sundays and Sunday school and lots of walks in the country. My stepfather was wont to say that Wiltshire was "God's own county" and who am I to disagree? I joined the local Amateur Dramatic Society and we rehearsed in an upstairs room at the Fishes Inn. We performed in Highworth and the surrounding villages, travelling with our props in the back of Mr Cook's coal waggon, properly cleaned out of course. The highlight of the year was the Waifs and Strays fancy dress dance on New Year's Eve in the school hall – children in the afternoon and adults in the evening. Highworth is a small town but there was a lovely friendly feeling there, always. Of course, there was no television in those days, so perhaps that made for more communication between people – there was only the occasional magic lantern show, in the school hall.'

'After the Second World War a local pantomime was performed annually at Donhead. It was organised by two teachers who lived at Yew Tree. One teacher wrote the script and the lyrics while the other was in charge of costumes. It was performed at Donhead village hall and the Remembrance Hall. Many villagers took part including retired people, farmers and local children. Of course, jokes about specific people in the audience were all part of the show, much to the delight of all. Mr Ralph Coward's barn was the venue of a Nativity play too, which is still performed there.'

THE PAGEANT

'Splashed over the back page of the *Daily Sketch* on Thursday 23rd July 1925 was a report and photographs of a pageant held the day before, presented by the Redlynch Morgans Vale and Woodfalls Women's Institute, with over 100 performers. This took place in the grounds of New House, Redlynch and was a great success; despite occasional showers of rain the pageant carried on as umbrellas went up.

This grand event is remembered by many of the performers who at the time were children. They were dressed in period costumes of the 16th century and gathered to see Sir Walter Raleigh pass through the village of Downton, which is approximately two miles from Redlynch.

The first scene was AD 640, "The Outskirts of a Saxon Forest", followed by several more scenes ending with a procession and tableau of all the characters. Miss Elsie Graham's choir from Salisbury, assisted by the Landford and Morgans Vale choirs sang *Land of Hope and Glory*. The producer was the local medical practitioner, Dr Brian Whitehead, and the pageant was written by Miss G Hope. Admission: afternoon performance four shillings and threepence; evening two shillings and fourpence, the proceeds for Salisbury Infirmary. It was first performed the previous year on Wednesday 16th July 1924.'

COME AND HEAR THE WIRELESS

'There were two people in Horningsham that had the wireless. They had an open evening for people to come and hear the wireless in the old village hall. It went on a bit, then music would come, then "brrr . ." noises, then a bit more music and talking. Lady Mary was going to play on the piano if it shouldn't carry on. She played a bit and they fiddled around and a voice came through to say that the weather forecast would come in two minutes, but nothing came out.

Mother said as we were leaving that she thought she'd hear the weather forecast and a man next to her said, "Gawd's truth, Missus, you got to get outside to know what the weather's going to be."

When the King opened the Exhibition at Wembley in 1924, Lady Bath fixed it so that all we kids could go down and hear it on the wireless. They got the men to fix up the aerial in the oak trees in the corner of the house at Longleat because that used to be her room and she had the windows open so that we could hear it. What a voice came through; we couldn't hear a word but we could say we'd heard the King so we were satisfied.'

A QUICK GETAWAY

'When Kington Langley played Colerne at football before the First World War they went by horse and cart. If Langley were winning, the cart had to be moving to get them safely away on the final whistle.'

THE TENNIS CLUB

'In the early 1930s a group of young people decided we would like a Tennis Club in our village. We made an appointment with Mr Hony (who owned Hallam) and called a meeting to see if the village wanted a Tennis Club. We had a good attendance and formed a committee. Now it was a question of cash! So we decided to have sixpenny hops, each Friday evening.

Mr Hony had let us have a piece of a field for one shilling a year. We ran the dances. My mother, Mrs Winchcome, and friends ran the refreshments for us. We raised enough money to buy netting wire, marker, mower, net etc and my father built us a small open pavilion. That spring we all (girls as well) helped with the work, and opened our club that summer.

We soon became invited to play against other clubs, one being Aldbourne, to which we had to climb the Aldbourne Hill. We had an old Clyno car, which we had bought for £6 from Mr Friend, Mayor of Marlborough, and this car would take the whole team as my father had made stools for extra seats. Now the problem was the car had a broken bottom gear, so we had to go up in *reverse* and did not know on which side of the road to travel.

The club lasted until 1939 when war broke out and the court became allotments – "Dig for Victory".'

THE INSTITUTE

'Gastard Women's Institute was an afternoon meeting when it started in 1926, my mother being a founder member. The meeting was held in what is still called the "Institute" and is now my garden shed, an old stone building.

My grandfather's job on the day would be to fill the black iron kettles with water and get the old black range fire going and fill the coal buckets. I always arrived home from school at the ladies' tea time. I remember the pot was always emptied afterwards on the garden outside. The tall yellow daises seemed to thrive with their feet in tea leaves.

In warm weather the door would be open and inside the members, about ten or twelve in those early days, all Gastard folk, could be seen sitting around a long table down the middle of the room on backless benches. "Granny Jones", now long gone, my mother and the others all knitting away at socks and gloves for their families.

I can't ever remember seeing a speaker, they always seemed to be chatting, knitting and drinking tea. They did quite a lot of "skits" for fund raising. Magic lantern shows were held in the local school because it was larger. On one occasion at about the age of nine I was drafted in to be the page in "Good King Wenceslas", dressed in a blue paper suit and dared to move in case it split. Another favourite was "The Raggle Taggle Gipsies O". We practised for these events at the home of Lord and Lady Middleton, she being president at the time. This we enjoyed because the butler would bring us cakes and lemonade afterwards!'

WHEN WE HAD A CINEMA

'My father ran the cinema in Gas Lane, Cricklade in the 1920s and Mother played the piano, as films then were silent. The only one that I can recall was *The wreck of the Hesperus*. The cinema closed when the talkies came along at cinemas in Swindon and Cirencester.'
'When I came to Pewsey in the early 1950s there was a cinema in the village. It was a large 1930s-type building, shoulder to shoulder with a pair of half-timbered thatched cottages by the river. A flight of wide steps led up to quite an imposing entrance, where a pretty young woman sold the tickets in the booking office, and also showed customers to their seats. However, within a few years the cinema audiences had dwindled to the point where it had to close.'

233

MEMORABLE OCCASIONS

Royal jubilees and coronations have been celebrated with great enthusiasm in Wiltshire through the century – and how many of us remember Coronation Day in 1953 because it was the very first time we had seen a television set!

THAT NURSE . .

'The mother of a neighbour of mine in Odstock recalled going as a schoolgirl to a funeral at East Wellow church. She said to me, "You remember that nurse – Florence Something." "Do you mean Florence Nightingale?" "Yes, that was the one – and what a lot of important gentlemen were there!" The year was 1910.'

1911 CORONATION

'I can remember the Coronation of George V and Queen Mary in 1911. I still have my husband's and my own coronation cups. In my village of Bromham we had a big get together in a field. The band played, there were all sorts of things on and we all had a free tea. What I remember most is a chip van outside the field and we were all treated to a pennyworth of chips done up in newspaper. My mother never cooked any chips so they were a treat.'

1935 AND 1937 JUBILEE AND CORONATION

'In 1935 the villages of Bishops Fonthill and Berwick St Leonard celebrated the Jubilee of King George and Queen Mary. There was a fancy dress competition for the children who paraded from the village to the Terrace field. Children not in fancy dress helped Mr Burt, the Estate head woodman, plant three copper beech saplings near the centre of the village, after which they joined the crowd at the Terrace field for races and a grand tea party and there was a beer tent for the grown ups to celebrate with a drink! Hindon Band played. Unfortunately, one tree only survived a few years. However, some years later the members of Bishops Fonthill, Berwick St Leonard, Chicklade and Pertwood Women's Institutes replaced the loss – when a copper beech sapling was planted in 1965 to mark 50 years of the WI formation in Britain. Today, these magnificent trees

The Jubilee Beacon on Strawberry Hill 1935. A chain of beacons was lit across Salisbury Plain on Jubilee night, visible for miles.

are a landmark of the village.

In 1937 and 1953 similar parties were held to celebrate the Coronations. In 1937 money-raising functions were held and in 1953 villagers paid so much a week toward the cost of these events. Major and Mrs John Morrison were very generous with money and food, so that the workers' wives and families would have a really good day of fun and frivolity.'

'At last the big day was here; every cottage in our small hamlet on Coronation day 1937 was decorated with red and blue. The old farmhouse where I lived was especially splendid; it had two big Union Jacks flying from the attic windows and red, white and blue bunting was draped all along the long stone wall surrounding the house and garden.

We had all worked very hard decorating our home and were delighted when Father told us (with a twinkle in his eye) that he had actually passed it on his way home from market and not even recognised it!

I could hardly wait until it was time for me to get dressed in the fancy dress costume my mother had made me. I was Little Bo Peep and had a smock dress of blue and white, a white mob cap and a shepherd's crook with a big red bow of ribbon tied on it. Two of my friends were dressed in costume, one a rather large fairy with yards of tinsel and silver paper wand, the other a milkmaid. We all stood proudly as Mother filmed us with her Brownie camera.

We joined the children in the nearby village where later we all paraded, showing off while our mothers sighed and told each other how sweet we all were and sniffed into their hankies!

The big event for us was to walk to the Abbey and, in line, ascend the steps where Miss Talbot was waiting to hand us our Coronation mugs – these were then returned to our mothers for safe keeping while we tucked into our free tea, provided for us on trestle tables in the wide village street. Lemonade, buns and sandwiches had never tasted so good.

In the evening the grown ups danced to a local band while we watched, wishing we were old enough to join them. The most exciting time was later when there was the firework display. How we "oohed and aahed" as each rocket exploded in a burst of stars.

Then it was all over and we were home and in bed with happy memories and our Coronation mugs safely beside us.'

'In 1935 we had a big celebration for the Silver Jubilee at Cricklade. A rostrum was erected in the High Street and singing for the pig took place. The contestants had to pick up the pig and sing a song, without making the pig squeal. I'm sure the RSPCA would have been against the methods used!

At the Coronation of George VI in 1937 there was an ox roast presided over by the local butcher in Pauls Croft. All the locals went with dishes and basins to collect their slices of meat. When I went and asked for twelve slices (I was one of twelve children) someone I knew had to vouch for me! There is a picture in the Town Hall depicting the ox roast, painted by Mr Edward Butler, who used to have rooms with my Aunt Win.'

1953 CORONATION

'In May 1953 I was chosen by my aunt, who had been elected Mayor of the then Borough of Camberwell, London, to be her Mayoress. I was 19 and the youngest of the Mayoresses of the 28 London boroughs. Having lived my 19 years in Monkton Farleigh, near Bradford on Avon and having visited London not more than two or three times, this was a great honour and was to be an incredible experience.

Of the many, many wonderful occasions during my year of office, Coronation Day, 2nd June 1953, was perhaps the most outstanding. The grey, misty and decidedly chilly dawn was disappointing and gave no hint of the excitement to come. However, as we had to be in our seats at 5 am there was no time to worry. The official car took us to the allocated dropping off point. My aunt had a seat in the Abbey and I was seated in a stand just outside, accompanied by an Alderman. There was already tremendous activity, people arriving to stand on the pavements, the soldiers to line the streets. The hours passed quickly until the carriages began to arrive, Lords and Ladies, Kings and Queens, the British Royal family and, finally, the Queen in her golden coach, looking so many things – petite, frail, calm and proud in her simple but exquisite white gown.

The service was broadcast and was followed intently by the people in the stands and on the streets, everything hushed as the solemn, holy, and age-old ceremony unfolded. At the conclusion of the service, the people waited expectantly for the young, newly-crowned Queen. Fanfares and tumultuous cheering greeted her as she appeared under the canopy at the great door of the cathedral, contrasting greatly with the recent sombre music of the service. Raw emotion showed on the faces of the watchers as they cheered themselves hoarse. The return procession of carriages was spectacular, dominated by the very plump, happy, laughing Queen of Tonga waving enthusiastically to everyone and enjoying every minute.

The time came for us to leave our places and proceed to the picking up point. We were ushered down the canopied walkways, jostling shoulder to shoulder with Peers and Peeresses of the Realm in ermine robes and tiaras. The organisation worked with military precision. We linked up with my aunt during the exit and as we emerged on Horseguards Parade, our car came forward and collected us.

We returned to Camberwell, had a quick snack and then going our separate ways, we toured dozens of street parties. At midnight on that historic day, we met up again and went to the top of One Tree Hill, the highest geographical point in the borough, and lit a beacon prepared by the Boy Scouts.

Forty years on, my memories of Coronation Day are of activity, colour, gaiety, solemnity, laughter, noise, the clip clop of horses, camaraderie, pageantry, the robes and the dresses, all pervaded by a deep emotion that the writing of history and the beginning of a new Elizabethan era was being witnessed.

A privilege I shall never forget.'

'Having no television set of our own, my family joined neighbours to watch the Coronation on their black and white set. I took sandwiches so as not to miss any of the celebrations. The older people sat in chairs and the children sat on the floor. The day after, there was a Coronation Tea held at Rutland Garage, Bradley Road, Trowbridge for all schoolchildren in the area.'

'A family who had come from London as a result of the MOD Admiralty move to Bath, lived in a small hamlet about two miles from Box. They were the only household with a television set in the summer of 1953, so all the neighbours were invited to view the Coronation ceremony in their home. The viewers included the local "grande dame" from the big house and her retainer (who was her "retired" nanny), farm workers and their wives and others from nearby cottages. This was the first time they had met together as a

Dancing in the High Street at West Lavington on Coronation Day 1953.

community in the home of one of their members, such was their Victorian sense of hierarchy. The length of this TV broadcast, which lasted for the major part of the day, provided an excellent opportunity for breaking down social barriers.'

ALL THROUGH THE YEAR

Every year brought its round of red letter days, whether they were the universal holidays of Easter and Christmas or more local events such as the summer solstice at Stonehenge or Wilton Race Day. All were eagerly anticipated in the days when holidays were few and far between. Some have now disappeared from the calendar, such as Empire Day which has gone the way of the empire it celebrated.

EASTER

'We loved Easter time. On Good Friday before nine o'clock we went to a bakery at Devizes to buy hot cross buns. All the shops were closed so it was exciting to go into the actual bakehouse behind the shop and savour the delicious smells. We went to church before a lunch of boiled fish, which we detested. Then we walked to Stert Valley carrying our hot cross buns. We loved jumping the streams and picking primroses as a gift for Mother. The buns tasted great. My two young sisters and I always had new clothes for Easter – a straw hat with flowers, black patent kid shoes and a dress hand-sewn by Mother. An aunt who worked at Bourneville sent us a large chocolate egg filled with pink cream and decorated with beautiful ribbons.'

CLUB DAY

'East Knoyle Club Day was on the Thursday after Whit Sunday. They used to have a big maroon flag – I know two of the men that used to carry it. There was the band and all that. They assembled down there, either by The Seymour Arms or just down Leigh Lane, by Lever's Garage. March up through, up here, up through Holloway, up to the front of the Rectory to summon the Rector, then back down here to the church. Go in and have a service, come back out and march on up round, then come into the schoolyard, go in there and have a dinner.

One man, his name was Alfie F, he lived on the Turnpike, and he were drunk before he marched up through here, to go up to the whatisit. Canon Milford didn't like that, but there, then he had to put up with it. Down here, as you come into the yard, over on the left hand side as you're goin' in, there was this fellow come there from Peacemarsh, down Gillingham, with a donkey and cart and sells nuts. Used to 'ave the band. Oh, yes, yes, t'was a real do an' that. Oh yes, they used to 'ave club sticks, they were dark blue and red. They 'ad a little top on 'em, round on here and then a smaller round on 'em, and some of them had streamers, red, white and blue that had to stay on 'em, the red and the blue.

I would say that I can't really remember it carrying on after the First World War. No, I don't think so for, you see, I can only just really remember it.'

OAK APPLE DAY

'Every year on 29th May at Wishford we celebrated Oak Apple Day, which meant going to the woods early in the morning to cut oak

Wishford celebrated Oak Apple Day and May Day combined on 29th May. Schoolchildren selected their May Queen and (opposite) houses were decorated with oak boughs.

240

boughs. People of Wishford were allowed to cut dead wood all the year round from Grovely but on 29th May they could bring away green wood (beansticks). The boughs were carried home and stood in front of the houses. At twelve o'clock the schoolchildren, headed by the May Queen, walked to the Town End and joined with people and children in fancy dress and with decorated wood carts and proceeded to walk around the village. A local band brought up the rear and the route was down the street over Stoford Bridge and back via West Street to the Oak Apple field (now a site with council flats and bungalows).'

EMPIRE DAY

'I have an old black and white photo of a smiling little girl all dressed up for Empire Day. It was taken many years ago, probably by my big brother as my father had no camera. I am wearing a white dress trimmed with bunches of wild daisies – a bracelet of them round my wrist, a chain round my neck and flowers around my head. I also have a decorated wand. I can remember being envious of a friend, Hazel, who wore large pink garden daisies on *her* dress.

We celebrated Empire Day in May and my husband thinks he can remember marching up the town waving a Union Jack – perhaps

241

that's what the little boys did. Our school in College Street, Swindon was adjacent to the big girls school. It just had an asphalt playground where we played at break and did our exercises when the weather was fine. The lavatories were across the yard with no such refinements as hand washing facilities.

No doubt our excellent head teacher Miss Pickett told us stories of our glorious Empire – all those pink splodges on the map of the world. Now 70 years on all I can recall is Mother making the daisy chains, dancing in a circle in the playground with the other little girls in our pretty dresses, and being given a half holiday.'

SWINDON TRIP WEEK

'When I was a child, almost 60 years ago, Swindon had its Trip week. All who worked "inside" were transported to seaside destinations by special Trip trains. The longest journeys to Penzance and St Ives left late in the evening and arrived before breakfast. The trains were met by landladies with vacant rooms seeking trippers who had not booked and also by the ones who regarded their Swindon guests as friends of many years standing. There were so many trains to be organised that the evening ones left from St Mark's sidings – no station, no platform, just short stepladders. My grandfather, who lived with us and was still working "inside" as a coach finisher, had done a recce so we knew where to find a pair of steps. Once ensconced we were often delighted to find that we knew our travelling companions and even if we didn't our common destination proved a ready made topic of conversation. The highlight of the journey was food, sandwiches, tea in a Thermos for the grown ups and lemonade made with Eiffel Tower crystals for the children (no buffet cars on Trip trains) – and delight of delight, Butter Puffs and triangular cream cheeses. Even today a packet of Butter Puffs will send me off into the story of the Trip journey to St Ives.'

SUMMER SOLSTICE AT STONEHENGE

'Before the days of the hippies and the new age travellers, access to Stonehenge was not restricted and the general public were allowed to walk around and touch the stones.

In the early 1950s when I was about five or six years old, my parents decided to visit Stonehenge for the summer solstice celebration. I was woken at some unearthly hour when it was still dark, dressed, wrapped in a blanket and carried to the car. The drive took about an hour but I imagine I slept the whole way as I have no recollection of the journey. When we arrived in the early dawn I could see the stones silhouetted against the grey sky and as we approached them on foot their size was awesome. The atmosphere was eerie but not frightening. My father had explained the history of the stones to me and described what was going to happen that morning. I was excited but somewhat apprehensive.

There were probably about 50 or 60 people there but I remember the overwhelming feeling of peace, quiet and contentment. I have no idea why all these people had decided to visit, whether the Druids' ceremony was important to them or whether like my parents, they thought it would be an interesting experience.

It was going to be a beautiful day and as the sun started to rise I remember turning my face to it and feeling its warmth. As the sun came fully above the horizon the ceremony began. I don't remember the details of the ceremony, just the men in long white robes performing some sort of ritual around the altar stone. When the sun rises on Midsummer's Day it shines between the two largest stone arches and plays on the altar stone. Whether through design or coincidence is not known but it is very impressive. Throughout the ceremony everyone was very still and quiet and even at that young age I could sense its importance.

After the ceremony was over and the Druids had left we went to look at the altar stone. I sat on it and my father explained to me that in days gone by young fair maidens were sacrificed to the sun god, and had I lived then it may well have been me as I was the youngest at the gathering. We examined all the other stones and stood for a while just drinking in the atmosphere. By this time the sun had risen fully and the magic of the early morning was fast disappearing. I don't remember the rest of the day and we never went to another solstice ceremony, but the memory of that morning has remained with me. I can still feel the warmth of the sun on my face and remember the inner peace.

It is a great pity that times have changed and that this simple ceremony can no longer be enjoyed peacefully.'

RACE DAY AND WILTON FAIR

'On Race days Wilton was full of people talking in what sounded to us a foreign language, shouting "Any race cards?", and people and horses being fetched from the station. A lot of horses were stabled at The Pembroke Arms. The boys would call out, "Any spare halfpennies in the river sir" and would then jump into the river for any that were thrown in (the river round the road). A lot of town people provided lodgings for the jockeys who stayed overnight. The horses came by train.

People used to tape up their windows because of the dust from the roads. There were a lot of brakes going to the station; Brakes were a sort of waggon with seats along the sides. We used to run behind them asking for halfpennies.

On Sheep Fair days the streets would be full of flocks of sheep. Some would have stayed in and around the town overnight. On the day of the September fair Mr White put a lot of whole cheeses outside his shop with a notice which said "Come and have a cup of tea with us", inviting country people to his garden in South Street gate. We used to think the cheeses were really to protect the shop windows!

On Fair and Race days many people met old friends they hadn't seen since the last Fair or Race day.'

MARLBOROUGH OWN

'I was the eldest of eight children, so holidays were unheard of and no one expected them, as it was only the very rich who had such luxuries during the 1920s-1940s. I lived on the edge of Savernake Forest and was educated in Marlborough. So Marlborough was the area of my "High Days".

The one outstanding day of my year was the "Marlborough Own", a day trip to the seaside when Marlborough was virtually empty and even the shops closed for the day. This outing was by train, and if you had attended Sunday school often enough you'd go free. We'd go to either Weymouth, Weston-super-Mare, Teignmouth or Barry Island, all seaside towns on the GWR line.

We'd wake very early on this special day and walk down the Forest Hill to see a huge train waiting at the station, usually about twelve carriages.

Mother had previously loaded the well of our huge pram with our swimming paraphernalia, buckets and spades plus enough food for us all for the day. All the prams would be loaded in the guards van. We'd dash for the nearest empty carriage and draw the blind, "reserved for us".

With much cheering we'd start but quickly we'd arrive at Marlborough Tunnel and close all of the windows or be covered in smuts. We'd explore the length of the train finding our school friends. I can't ever remember a wet day, we always had such a wonderful time, but looking back this train journey was the highlight of the day.

During August Marlborough had its sheep fair, held on the

common. Drovers would drive the flocks over the Downs. They'd also arrive by train loads at the station. We children would meet the trains and help the shepherds through the street with his flocks. The auction would take all day, then we'd make the return journey with his new flock, rewarded by a few pennies.

Also in October Marlborough has its famous fair occupying the High Street, but when we were young it was another High Day. We'd save pocket money for weeks beforehand and it was such a fun evening. We'd meet friends, buy bags of confetti, and balls filled with sawdust attached to elastic, flicking them at everyone. The Fair ladies made sweets like winding skeins of wool, around and around their plump arms in glorious striped mixed colours and they tasted delicious. After rides on the helter skelter, whales, horses etc we'd try our luck at the many stalls and go home happy with our winnings and, of course, always a coconut.'

FAIRS AND FETES

'In my early childhood in the 1930s there was one day of the year that everyone looked forward to – on the second Saturday in August the GWR held a fete at The Park, Faringdon Road, Swindon. If your father worked for the railways you went free; if not you bought a ticket which entitled you to one cup of tea (children used to carry their cups on string around their necks), one slab of fruit cake and one free ride on the roundabouts. There were fireworks in the evening and everyone seemed to have a wonderful time.'

'The Market Place was a focal point in the life of Devizes, with its weekly market, the Salvation Army band playing there on Sunday evenings, and the big carnival parade in Carnival Week. I especially remember in Carnival Week the placing of little blue, green and amber glass pots on window ledges in which lighted candles glimmered – there were no electric lights in the town until the 1930s. Ice cream and a ride in Mr Joliffe's cab to the Mayor's Soirée for children was a highlight of the Christmas holidays.'

'How we counted the days as October came and with it Salisbury Fair. How often it brought wind and rain and the grown ups called it "Salisbury Fair Weather". Scarlet fever and diphtheria were rampant before the Second World War and my friend and I always had to suck iodised throat tablets on the way down across the Greencroft to the Market Place. I was really rather frightened by the noise and would only go on the big roundabout with seats and horses. Always an optimist, I spent my money on those cranes in

245

glass cages which were going to lift up such treasures – and then tears nearly came as the treasure slipped down again. We were never allowed to buy the enticing toffee apples or brandy snaps – too much risk of infection! But on the way home up Bedwin Street we were allowed to purchase a brandy snap each at Fry's Bakers, also famous for their delicious dough cakes.'

'In the early days at Salisbury, the fair people lined up outside the city as they were not allowed in until after midnight on Monday and had to be out by midnight on Tuesday, the first Tuesday after 15th October.'

'The feast of St Mary Magdalene has been celebrated for centuries past at Aldbourne, taking the form of an annual market and fair. This tradition enabled families, many travelling miles with their children, to visit grandparents and meet up with old friends. Feast Sunday, the first after 22nd July, later became the Methodist Camp Meeting day, with three services out of doors (usually in a meadow), then the fair would arrive causing great excitement among the children who were allowed a late night to enjoy Feast Monday! Although this tradition no longer has the same significance, with family ties diminishing, it still happens, the fair being extended to Tuesday as well.'

'The second Thursday in August was a very special day in Britford some 60 years ago, and eagerly awaited by all. Thousands of sheep from miles around were driven by shepherds and their dogs along the old droves to the Fair Field for the great sale.

After a hurried breakfast and a "Don't be late for dinner" from Mother, my sister and I ran up the lane, across a field called Paradise, through a barbed wire fence and we were there!

A great hubbub of noise greeted us, the sheep bleating and the loud voice of Mr John Jeffries, the auctioneer, whacking down his stick after each sale. We wandered between the raised pens, pitying the lambs separated from their mothers and admiring the splendid rams. These had been carefully prepared with their chipped flat backs dyed a bright yellow.

But perhaps the bigger attraction was the strong sweet smell of Stainers Stall. A fascinating display of brightly coloured unwrapped sweets, liquorice laces, sherbet dabs etc – all a-buzz with wasps! What to choose, that was the problem. A lot of thought was needed before parting with our twopence a week pocket money.

Finally clutching our sticky selection – all wrapped in a paper cone – we reluctantly went home. There we would find Great Uncle

Frank, a sheep farmer from Martin, sitting at the scrubbed kitchen table having a bite of bread and cheese. He was a very large man who seemed to fill his flimsy little pony trap which had brought him to Britford. The pony was fed and rested in our stable until the return journey.

The fair is no longer held in our village but at Wilton where it is still known as "Old Britford Fair".'

THE AIR CIRCUS

'Sir Alan Cobham's Air Circus came to Rowde several times in the 1930s and Father paid seven shillings and sixpence for me to have a flight on my birthday. He came up with me but Mother stayed safely on the ground while we had a ten minute trip over Devizes and the surrounding area. The canal looked like a ribbon, and on a poultry farm the hens were white dots.'

THE FLOWER SHOW

'I spent my childhood on a Wiltshire farm. Born in 1920, those early days now appear to be one long idyllic period in both my life and that of my twin sister Peggy. The annual Heddington and Stockley Flower Show was the biggest village event and we enjoyed every moment of it.

We were up early on Flower Show day — Mother would have made several entries in the various classes and for days would have been selecting, discarding, reselecting and finally her ultimate choice would be lined up in the dairy. Bright aster heads, pushed through cardboard covered with black velvet, their stems in little meat paste pots, out of sight, behind the cardboard. Sweetpeas, in long thin glass vases. The maidenhair fern in the green china jardinière, looking green and fresh, as its dead fronds had been carefully cut away with nail scissors. Brown eggs on a white doily, white eggs on black velvet and a dish of beautifully floury potatoes, garlanded with sprigs of parsley. The exhibits would be carefully loaded onto the floor of the pony trap — we nursed the more fragile entries. The little brown pony, Frolic, set off at an unusually sedate pace.

In the large Flower Show tent, it was a hive of activity, with everyone hurrying to finish before the judges arrived at 11.30 am. Peggy and I amused ourselves by watching the exhibitors completing their large table decorations. Everyone used an "epergne" in the centre of the table with four little vases at each corner. Most of the flowers used were very dainty ones — lots of asparagus fern and pastel shaded sweetpeas with gypsophila.

When we got fed up with the inside of the tent we sat outside by the entrance, leaning up against the heavy guy ropes and watched the people coming and going. Tommy Gartside the roadman would arrive, a large dahlia in his buttonhole; he would be carrying two large vegetable marrows and always had a beaming smile on his face. The rector's wife left, carefully pushing her high bicycle with its dress guards across the grass to the road gate, secateurs and unused flowers in the basket over the front wheel.

On the way to the gate were the caravans – romantic they seemed when the half doors were open and one glimpsed all the brightness of the brass and glass and colourful fittings inside. In contrast the fair folk seemed drab – the children silent and watchful and looking like tiny adults in their long skirts. The womenfolk were washing their clothes, hanging them over the thick hedge, transforming it into a colourful patchwork quilt. At night, behind the hoop-la and the coconut shies, these women would seem different, younger, more glamorous, with flashing earrings and gaudy beads, accentuated by the flickering naphtha lights. With smiling faces they would laugh and joke with the crowd and with one another, but now they seemed sullen and ill humoured.

It would seem ages from the time we reached home in the morning, until we could go back to the show at 2.30 pm for the

Gathering at the War Memorial for Cricklade's Armistice Day service in the 1920s. This solemn occasion brought life to a standstill for the two minutes silence, strictly observed.

official opening. The sports were scheduled to start at three o'clock but we planned to walk around the flower tent and view the prize cards before we took part. There would be many villagers doing the same thing – some happy with results, beaming as they stood near the entrance, ready for the congratulations. Others were not so pleased with either the judging or the results. "They taters ben't worth a fust, be 'un", someone grumbled. "If they say h'annuals they do mean h'annuals not b . . . . p'renuls," from another.

The sports started at three o'clock. Peggy and I relied on the prize money from these to finance the rest of the day. Most years, we had got prizes for our wildflowers – jamjars full of willowherb, meadowsweet, ragged robin and wild orchids, scabious and round-headed rampions from the downs. Unfortunately the prize money for this would not be delivered until the following week so it was imperative to get a few prizes with the sports – this was presented at the finishing tape, a very satisfactory arrangement.

We were fairly sure of winning first prize for the three-legged race. For at least a fortnight we had practised hard – running up and down the rickyard with one of Dad's handkerchiefs tied firmly around our legs, until we became proficient. We could even leap over fallen competitors lying on the ground without losing our rhythm. Later on there were the adults' sports. The motor cycling races were the most exciting – the competitors roared into the ring on their old James, Matchless or Douglas machines, revved up and away, smoke billowing from the exhaust. There would also be a tug of war and one year a pillow fight on a greasy pole. The men's sports always finished with "the marathon". At least it was called by that name, although the competitors actually ran the distance around the roads of Heddington and Stockley, starting and finishing with the show ground. By the time the winner arrived and breathlessly staggered the last few yards into the field, dusk would be falling.

The end of the sports meant we could devote all our time and interest to the fair ground. The roundabouts were our favourites. They had had quite a slack time whilst people were watching the sports but, now, there would be a queue waiting for the horses to slow down and stop. Bromham Brass Band which had been playing non stop throughout the afternoon had finished all their stirring marches and the members had repaired to the beer tent and the music from the fairground organ took over. The brightly coloured carved figures moved jerkily and not quite in time with the music. One got an entirely fresh view of the field from the back of the horses. Climbing high above the colourful canopy, a shuddering jerk when one felt the wooden charger was going to break away from the golden plated rod and then the plunge back down towards the revolving dais. When one was high in the air, the stalls took on a different aspect. Looking down on the sweet stall, there seemed to be a sea of candy floss with mounds of brown and cream barley sugar forming little islands. On the other side, the celluloid windmills and the balloons on sticks formed an ever changing kaleidoscope of colours. The swinging boats were doing a roaring trade now. In the afternoon they had been mainly occupied by young children, being gently swung to and fro by parents or the man in charge. Now they had a different clientele. Youths and girls swung higher and higher until it looked that they would go over the top, some of the more brave standing up in the boats to get more leverage on the ropes.

The field seemed full of people now. Mothers trundled their deep prams with the small wheels, that were so popular in those days, their tiny occupants peering over the high sides. Older brothers and sisters drooped on their fathers' shoulders, fighting to overcome sleep that threatened to overtake them.

Beyond the circle of light and colour were the grey fields, their hedges black in the night, and shadowy cattle stood by the dividing gate, motionless in the darkness, puzzled by the intrusion into their solitude. Everywhere there was laughter, deep throated guffaws from the beer tent, shrill bursts of excited mirth from the funfair.

Eventually Mother gathered up her brood and we made for home, across the common and down the hill. Before we went to sleep, we leant out of our bedroom window – we could still hear faintly in the distance the noise of the fair and see the faint glow in the sky from the lights. It seemed a long time to next August and the next Flower Show.'

HOSPITAL WEEK

'Every year in the 1920s a Hospital Week was held at Bromham in aid of Devizes Hospital. It culminated with a procession led through the village by the village band, and we ended up dancing in the field.'

HARVEST HOME

'A Harvest Home of a hundred years ago was a very busy and happy time. The farmer's wife with the help of her one domestic help (who lived in) and the carter's wife (the carter looked after the horses) would do all the cooking for the supper. All those who worked on the farm plus wives and children and near neighbours were invited to a supper of meat pasties, boiled ham and roast fowls with baked potatoes, followed by beastings pudding which was very rich, thick milk taken from a freshly calved cow. All the goodness was in this milk to help protect the newborn calf from diseases. Apple and plum pies and cream, and cider and beer to drink.

When all had had their fill, music and a sing-song followed. The farmer's wife played the spinnet and one of the invited company played the fiddle. Everyone left the party by nine o'clock, the carter to "rack up" his horses (give them hay), the cowman to look at the cattle and the shepherd his sheep before going to their beds. I can remember the men doing these last chores when I was a girl.

Today's Harvest Supper in our village of Chitterne is a community affair held in the village hall. So few people are employed on farms today because of the amount of machinery used. Harvest Festival takes place on the last Sunday in September. Afterwards the produce is taken into the village hall.

The supper is held in the evening of the same day and consists of beef casserole or shepherd's pie with hot vegetables followed by apple and plum pies, chocolate mousse, meringues – all served with cream. Cheese board and coffee round off the meal, red and white wine served during the repast.

When everyone is replete, the produce etc is auctioned. We don't get to our beds much before midnight! The produce from the festival used to go to a children's home but this no longer exists and now the money goes to the upkeep of All Saints church, Chitterne.'

ARMISTICE DAY

'My mother remembers the first Armistice Day service to be held at St Andrew's church, Chippenham in 1918. As a child, she recalls attending with her classmates from the nearby school. She was impressed by the sadness of the occasion and the two minutes silence at eleven o'clock. This practice continued for many years, when even the traffic came to a halt.'

CHRISTMAS

'Christmas was the most special time of the year. Weeks before there were exciting preparations. Christmas puddings took hours to prepare. Candied peel had to be chopped into small pieces and we were allowed to crunch the large lumps of crystallized sugar. Suet had to be grated, raisins stoned and lemons squeezed. The mixture was stirred by everyone and a wish made but kept secret. The puddings were covered with snowy white cloths and boiled all the next day. There were many whispers about presents and secret things to be hidden.

Santa Claus used to arrive at Devizes station about two weeks before Christmas. He tossed out shiny new halfpennies to all of us waiting to see him and oh! the delight if you caught a coin. He proceeded to a large store called Slopers where he sat in splendour handing out sixpenny gifts.

We made decorations at school and at home using fir cones and coloured paper. Fairies were said to live in the bells hanging from the ceiling if the bells twisted around. Christmas Eve the fir tree was planted in a large bucket. The tree was decorated with metal candle holders and small candles and sparkling glass baubles. My father always took me shopping on Christmas Eve and it seemed traditional to buy leather gloves and ankle strap slippers plus good port and burgundy. We hung up stockings by the open fire and went to bed early. My long hair was tied up in strips of cotton so that I would have corkscrew curls the next day. Traditionally our stockings contained nuts, oranges, apples, sweets, painting books and pencils, and what happiness to have new books to read. It was wonderful to give our parents surprise gifts for which we had saved threepence weekly in a church fund. Neighbours called with gifts and we sang carols.'

'At Christmas at Rushpool my uncle and aunt used to walk down from Maiden Bradley. There wasn't much room so uncle and son slept in the chairs and aunt used to turn in with me. At Rushpool we had turkey for Christmas, as I used to rear them. They were bronze ones, I never saw a white one until years later. Dad and Mum used to kill on the 18th December. Mother cleared everything out of the kitchen bar the table and seats. I've been sitting up till two or three in the morning picking turkeys and she used to keep me supplied with hot drinks. I never got sore fingers, Mother bought white tape to go round them. Dad used to truss the turkeys and keep their heads on – we didn't draw them – and wrap them all in paper.

As children we used to hang up our stockings and we'd get an apple and an orange. It used to be apples with a stripey bit and a real golden yellow one in the toe of our stocking and it wasn't till I came to Rushpool that I found out that my aunt down at Stalls used to grow them. They were so nice. We mostly got a game for Christmas. I had several dolls and Henry used to have Meccano.

During the First World War years, Mother had basins of rendered down yellow fat and she made a cake and couldn't you ever taste that old hen.'

'The school at Lydiard Millicent being C of E was closely connected with the church both spiritually and geographically – the schoolhouse garden adjoined the churchyard. This meant that the pupils were a very useful source of talent for the yearly Nativity tableaux that were staged in the church under the direction of Lady Richmond and Mrs Robertson. In early November selection would start to fill the roles of shepherds, wise men, angels, the Virgin Mary, King Herod and a cast of what seemed like thousands.

After a couple of rehearsals there came the most exciting part, the visit to Lady Richmond's upstairs sitting room in Netherhampton House for the selection of garments for the various members of the cast. There were several large trunks full of exotic items of clothing from many Middle Eastern countries collected in Her Ladyship's travels. There was lots of trying on, pinning up and alterations to be done before everyone was fully equipped for the first dress rehearsal.

The raised section of the aisle between the choir stalls was the stage, a pair of heavy curtains rigged up on poles for easy sliding, and stage lighting made from biscuit tins on stands with bulbs inside and sheets of various coloured cellophane for different scenes. Improvisation was important with most things difficult to get during the war. One rock-hard bread roll made three annual journeys up the aisle from behind the font as one of the "gifts" from the Three Wise Men.

The shepherds, wise men and kings were the only moving members of the cast, making the journey up the aisle to the crib, all the other scenes were in tableau form. These still scenes were most impressive when suitably lit with members of the choir singing an appropriate carol accompanied by Sir Bruce Richmond on the dulcitone. There were two performances each year and the church was always full with people coming from miles around. After the last performance a tea was laid on in The Victoria and Albert on the following Saturday as a reward for all our efforts.'

'Every Christmas morning the residents of the village are awakened by carols being played by the Aldbourne Band, who meet at 4 am and tour every street. This is a tradition which has been kept going for well over 100 years, the reason for the early start being that in the early days some of the band members were also bellringers who were due at the belltower by 6 am. Although this does not apply in modern times, the bandsmen are loath to break with tradition, and Christmas would not be the same without their early morning call.'

Index

255